# Land Education

This important book on Land Education offers critical analysis of the paths forward for education on Indigenous land. This analysis discusses the necessity of centring historical and current contexts of colonization in education on and in relation to land. In addition, contributors explore the intersections of environmentalism and Indigenous rights, in part inspired by the realization that the specifics of geography and community matter for how environmental education can be engaged.

This edited volume suggests how place-based pedagogies can respond to issues of colonialism and Indigenous sovereignty. Through dynamic new empirical and conceptual studies, international contributors examine settler colonialism, Indigenous cosmologies, Indigenous land rights, and language as key aspects of Land Education. The book invites readers to rethink 'pedagogies of place' from various Indigenous, postcolonial, and decolonizing perspectives.

This book was originally published as a special issue of *Environmental Education Research.*

**Kate McCoy** is Associate Professor of Educational Foundations and affiliated faculty of Women's, Gender, and Sexuality Studies at SUNY New Paltz, NY, USA. Her scholarship focuses on qualitative research methods and representation, cultural studies of addiction and drug use, and historical and contemporary uses of drug-crop agriculture in colonial processes.

**Eve Tuck** is Associate Professor at the Ontario Institute of Studies in Education, University of Toronto, Canada. Her scholarship focuses on the ethics of social science research and educational research, Indigenous social and political thought, decolonizing research methodologies and theories of change, and the consequences of neoliberal accountability policies on school completion.

**Marcia McKenzie** is Associate Professor of Educational Foundations and Director of the Sustainability Education Research Institute at the University of Saskatchewan, Canada. Her scholarship focuses on the intersections of environment and education, educational policy and practice, youth identity and place, and the politics of social science research.

# Land Education

## Rethinking pedagogies of place from Indigenous, postcolonial, and decolonizing perspectives

*Edited by*

**Kate McCoy, Eve Tuck and Marcia McKenzie**

LONDON AND NEW YORK

First published 2016
by Routledge

2 Park Square, Milton Park, Abingdon, Oxfordshire OX14 4RN
711 Third Avenue, New York, NY 10017

*Routledge is an imprint of the Taylor & Francis Group, an informa business*

First issued in paperback 2017



*British Library Cataloguing in Publication Data*
A catalogue record for this book is available from the British Library

ISBN 13: 978-1-138-99999-2 (hbk)
ISBN 13: 978-1-138-30905-0 (pbk)

Typeset in Times
by RefineCatch Limited, Bungay, Suffolk

**Publisher's Note**
The publisher accepts responsibility for any inconsistencies that may have arisen during the conversion of this book from journal articles to book chapters, namely the possible inclusion of journal terminology.

# Contents


*Citation Information* vii
*Notes on Contributors* ix

Introduction – Land education: Indigenous, post-colonial, and decolonizing perspectives on place and environmental education research 1
*Eve Tuck, Marcia McKenzie and Kate McCoy*

1. Speaking back to Manifest Destinies: a land education-based approach to critical curriculum inquiry 24
*Dolores Calderon*

2. Muskrat theories, tobacco in the streets, and living Chicago as Indigenous land 37
*Megan Bang, Lawrence Curley, Adam Kessel, Ananda Marin, Eli S. Suzukovich III and George Strack*

3. Sea Country: navigating Indigenous and colonial ontologies in Australian environmental education 56
*Hilary Whitehouse, Felecia Watkin Lui, Juanita Sellwood, M.J. Barrett and Philemon Chigeza*

4. An African-centred approach to land education 70
*Salvatore Engel-Di Mauro and Karanja Keita Carroll*

5. Manifesting Destiny: a land education analysis of settler colonialism in Jamestown, Virginia, USA 82
*Kate McCoy*

6. Hoea Ea: land education and food sovereignty in Hawaii 98
*Manulani Aluli Meyer*

7. Between the remnants of colonialism and the insurgence of self-narrative in constructing participatory social maps: towards a land education methodology 102
*Michèle Sato, Regina Silva and Michelle Jaber*

8. A ghetto land pedagogy: an antidote for settler environmentalism 115
*La Paperson*

9. Eco-heroes out of place and relations: decolonizing the narratives of *Into the Wild* and *Grizzly Man* through Land education 131
*Lisa Korteweg and Jan Oakley*

*Index* 145

# Citation Information

The chapters in this book were originally published in *Environmental Education Research*, volume 20, issue 1 (February 2014). When citing this material, please use the original page numbering for each article, as follows:

**Editorial**

*Land education: Indigenous, post-colonial, and decolonizing perspectives on place and environmental education research*
Eve Tuck, Marcia McKenzie and Kate McCoy
*Environmental Education Research*, volume 20, issue 1 (February 2014) pp. 1–23

**Chapter 1**

*Speaking back to Manifest Destinies: a land education-based approach to critical curriculum inquiry*
Dolores Calderon
*Environmental Education Research*, volume 20, issue 1 (February 2014) pp. 24–36

**Chapter 2**

*Muskrat theories, tobacco in the streets, and living Chicago as Indigenous land*
Megan Bang, Lawrence Curley, Adam Kessel, Ananda Marin, Eli S. Suzukovich III and George Strack
*Environmental Education Research*, volume 20, issue 1 (February 2014) pp. 37–55

**Chapter 3**

*Sea Country: navigating Indigenous and colonial ontologies in Australian environmental education*
Hilary Whitehouse, Felecia Watkin Lui, Juanita Sellwood, M.J. Barrett and Philemon Chigeza
*Environmental Education Research*, volume 20, issue 1 (February 2014) pp. 56–69

**Chapter 4**

*An African-centred approach to land education*
Salvatore Engel-Di Mauro and Karanja Keita Carroll
*Environmental Education Research*, volume 20, issue 1 (February 2014) pp. 70–81

**Chapter 5**
*Manifesting Destiny: a land education analysis of settler colonialism in Jamestown, Virginia, USA*
Kate McCoy
*Environmental Education Research*, volume 20, issue 1 (February 2014) pp. 82–97

**Chapter 6**
*Hoea Ea: land education and food sovereignty in Hawaii*
Manulani Aluli Meyer
*Environmental Education Research*, volume 20, issue 1 (February 2014) pp. 98–101

**Chapter 7**
*Between the remnants of colonialism and the insurgence of self-narrative in constructing participatory social maps: towards a land education methodology*
Michèle Sato, Regina Silva and Michelle Jaber
*Environmental Education Research*, volume 20, issue 1 (February 2014) pp. 102–114

**Chapter 8**
*A ghetto land pedagogy: an antidote for settler environmentalism*
La Paperson
*Environmental Education Research*, volume 20, issue 1 (February 2014) pp. 115–130

**Chapter 9**
*Eco-heroes out of place and relations: decolonizing the narratives of* Into the Wild *and* Grizzly Man *through Land education*
Lisa Korteweg and Jan Oakley
*Environmental Education Research*, volume 20, issue 1 (February 2014) pp. 131–143

# Notes on Contributors

**Megan Bang** is of Ojibwe and Italian descent. She is an Assistant Professor in Learning Sciences and Human Development at the University of Washington, Seattle, WA, USA, and focuses on culture, learning, and development, with a specific focus on science education.

**M.J. Barrett** is a Canadian animist scholar who teaches in the College of Education at the University of Saskatchewan, Saskatoon, Canada.

**Dolores Calderon** is an Assistant Professor in the Department of Education, Culture, and Society, and in the Ethnic Studies Program, at the University of Utah, Salt Lake City, UT, USA. Her research focuses on Indigenous education, culturally relevant/multicultural education, Chicana(o)/Indigenous student success, and coloniality and critical race theories. She is Principal Investigator of 'The Role of Home in Chicano/Indigenous Student Success', a research project documenting the educational trajectories of Chicana/o and Indigenous student graduates from highly selective universities.

**Karanja Keita Carroll** is currently an Associate Professor of Black Studies at SUNY New Paltz, NY, USA. His teaching and research interests revolve around African-centred theory and methodology, with an emphasis on social and psychological theory. His publications have appeared in the *Journal of Pan African Studies*, *Journal of the International Society of Teacher Education*, *Critical Sociology*, and *Race, Gender and Class*. He is also Associate Editor of the *Journal of Pan African Studies*. He is committed to 'academic excellence and social responsibility' as originally articulated by the National Council for Black Studies.

**Philemon Chigeza** combines mathematics and science education scholarship and teaching with explorations in cultural studies in the School of Education at James Cook University, Cairns, Australia. His family links are to regional Zimbabwe.

**Lawrence Curley** (Ojibwe and Dine) is a Hydrogeologist and is currently working on his master's degree in Restoration Ecology at the University of Washington, Seattle, WA, USA. His work is focused on restoring wetlands and estuaries as well understanding contaminant transport and its impact on salmon populations.

**Salvatore Engel-Di Mauro** is an Associate Professor in the Geography Department of SUNY New Paltz, NY, USA. His recent teaching subjects include physical geography, gender and environment, people-environment relations, and soils. The principal interests of his current work include soil degradation, urban soils, heavy metals contamination, and society–environment relations, but he has also published on critical geographies, the European Union, ethnopedology, Indigenous peoples' struggles, and pedagogy. He is Chief Editor of the journal *Capitalism Nature Socialism*.

**Michelle Jaber** is Professor in the Institute of Education at the Federal University of Mato Grosso, Brazil. She is a member of the Environmental Education, Communication and Art Research Group, and develops educational activities with social movements, mainly through popular education. She is also a member of the Human and Earth Right Commission, and the Portuguese language Environmental Education Network (Redeluso).

**Adam Kessel** (Lakota, Italian, German) has extensive experience as a teacher in urban ecology education programs in Chicago, USA. He currently works as an Outreach Naturalist with the Forest Preserves of Cook County, Illinois, USA. He holds a teaching certificate with the state of Illinois, an arborist certificate through the International Society of Arboriculture, and an Interpretive Guide certificate through the National Association for Interpretation.

**Lisa Korteweg** is an Associate Professor in the Faculty of Education, Lakehead University, Thunder Bay, Ontario, Canada, and an Associate Editor of the *Canadian Journal of Environmental Education*. The overarching goal in her research, teaching, and service is to work with others to actively improve the Indigenous-non-Indigenous relationship in Canada through education.

**Ananda Marin** is of African American, Choctaw, and European American descent. She is a Postdoctoral Fellow in the Department of Psychology at Northwestern University, Chicago, IL, USA. Her research focuses on the intersections between culture, orientations to the natural world, and science education.

**Kate McCoy** is Associate Professor of Educational Foundations and affiliated faculty of Women's, Gender, and Sexuality Studies at SUNY New Paltz, NY, USA. Her scholarship focuses on qualitative research methods and representation, cultural studies of addiction and drug use, and historical and contemporary uses of drug-crop agriculture in colonial processes.

**Marcia McKenzie** is Associate Professor of Educational Foundations and Director of the Sustainability Education Research Institute at the University of Saskatchewan, Canada. Her scholarship focuses on the intersections of environment and education, educational policy and practice, youth identity and place, and the politics of social science research.

**Manulani Aluli Meyer** works in one of the most radical, progressive community colleges in the world, Te Wānanga o Aotearoa, based in New Zealand, and with more than 35,000 students. She sees direct application of her work in Indigenous epistemology applied in all degrees and policies and enjoys the lessons from her Maori cousins. She is currently the lead teacher for He Waka Hiringa, and has a master's degree in Applied Indigenous Knowledge. She is committed to food sovereignty, cultural and place-based education, and to truthful, clear, and kind thinking with others. Ho'olu lahui o Hawaii-nui-akea: Let our peoples and nations rise together to be of service to *loving*.

**Jan Oakley** is Adjunct Professor in the Faculty of Education, and sessional Lecturer in the Department of Women's Studies, at Lakehead University, Thunder Bay, Ontario, Canada. Her research interests include environmental education and social justice pedagogies. She is an Editorial Assistant for the *Canadian Journal of Environmental Education*.

**La Paperson** is concerned with coloniality in urban ghettos, and its connections to settler colonialism and imperial projects at large. S-he is the author of the article, 'The Postcolonial Ghetto: Seeing her shape and his hand'.

**Michèle Sato** is Professor in the Institute of Education at the Federal University of Mato Grosso, Brazil. She is a member of the Environmental Education, Communication and Art Research Group, and develops educational activities with social movements, mainly through popular education. She is also a member of the Human and Earth Right Commission, and the Portuguese language Environmental Education Network (Redeluso).

**Juanita Sellwood** is a Torres Strait Islander scholar who teaches in the School of Education at James Cook University, Cairns, Australia. Her family links are to Masig Island in the Torres Strait.

**Regina Silva** is Professor in the Institute of Education at the Federal University of Mato Grosso, Brazil. She is a member of the Environmental Education, Communication and Art Research Group, and develops educational activities with social movements, mainly through popular education. She is also a member of the Human and Earth Right Commission, and the Portuguese language Environmental Education Network (Redeluso).

**George Strack** (Miami) is a teacher and grandfather, and is deeply committed to language and cultural revitalization. George has worked for his tribe in a variety of capacities, including as historic preservation officer.

**Eli S. Suzukovich III** (Little Shell Chippewa-Cree) is a Postdoctoral Fellow in the Department of Psychology at Northwestern University, Chicago, IL, USA. His research focuses on ethno-biology, ethnography, and cultural resource management.

**Eve Tuck** is Associate Professor at the Ontario Institute of Studies in Education, University of Toronto, Canada. Her scholarship focuses on the ethics of social science research and educational research, Indigenous social and political thought, decolonizing research methodologies and theories of change, and the consequences of neoliberal accountability policies on school completion.

**Felecia Watkin Lui** is the Director of Research Training, a teacher in the School of Indigenous Australian Studies and a researcher with the Cairns Institute, at James Cook University, Cairns, Australia. She is a leading Torres Strait Islander scholar, with family links to Badu and Erub Islands.

**Hilary Whitehouse** is the Director of Research, a teacher in the School of Education, and a researcher with the Centre for Research and Innovation in Sustainability Education (CRISE), at James Cook University, Cairns, Australia.

# INTRODUCTION

## Land education: Indigenous, post-colonial, and decolonizing perspectives on place and environmental education research

> The land is always stalking people. The land makes people live right.
> The land looks after us. The land looks after people.
> -Annie Peaches quoted in Basso, *Wisdom Sits in Places,* 1995

This special issue features new empirical and conceptual studies that suggest a range of considerations and practices of land education. In examining and articulating land education, the authors in the issue discuss both the role of Indigenous cosmologies in practices of land education, as well as the necessity of centering historical and current contexts of colonization in education on and in relation to land. In particular, the issue focuses on land education in relation to settler colonial territories: that is, in territory that is Indigenous and which has been and continues to be subject to the forces of colonization through land-based settlement (e.g. the US, Australia, and Brazil). The articles in the special issue delineate how the ongoing colonization of land and peoples are in fact embedded within educators' and researchers' practices and understandings of (environmental) education around the globe. Thus, the audience for this special issue includes all practitioners and researchers concerned with education and, in this venue, specifically those concerned with environment and education.

The special issue also arises as a conversation in relation to the building momentum of place-based education, including how it has been mobilized within the field of environmental education. In part inspired by a recognition that the specifics of geography and community matter for how (environmental) education can and should be engaged, place-based forms of education are steadily evolving with increasing curricular uptake and empirical research. Many authors in the current collection, however, draw attention to concerns with place-based and other forms of environmental education that position themselves as culturally or politically neutral while perpetuating forms of European universalism (Mignolo 2003) and settler colonialism, including understandings of Indigenous peoples as repositories of static forms of cultural knowledge (Friedel 2011).

In this introductory essay we will elaborate on these themes after providing an overview of the nine pieces included in the issue. The articles in this collection were selected from among those that were submitted in response to an open call for articles on the topic of 'Land education: Indigenous, post-colonial, and decolonizing perspectives on place and environmental education research.' The majority of articles are written on or in relation to land located in the US (e.g. New York, Illinois, Virginia, Hawaii, California, Alaska, and cross-state), as well as one paper about Australia and one about Brazil. Authors cross nations in their origins, locations, and writing focus. Many of the articles' authors belong to Indigenous nations

(Ojibwe, Lakota, Choctaw, Little Shell Band of Chippewa-Cree, Miami, Diné, including others). In other cases, authors based in Canada write mainly about events in Alaska (Korteweg and Oakley); authors writing on the Australian curriculum reside in Australia and Canada (Whitehouse et al.); authors writing about an African-centered curriculum write in the context of the US (Engel Di-Mauro and Carroll).

While topical themes of similarity and divergence crisscross the articles, the first half of the issue features articles on the possibilities of land education in relation to particular disciplinary and formal education domains: of K-12 social studies education (Calderon), K-12 science education (Bang et al.), K-12 cross-curricular education (Whitehouse et al.), and Africana Studies and Geography post-secondary education courses (Engel di-Mauro and Carroll). The remaining articles focus on education more generally and/or in relation to popular and non-formal contexts, and are grouped together because they offer more specific examples of land education pedagogy at work: through historical analysis (McCoy), food sovereignty (Meyer), social mapping (Sato et al.), critical cartography and ethnography (Paperson), and film analysis (Korteweg and Oakley). The range of research and teaching methodologies represented here is also of note – including social mapping, critical cartography, ethnography, historical analysis, community-based design research, document and film analysis, and conceptual essay, and will be discussed further towards the end of the introduction.

Though some may attempt to dismiss discussions of settler colonialism as overly concerned with the past, settler colonialism is important to analyze because it 'relies upon assumptions about other cultures that are alive and well in the most powerful societies in the contemporary world' (Hinkson 2012, 1). As Indigenous (Eve Tuck) and non-Indigenous (Kate McCoy and Marcia McKenzie) co-editors of the issue, writing from settler colonial countries of the US and Canada, we embarked on editing this special issue because of our commitment to the issues discussed herein. Bridging fields and considerations of settler colonial studies, Indigenous studies, and environmental education is a challenging but necessary task, and we appreciate the work of the authors and readers of this issue towards furthering the important considerations and practices discussed in this collection. As Calderon (this issue) outlines, the intersections of environmentalism and Indigenous rights have long been articulated by Indigenous communities, scholars, activists, and allies, with recent global Indigenous social movements demanding broader dialog and action on these intersections. This issue contributes to these intentions, suggesting why and how education, including environmental education, might better account for the history, present, and future by attending to its embedded issues of colonialism and Indigenous rights and sovereignty.

## Overview of the articles

The first four articles of the special issue discuss and provide examples of land education in the context of K-12 education (social studies education, science education, and cross-curricular), post-secondary education, and community-based education. In the first article, 'Speaking back to Manifest Destinies: a land education-based approach to critical curriculum inquiry,' Dolores Calderon suggests how land education can move place-based education forward, 'especially its potential for centering indigeneity and confronting educational forms of settler colonialism'

(24). She outlines how through the US social studies curriculum, K-12 schooling transmits a settler colonial land ethic and suggests that a limitation of much place-based education has been a lack of meaningful engagement of such colonial legacies in education, including through conceptualizations of place. Land education, according to Calderon, should involve an analysis of territoriality and settler colonialism; center Indigenous realities (e.g. include a history of the land as Indigenous, require that Indigenous peoples lead discussions regarding land education in communities, and be infused with Indigenous metaphysics); and destabilize the focus on local (i.e. acknowledge how global histories and broader ideologies shape the local). Building on the language of 'decolonization' and 'reinhabitation' used in much recent place-based work (Gruenewald 2003), Calderon emphasizes that 'land education takes up what place-based education fails to consider: the ways in which place is foundational to settler colonialism' (33). She suggests that environmental education has an overdue responsibility to make visible and begin to address the assumptions of settler colonialism within the field.

The second article by Megan Bang, Lawrence Curley, Adam Kessel, Ananda Marin, Eli Suzukovich III, and George Strack is titled 'Muskrat theories, tobacco in the streets, and living Chicago as Indigenous land.' Framed in relation to science education as environmental education, Bang and colleagues offer powerful descriptions and examples of 'urban Indigenous land-based pedagogies' (39). The authors advocate for the necessity of science education given current socio-scientific realities (such as climate change) that are shaping the land and the lives that the land supports, including those of both Indigenous and non-Indigenous peoples. They propose science education as a site of potential transformation due to its relationships to epistemologies and ontologies of land and Indigenous futurity. They suggest, however, that achieving this potential requires 'desettling dynamics of settler colonialism that remain quietly buried in educational environments that engage learning about, with and in the land and all of its dwellers' (39). Questioning the possibilities for Indigenous peoples in current forms of place-based education, Bang et al. express concerns about the reification of western intellectual traditions. Their article, in contrast, describes the theoretical and practical tools they developed to collaborate with Native youth, families, and community members in relation to urban science and environmental learning environments in order to (re)story Chicago as Indigenous lands. Informed by the work of Smith (1999), Bang and her co-authors aspire to 'work within a methodological paradigm of decolonization' (39) in undertaking community-based design research. The article does important theoretical work in enacting critical readings of place-based education that are informed by settler colonial studies, establishing Indigenous presence in urban educational contexts, and disrupting settler zero point epistemologies – those epistemologies that deny other perspectives and truths – in environmental education.

Changing continents with 'Sea Country: navigating Indigenous and colonial ontologies in Australian environmental education,' authors Hilary Whitehouse, Felecia Watkin Lui, Juanita Sellwood, Mary Jeanne Barrett, and Philemon Chigeza analyze the positioning of Torres Strait Sea Country and Torres Strait *Ailan Kastom* (Island Custom) in relation to Australian K-12 environmental education curriculum and practice. Importantly, this paper identifies the ways that sea is part of 'land,' and also embedded within cosmology and history (Styres, Haig-Brown, and Blimkie 2013). The authors provide a rich description of Indigenous Torres Strait Islanders' understandings of 'Sea Country,' as not categorized by a binary opposition between 'people' and 'environment,' but rather as a totality of complex relationships. Likewise, *Ailan Kaston*, or native title derived from customary law, sets out particular relationships of connection with and care for the sea. The article describes how colonial settlement, supported by the 'legal fiction of *terra nullius*' (61), introduced the concept of the sea as a public commons and the related impacts on relationships and the 'management' of the area. Turning to the pedagogical implications of and for Sea Country, the second half of the article exposes the ways that Indigenous cosmology is simultaneously supported and ignored in the cross-curricular priorities in the first 11 years of the Australian national school curriculum, including in the 'Sustainability' priority area.

Focusing on post-secondary level classrooms in the US, Salvatore Engel-Di Mauro and Karanja Keita Carroll offer 'An African-centered approach to land education.' The paper discusses the role of the 'native-slave-settler triad' in the settlement of the US and other settler colonial contexts (Wolfe 2006) and outlines the necessity of also examining the history of chattel slaves (mostly from Africa) who were kept landless and made into property along with Indigenous land as part of the settlement process in the US and elsewhere. Offering examples of place-based and environmental education that the authors find problematic, they suggest that 'Eurocentrism must be exploded at its roots,' with African-centered environmental education curricula making contributions in this respect. They utilize examples from Africana Studies and Geography to illustrate the contributions an African-centered approach can make to land education in the context of college-level environmental education. Such an approach, the authors argue, promotes an integrative view of nature and people, histories, power relations, and community that can challenge settler colonial assumptions that undergird much of environmental education.

The second half of the special issue is comprised of five articles that enact land education through various types of analyses in particular locations. Kate McCoy's article, 'Manifesting Destiny: a land education analysis of settler colonialism in Jamestown, VA USA,' maps the discursive and material relations that produce(d) Manifest Destiny and the settler colonial triad in the US. The paper outlines how discourses arising from the emerging modernism of seventeenth-century Protestant Christianity articulated a new interpretation of the creation story, calling for human dominion over the earth and its creatures. These and other discourses, McCoy suggests, joined with the practices the English created as they established capitalist enterprise in what they called Jamestown, Virginia. Such enterprise included growing commercial tobacco for export, creating the material conditions and justifications for taking Indigenous land and introducing slavery. These discourses, practices, and relations, McCoy argues, established the settler colonial triad in the English colonies that became known as the US. Settlers still undertake large-scale monoculture and environmental degradation in areas around the globe and continue to cover their tracks using Manifest Destiny – in discourse, practice, and relation – in the contemporary name of 'development' to justify settler colonialism past and present. McCoy's study exemplifies how historical analysis of settler colonialism in the US can inform land education and environmental education.

In 'Hoea Ea: land education and food sovereignty in Hawaii,' Manulani Meyer uses photographs and accompanying narratives to share two land education efforts in the Hawaiian Islands. In the Limahui valley in the *ahupua'a* of *Hā'ena* on the island of Kauai, the ancient Hawaiian staple food taro (*lo'i kalo*) is being grown utilizing traditional land, methods, and management practices (established

700–1000 years ago). It is used to sustainably feed a large population and honor taro's cosmological role in Hawaiian origin stories. Meyer describes the methods used and their importance, highlighting the threat of encroachment as profit-driven systems close in. The second photograph depicts the Kaiao Youth Community Garden in Hilo Ho'ea, as part of a food sovereignty movement in Hawaii. She describes the history and aims of the project as it works to promote a native Hawaiian view of land and sustenance as land education.

A social mapping methodology for land education research and practice in settler colonial Brazil is articulated by Michèle Sato, Regina Silva, and Michelle Jaber in their article 'Between the remnants of colonialism and the insurgence of self-narrative in constructing participatory social maps: towards a land education methodology.' Sato and colleagues discuss maps as weapons of imperialism, but also as tools that can be used to better understand settler colonialism, including its ongoing effects on vulnerable communities. The article reports on a large-scale empirical study undertaken with 239 participants from diverse groups from the Mato Grosso Region in Brazil, a territory initially colonized by the Portuguese. Study data were gathered through interviews, discussions of mapped results, photo and video material, and participant observation, using a process of iterative mapping of participants' self-narratives. The authors suggest that this process is a powerful tool for land education in that it allows the mapping of social identities, 'recognizing land as an epistemological basis for understanding people's lives' (108). They use the methodology to map the identities of vulnerable groups and the social and environmental conflicts that affect them, in efforts to render these groups and the challenges they face visible. In doing so, the project aims to contribute to responsive and participatory land and environmental policy, and provides an example of social mapping as environmental education.

In 'A ghetto land pedagogy: an antidote for settler environmentalism,' Paperson draws on ethnographic research and historical analysis to provide a 'critical cartography' of the San Francisco Bay area of California. Weaving together stories of the histories of Indigenous land and settlement, Paperson provides an unsettling land education that examines the San Quentin prison, student responses to an Urban Ecology lesson, and an analysis of the 2011 Occupy movement. Paperson characterizes the settler view of 'ghetto' land as *terra sacer*, the contemporary mutation of the colonial fiction of *terra nullius* or empty land that justifies the doctrine of colonial discovery. *Terra sacer* is theorized as simultaneously sacred and accursed land, ripe for re-settling through gentrification, the way paved in part by environmental education that aims toward settler sustainability. In contrast, Paperson outlines the ways that storied land can serve as 'an important connecting node between Indigenous struggle and black resistance' (126), and through the vignettes shared, outlines how youth and communities enact agency and resistance in the face of settler (and environmentalist) assumptions of land and occupation. Critiquing the language of 'reinhabitation' used in place-based education, Paperson works to exemplify the ways in which 'decolonization is not just symbolic; its material core is repatriation of native life and land, which is incommensurable with settler re-inhabitation of native land' (124).

Finally, Lisa Korteweg and Jan Oakley critically analyze the eco-heroic quest as depicted in Hollywood movies in their article 'Eco-heroes out of place and relations: decolonizing the narratives of *Into the Wild* and *Grizzly Man* through Land education.' This kind of criticism, at the intersection of post-colonial/decolonizing methodologies and Indigenous studies, gestures toward a land education critical of such representations and attentive to Indigenous stories and teachings of land already in place in order to interrupt settler fantasies of becoming native. They propose to offer a counter-narrative of how environmental education might enter into more respectful relations with Indigenous peoples in protecting Indigenous lands. The paper also elaborates the ways in which 'environmental damage to the land/ animals (through resource extraction, animal extinction, land clearance, and pollution) [is] intertwined inextricably with socio cultural genocide to the Indigenous peoples of the land' (132). The conflicting representations of the films' protagonists as offering both examples of 'good inhabitance' of place and at other times of being 'dangerously out of place' suggests the tensions in the aspirations of 'reinhabitation through environmental place-based theories' on and in relation to Indigenous land (140).

## Key contributions of the collection: descriptions and departures

Having provided a preliminary introduction to the various contributions of the issue, we now turn to drawing out further some of the key issues that are raised in the articles. In particular, we elaborate on settler colonial studies as discussed in the articles as central to land education, meanings of 'land' as mobilized in the issue, the agency in old and new movements to recognize land and Indigenous claims to land, and the role of naming as part of land education. We conclude with sections addressing the question 'Why land education?' in relation to place-based and environmental education, and discussing modes and methodologies of what counts as environmental education research.

### *Land and settler colonialism*

Theories of colonialism have largely focused on what is sometimes called exogenous domination (Veracini 2011), exploitation colonialism, or external colonialism – three names for the same form. In this form of colonization, small numbers of colonizers go to a new place in order to dominate a local labor force to harvest resources to send back to the metropole, for example the spice and opium trade that impelled the colonization of India by several different European empires. Exploitation colonialism, its nature, consequences, endgame, and post-possibilities have been the focus of (what would become) the field of post-colonial studies for the past 50 years.

It has only been in the last two decades that *settler* colonialism has been more comprehensively theorized, mostly via the emergence of the field of settler colonial studies. As already indicated, *settler* colonialism is a form of colonization in which outsiders come to land inhabited by Indigenous peoples and claim it as their own new home (see also Hinkson 2012). Subsequent generations of settlers come to the settler nation-state for many reasons, under many circumstances – but at the heart of all of those rationales is the need for space and land. This form is distinct from the exploitation colonialism that has been so deeply theorized in post-colonial studies, because, in settler colonialism, settlers come to the new land seeking land and resources, not (necessarily) labor (Wolfe 2011). Though there are many important parallels and connections between these forms of colonialism, especially as settler colonial nation-states also occupy and colonize other lands, there are important differences to be teased apart (see also Hinkson 2012). For example, Veracini (2011) observes that exploitation colonizers and settler colonizers want very different things: the exploitation colonizer says to the Indigenous person, 'you, work for me,' whereas the settler colonizer – because land is the primary pursuit – says to the Indigenous person, 'you, go away' (1). Of course, in reality, settler colonizers communicate an amalgamation of these messages to Indigenous peoples; Veracini observes that the accumulating sentiment may be more like, 'you, work for me while we wait for you to disappear,' or 'you, move on so you can work for me,' but the base intention of settlers has been to disappear Indigenous peoples from the land to make it available for settlement (2).

One of the notable characteristics of settler colonial states is the refusal to recognize themselves as such, requiring a continual disavowal of history, Indigenous peoples' resistance to settlement, Indigenous peoples' claims to stolen land, and how settler colonialism is indeed ongoing, not an event contained in the past. Settler colonialism is made invisible within settler societies, and uses institutional apparatuses to 'cover its tracks' (Veracini 2011). For example, most non-Indigenous people living in settler societies, if they think of colonizers and/or settlers at all, think of Captain James Cook, Christopher Columbus, colonies, and forts (Donald 2012; see Hinkson 2012 for a discussion of the colonization of Australia). They think of colonization as something that happened in the distant past, as perhaps the unfortunate birthpangs of a new nation. They do not consider the fact that they live on land that has been stolen, or ceded through broken treaties, or to which Indigenous peoples claim a pre-existing ontological and cosmological relationship.[1] They do not consider themselves to be implicated in the continued settlement and occupation of unceded Indigenous land. Indeed, settler colonial societies 'cover' the 'tracks' of settler colonialism by narrating colonization as temporally located elsewhere, not here and now (Veracini 2011).

Another of the general characteristics of settler societies is that settlers are located at the top and at the center of all typologies – as simultaneously most superior and most normal (Tuck and Yang 2012). These typologies include settler/Indigenous, but also the hegemony of settlers over non-Indigenous workers. These hierarchies are established through force, policy, law, and ideology, and are so embedded that they become naturalized. Morgensen (2011) theorizes settler colonialism as biopower, observing that 'the biopolitics of settler colonialism arose in the Americas by perpetuating African diasporic subjugation and Indigenous elimination simultaneously,' (57). Thus, in several contexts, settler colonialism has simultaneously taken form as 'Slave estates' (Spillers 2003; Wilderson 2010) requiring the forced labor of stolen peoples on stolen land. In these cases, settlement require[d/s] the labor of chattel slaves and guest workers, who must be kept landless and estranged from their homelands. For example, as detailed in Kate McCoy's article in this special issue, Tsenecommacah peoples were killed, displaced, and otherwise removed from areas surrounding colonies in Virginia, as Black men and women were brought from Africa to be bought and sold to labor the land. Indeed, as discussed in several of the articles in the issue (Engel-Di Mauro and Carroll, McCoy, Paperson), settler colonialism 'works' by making Indigenous land into property, and designating the bodies of slaves as property, or chattel (Tuck and Yang 2012). This same 'triad' dynamic continues to operate in North America and elsewhere in the working and living conditions of migrant workers (Byrd 2011; Patel 2012).

A final general characteristic of settler colonialism is its attempt (and failure) to contain Indigenous agency and resistance. Indigenous peoples have refused settler encroachment, even while losing their lives and homelands. Writing about Aotearoa/New Zealand, Smith (2011) cites the long history of Maori resistance to settler invasion, describing the settler nation's need to 'continually code, decode, and re-code social norms and social spaces so as to secure a meaningful (read: *proprietary*) relationship to the territories and resources at stake' (112, parentheses original). Thus, when we theorize settler colonialism, we must attend to it as both an ongoing and incomplete project, with internal contradictions, cracks and fissures through which Indigenous life and knowledge have persisted and thrived despite settlement.

In attending to these conditions of settler colonialism, land education calls into question educational practices and theories that justify settler occupation of stolen land, or encourage the replacement of Indigenous peoples and relations to land with settlers and relations to property. The articles in this special issue instead seek to intervene upon settler colonialist narratives of land by refusing accounts of the past, present, and future that are only accountable to settler futurities. That is, in land education settler futurities are dislocated as the central referent for the effectiveness of an interpretation, the viability of a theory, or the possibility of reinvisionings or reimaginations. Instead, land education is accountable to Indigenous futurities, as is discussed further below.

### *Land and Indigenous cosmologies*

A second key consideration of the special issue that we want to highlight is how 'land' is understood and engaged in the articles of the collection. These understandings and practices draw on long and vibrant trajectories of Indigenous practice and theory that understand land as encompassing all of the earth, including the urban, and as much more than just the material. In this section, we discuss these considerations of land as they link to Indigenous cosmology and land education.

'Land' is used in the special issue as shorthand for land, water, air, and subterranean earth – for example, in discussions of wetlands (Bang et al.) and Sea Country (Whitehorse et al.). Among Indigenous peoples, relationships to land and place are diverse, specific, and un-generalizable (Lowan 2009):

> Every cultural group established their relations to [their place] over time. Whether that place is in the desert, a mountain valley, or along a seashore, it is in the context of natural community, and through that understanding they established an educational process that was practical, ultimately ecological, and spiritual. In this way they sought and found their life. (Cajete 1994, 113, as cited in Lowan 2009, 47)

'Land' is imbued with these long relationships and, as we discuss below, the pedagogies and knowledges that have emerged from those relationships.

Significantly, authors in the collection also include the urban in their understandings and practices of land. Land and land education are not considered to occur only outside cities, or in 'green spaces' within the urban. Rather, several articles focus specifically on urban land, making the case for the need for pedagogies that examine and experience the urban as storied Indigenous land. In (re)storying Chicago as Indigenous land through 'urban Indigenous land-based pedagogies,'

Bang and colleagues write, 'A critical dimension of the work was making visible settler colonial constructions of urban lands as ceded and no longer Indigenous' (39). Likewise, Paperson (this issue) focuses on the urban context in hir discussion of 'ghetto colonialism' as an active specialization of settler colonialism in North America and as an important focus for land education.

As Styres, Haig-Brown, and Blimkie (2013) recently articulated in discussing a 'pedagogy of Land,' (echoing Cajete 1994; Lowan 2009) 'land' refers not just to the materiality of land, but also its 'spiritual, emotional, and intellectual aspects' (37). These scholars choose to signify consideration of these aspects in their capitalization of Land (as do Korteweg and Oakley; and Engel-Di Mauro and Carroll, this issue) and indicate they build on the work of Styres and Zinga (2013) in this respect:

> We have chosen to capitalize Land when we are referring to it as a proper name indicating a primary relationship rather than when used in a more general sense. For us, land (the more general term) refers to landscapes as a fixed geographical and physical space that includes earth, rocks, and waterways; whereas, 'Land' (the proper name) extends beyond a material fixed space. Land is a spiritually infused place grounded in interconnected and interdependent relationships, cultural positioning, and is highly contextualized. (300–301)

Thus, the word 'land' is also used in this special issue to convey these interwoven dimensions.

Relational pedagogies of land are not new, as Bang and colleagues discuss in their article in this issue. They write,

> Indigenous scholars have focused much attention on relationships between land, epistemology and importantly, ontology. Places produce and teach particular ways of thinking about and being in the world. They tell us the way things are, even when they operate pedagogically beneath a conscious level (44).

Or, in other words, land can be considered as a teacher and conduit of memory (Brooks 2008; Wilson 2005), in that it 'both remembers life and its loss and serves itself as a mnemonic device that triggers the ethics of relationality with the sacred geographies that constitute Indigenous peoples' histories' (Byrd 2011, 118).

Relationships to land are familial, intimate, intergenerational, and instructive. For example, special issue contributor Manulani Aluli Meyer writes elsewhere,

> Land is our mother. *This is not a metaphor.* For the Native Hawaiians speaking of knowledge, land was the central theme that drew forth all others. You came from a place. You grew in a place and you had a relationship with a place. *This is an epistemological idea* … One does not simply learn about land, we learn best *from* land. (2008, 219, italics original; ellipses inserted)

Land teaches and can be considered as first teacher (Styres, Haig-Brown, and Blimkie 2013). Yup'ik scholar Angayuqaq Oscar Kawagley writes that for Yupiaq people, land and nature are 'metaphysic' and pedagogical:

> It is through direct interaction with the environment that the Yupiaq people learn. What they learn is mediated by the cultural cognitive map. The map consists of those 'truths' that have been proven over a long period of time. As the Yupiaq people

> interact with nature, they carefully observe to find pattern or order where there might otherwise appear to be chaos. (2010a, 88)

He continues, 'It was meaningless for Yupiaq to count, measure, and weigh, for their wisdom transcended the quantification of things to recognize a qualitative level whereby the spiritual, natural, and human worlds were inextricably interconnected' (90). Kawagley's rendering of Yupiaq relations to land braids together the cosmological, pedagogical, pragmatic, and spiritual.

Relationships to land within Indigenous frameworks are not between owner and property, as typified in settler societies. As discussed in McCoy's paper in this issue, property is an enabling concept in a settler colonial framework, with property and property ownership being individualized. Instead, land is collective. Bang et al. invoke Burkhart's (2004) revision of Descartes' insistence, 'I think, therefore I am,' to 'We are, therefore I am,' to express the saliency of collectivity in Indigenous life and knowledge systems (this issue, 44). Bang et al. continue,

> Similarly, we might imagine that ontology of place-based paradigms is something like 'I am, therefore place is,' in contrast, the ontology of land-based pedagogies might be summarized as 'Land is, therefore we are.' (45)

Clearly, Bang et al. differentiate place-based education from land education because of the ontologies that animate them. Understandings of collectivity and shared (though not necessarily synchronous) relations to land are core attributes of land education. Further – and this is not a romantic point – the *land-we* ontology articulated by Bang et al. is incommensurable with notions of ownership that are so integral to notions of property.

Styres, Haig-Brown, and Blimkie (2013), Meyer (2008), and Kawagley (2010a) and others also warn against understandings of Indigenous knowledge of land as static or performable. Calderon (this issue) emphasizes embracing protocols 'that are mindful of how Indigenous knowledge has been co-opted and omitted' (28), including for example expectations that Indigenous peoples lead discussions on land education. This mindfulness of co-option also entails an acknowledgment that Indigenous identities and knowledge are not static, and that non-Indigenous desires for performances of 'authentic' Indigeneity are also problematic. Friedel (2011) outlines this concern well in her paper on 'urban Native youth's cultured responses to Western place-based learning' in western Canada. The youth in the study resisted the stereotypes and expectations of the white educators for them to 'get back to nature,' instead holding fast to their own desires for social experiences and connections, wanting to 'to learn to be Aboriginal without being in the woods' (535). Friedel (2011) writes:

> Of the pernicious representations of Indigeneity today, none is more equivocal than the trope of 'the Ecological Indian.' Borne from nineteenth-century romantic primitivism, this White construction (Bird 1996) has become a prevalent signifier in the environmental realm, an ideal to which Canadians and others look today for a critique of Western institutions (534).

As this point suggests, mindfulness of non-Indigenous desires to access assumed Indigenous knowledge also needs to extend to a mindfulness of non-Indigenous desires to adopt or use such knowledge (e.g. critiques of the formulations and uses of 'traditional ecological knowledge,' as in Agrawal 2002). This is difficult terrain in working both with Indigenous and non-Indigenous learners: to acknowledge and include Indigenous knowledge and perspectives but in non-determined ways that do not stereotype Indigenous knowledge or identities. The creative resistance of students and instructors are perhaps the best teachers in walking this path (Bang this issue; Paperson this issue; Friedel 2011; Styres, Haig-Brown, and Blimkie 2013).

### *Land and agency: Indigenous land rights and social movements*

In addition to elaborating on the special issue themes of settler colonialism and Indigenous cosmologies in relation to land, we also want to highlight the themes of agency and resistance in relation to land education and environmental education more broadly. The role of agency in environmental education can be manifested at the level of participating students (e.g. Paperson's discussion of youth resistance to educators' expectations of white middle-class environmentalism or as in Friedel's 2011 study discussed above), and a number of articles in the issue suggest forms of land education that are participatory and open-ended in ways that aim to center participant input and agency (e.g. Bang et al.; Sato, Silva and Jaber; Whitehouse et al.).

Articles in the special issue also highlight and exemplify agency and resistance through forms of land education that explicitly address settler colonialism in relation to futurities of Indigenous land and life. Discussing 'organizing rooted in storytelling,' Paperson provides a land-based ethnography of past and present Indigenous resistance to colonialism in the San Francisco Bay area. In contrast to narrations of 'Indian resistance … as a lost cause of a vanishing race and dying culture' (125), Paperson highlights past and present circumstances of resistance as land education curriculum. Likewise, Sato, Silva, and Jaber (this issue) offer as land education the mapping and distribution of the stories of land-based exploitation and resistance within the Mato Grosso Region of Brazil. Thus, countering the 'institutionalization of territoriality in settler colonialism' (Calderon this issue, 30), authors in the special issue offer compelling articulations and examples of agency towards more ethical relations on and with land.

This work builds on existing trajectories of Indigenous resistance and movement building. Describing a 1970 meeting of Indigenous scholars at Princeton, Cook-Lynn (1997) writes that the participants asserted the foremost concerns of the then-emerging field of Native American Studies as the 'defense of Indigenous land and rights' (9). Participants emphasized the '*endogenous* study of First Nations cultures and history,' (11, italics original) that is, the study of Indigenous lives and issues *by* Indigenous peoples. Smith (1999/2013), Wilson (2008), Kovach (2010), and Chilisa (2011) describe corresponding central commitments within Indigenous studies emerging in New Zealand, Australia, Canada, and Botswana. Likewise, the intersections of environmentalism and Indigenous rights have long been articulated by Indigenous communities, activists and allies (Calderon, this issue). As discussed in several of the articles, *Idle No More* and prior global Indigenous social movements have intensified the demands from Indigenous communities and allies for dialog and action on Indigenous land rights and sovereignty. Paperson theorizes how these very concepts of rights, sovereignty, and justice take on significantly divergent inflections in Indigenous movements and lexicons than in settler colonial lexicons: 'Aboriginal sovereignty is different from state sovereignty because it embraces diversity and focuses on inclusivity rather than exclusivity (Watson 2007, 20, as quoted in Paperson, 123). As part of, and allied with, these trajectories and movements, this special issue on land education prioritizes Indigenous theorizing, Indigenous land rights, and Indigenous sovereignty.

### *The significance of naming: language, thought, and land*

Yup'ik scholar Angayuqaq Oscar Kawagley said often that Mother Nature has a culture, and it is a Native culture (2010b). Connecting language and land, Rasmussen and Akulukjuk (2009) insist that when discussing environmental education, the crucial question is, *what language does the environment speak?* 'In Nunavut,' the authors say, 'the land speaks Inuktitut' (285). By this they mean that the land and sea have 'evolved' an Indigenous language to communicate with and through human beings, a language that 'grew in [an] area over thousands of years of interaction between the elements and the human and plant and animal beings' (285). Noting that this point is likely obvious to Indigenous readers, they go on to assure those who view it as a 'dislocated phenomenon' that language is not something developed in isolation in human brains, but in relationship to land and water (285).

In an example of the intimate relationships between land, language, and thought from Alaska, Iñupiaq scholar Edna Ahgeak MacLean speaks to life in a world that would appear to outsiders as barren and frozen:

> People use their language to organize their reality. Iñupiaq and Yup'ik cultures are based on dependence on the land and sea. Hunting, and therefore a nomadic way of life has persisted. The sea and land that people depend on for their sustenance are almost totally devoid of landmarks. These languages have therefore developed an elaborate set of demonstrative pronouns and adverbs that are used to direct the listener's attention quickly to the nature and location of an object. In place of landmarks, words serve as indicators about proximity, visibility, or vertical position and implies whether the object is inside or outside, moving or not moving, long or short. For example, Inupiaq has at least 22 stems that are used to form demonstrative pronouns in eight different cases and demonstrative adverbs in four cases. American English has two demonstrative pronouns [this and that] (plural forms these and those), with their respective adverbs here and there. (MacLean 2010, 49)

In a recent interview, Anishinaabe writer Gerald Vizenor asserted that language is among the most powerful forms of Indigenous resistance (Vizenor, Tuck, and Yang 2014). Many generations of Indigenous intellectuals have insisted on the power of words to make change and ensure self-determination and well-being (Deloria 1969; Smith 1999/2013), and along with Kawagley, MacLean, Rassmussen, and Akulukjuk, we see this power as derived from the rootedness of (Indigenous) languages in land.

All of the articles in this special issue are written in English, despite the limitations of the language that Indigenous authors have identified above (see also Chambers 2008). Indeed, 'Native languages contain the map of the common pot' – or the 'hollowed out places' formed by river intervales where Abenaki families lived in community – says Abenaki scholar Brooks (2008). '(B)ut writing in English is the means through which its boundaries have been maintained, asserted, and reclaimed' (254). This is to say that the work of making space for, and recognizing the sovereignty of Indigenous knowledges and languages can be accomplished in English, even if nuanced and sophisticated renderings of land-based concepts are made more possible within Indigenous languages. Bang et al. (this issue) argue that language work is necessary to confront the reification of settler colonialism and Western intellectual traditions in place-based pedagogies (see also Bowers 2003). These reifications, according to Bang et al., are akin to zero point epistemologies which erase and disavow all other perspectives; they perform an epistemic violence on Indigenous knowledges, eclipsing Indigenous points of reference. Thus, the authors argue that a focus on language is required in order to 'rupture' the cognitive imperialism of the zero point of Eurocentric universalism and its rule over ontology and epistemology. Likewise, other authors in the special issue point to the necessity of disrupting the 'rhetorical power of European universalism' (Mignolo 2003 in Sato, Silva, and Jaber this issue, 104) or the 'cognitive imperialism' (Battiste 2000) embedded in the language and assumptions of many forms of (environmental) education. The significance of naming and language is evident across all nine of the articles in this special issue, and thus can be understood as an important feature of land education.

### *Why 'land education'?*

Land education puts Indigenous epistemological and ontological accounts of land at the center, including Indigenous understandings of land, Indigenous language in relation to land, and Indigenous critiques of settler colonialism. It attends to constructions and storying of land and repatriation by Indigenous peoples, documenting and advancing Indigenous agency and land rights. We have highlighted these aspects of land education as they are built through and across many of the articles in this special issue, and suggest that these characteristics advance environmental education practice and research in important ways. In this section, we briefly outline some of the linkages in prior writing on these themes within (environmental) education, before turning to discuss in more depth how the characteristics of 'land education,' as discussed so far and as elaborated throughout the issue, relate to those of 'place-based education' as it has been evolving in the research literature to date.

Land education, as we have constructed it here, emphasizes educational research that engages acute analyses of settler colonialism as a structure, a set of relations and conditions. Certainly, work has been undertaken on colonialism and land in environmental education fora by Indigenous scholars. For example, the work of O'Riley and Cole (2009) has grappled with Indigenous and settler relationships to land and education in a Canadian context; Donald (2012) has theorized the centrality of the 'fort on frontier' as a signifier for the myth of civilization and modernity in the creation story of the Canadian nation-state; Le Grange (2009), Shava (2013), and others have written about colonialism and Indigenous knowledge in relation to environmental education research and practice in southern Africa.

Other work by Indigenous and non-Indigenous scholars has taken up a focus on decolonization in relation to environmental education, but typically not with a critique of how colonialism in many contexts has involved settlement and displacement as part of the land-based structure of colonialism in settler colonial contexts. For example, Chambers (2008), learning from collaborations with several First

Nations communities in Northwest Territories in Canada, writes that there are four dimensions of a 'curriculum of place.' They include (as section headings):

(1) A curriculum of place calls for a different sense of time.
(2) A curriculum of place is enskillment.
(3) A curriculum of place calls for an 'education of attention'.
(4) A curriculum of place is a wayfinding.

Together, these dimensions try to teach and learn how more than one people might call a place home (215). A curriculum of place is configured to redress settlement and determine a shared (long) future. Chambers quotes Andy Blackwater, a Kainai elder, who said 'The Blackfoot are not going anywhere; the newcomers are not going anywhere; now the same peg anchors the tips of both' (in Chambers 2008, 125). Chambers continues, 'It is not the grudge but the grief that matters, and what we are going to do about it' (125).

In contrast to Chambers' aims of a curriculum of place, articles in a 2012 special issue of the *Canadian Journal of Environmental Education* on *Decolonizing + Indigenizing: Moving Environmental Education Towards Reconciliation* (edited by Lisa Korteweg and Connie Russell) trouble notions of a shared future that is not preceded by a process of decolonization. Articles in the issue warn against temptations to try to 'skip ahead' to 'some neutralized ahistorical, guilt-free, pain-free, "romanticized" version of environmental education' (Korteweg and Russell 2012, 8). The articles in the special issue belie the seduction of claiming Indigenous land as 'our' (settlers') 'special places' where feeling connected to the natural world is possible; they also contravene claims that 'gifted/enlightened non-Indigenous environmental or outdoor educators are the chosen ones to learn and pass on Indigenous knowledge and traditions' (Korteweg and Russell 2012, 8). Korteweg and Russell emphasize the importance of decolonization and 'Indigenizing' – 'actively recognizing, centring, validating, and honouring Indigenous rights, values, epistemologies or worldviews, knowledge, language, and the stories of the people of the Land' (7) in environmental education toward reconstituting a shared future, or perhaps parallel futures, for settlers and Indigenous peoples.[2]

The aforementioned works withstanding, it is rare to find explicit discussions of settler colonialism, decolonization, and Indigenous conceptualizations of land within environmental education research. Much of the work in environmental education research that is most conversant or related to what authors in this special issue are distinguishing as land education is described under the banner of 'place-based education,' so it makes sense to speak to how and why, at least for now, land education is distinct from place-based education. Our hope, of course, is that place-based education practitioners and researchers take more seriously and address more explicitly the contexts of settler colonialism, the conditions and diversely articulated aims of decolonization, and the epistemologically and ontologically distinct understandings of land lived by Indigenous peoples. Toward this end, we now attend to some of the shared ground and departures between place-based education and land education.

One of the core occupations of place-based education is facilitating meaningful relationships to place. Indeed, because of human-caused carbon emissions and other dangers to climate and planetary stability, this work is necessary in part to cultivate the humility needed to ensure the *future* of places (see Gruenewald and Smith

2008, xix). Alan Gussow describes place as 'a piece of the whole environment which has been claimed by feelings' (quoted in Knapp 2008, 5). Gruenewald observes,

> For the most part, place-based educators use the term 'place' synonymously with 'community.' Indeed, both place-based and community-based educators advocate using diverse communities as 'texts' for curriculum development and engaging teachers and learners in direct experience and inquiry projects that lead to democratic participation and social action within the local environment. (2008, 143)

Gruenewald continues by noting that an important distinction between place-based education and community-based education is that place-based education is intentionally non-anthropocentric. Further, he clarifies, place-based education is committed to attending to what social and cultural theories overlook, including the land, natural environment, and non-human world (2008, 143).

The praxes of place-based education have forwarded important discussions that would otherwise have been silenced, particularly the works of David Greenwood/Gruenewald and others who have invoked descriptions of a critical pedagogy of place to attend to the need for decolonization and anti-oppression. Yet, though earnest in attempts to acknowledge colonial histories of particular places, the place-based and broader environmental education literature has replicated some of the very problematic assumptions and imperatives of settler colonialism (see Bang et al.; Calderon this issue). This collection draws readers' attention to these issues not to point fingers, but to underscore the need for works in land education that examine currents of settler colonialism as they course through environmental education and research. That is, the articles in this issue outline concerns about desires toward settler emplacement that are often embedded in environmental education and research (see discussions in Bang et al.: Calderon; Engel-Di Mauro and Carroll; Paperson this issue).

'"Settler" is a way to describe colonizers that highlights their desires to be emplaced on Indigenous land' (Morgensen 2009, 157). Settler emplacement, in Morgensen's analysis, is the desire to resolve the experience of dis-location implicit in living on stolen land. A core strategy of emplacement is the discursive and literal replacement of the Native by the settler, evident in laws and policies such as eminent domain (and similar constructs), manifest destiny, property rights, and removals, but also in boarding schools, sustained and broken treaties, adoptions, and resulting 'apologies' (See Coulthard 2007 for a discussion on the politics of reconciliation in Canada). 'Historically, a desire to live on Indigenous land and to feel connected to it – bodily, emotionally, spiritually – has been the normative formation of settlers,' writes settler-scholar Morgensen (2009, 157; see also Korteweg and Oakley this issue).

Here, we wish to differentiate the goal of settler emplacement, which is one way of resolving the colonial situation, from decolonization, which is another way. Settler emplacement, according to Morgensen (2009), can never lead to decolonization.

> Decolonization does not follow if settlers simply study and emulate the lives of Indigenous people on Indigenous land … [this] is relevant in particular to those for whom anarchism links them to communalism and counterculturalism, such as in rural communes, permaculture, squatting, hoboing, foraging, and neo-pagan, earth-based,

> and New Age spirituality. These 'alternative' settler cultures formed by occupying and traversing stolen Indigenous land and often by practicing cultural and spiritual appropriation ... They must ask, then, if their interest to support Indigenous people arose not from an investment in decolonization, but in recolonization (157).

Settler emplacement is incommensurable with decolonization, because at its basis is a drive to replace the native as the rightful claimant of the land. Replacement relies on fantasies of the extinct or becoming-extinct Indian as natural, forgone, inevitable, indeed, and evolutionary (see Tuck and Gaztambide-Fernández 2013). Replacement is invested in settler futurity; in our use, futurity is more than the future, it is how human narratives and perceptions of the past, future, and present inform current practices and framings in a way that (over)determines what registers as the (possible) future. Settler futurity, then, refers to what Andrew Baldwin calls the 'permanent virtuality' (2012, 173) of the settler on stolen land. Theorizing the significance of futurity for researching whiteness and geography, Baldwin (2012) examines whether a history-centered analysis paves the way for the faulty,

> teleological assumption that [settler colonialism] can be modernized away. Such an assumption privileges an ontology of linear causality in which the past is thought to act on the present and the present is said to be an effect of whatever came before [...] According to this kind of temporality, the future is the terrain upon or through which [settler colonialism] will get resolved. It cleaves the future from the present and, thus, gives the future discrete ontological form (174, insertion ours).

Replacement and emplacement, to be clear, are entirely concerned with settler futurity, which always indivisibly means the disruption of Indigenous life to aid settlement. Any form of justice or education that seeks to recuperate and not interrupt settler colonialism, to reform the settlement and incorporate Indigenous peoples into the multicultural settler colonial nation-state is invested in settler futurity.[3]

The resounding critique of place-based education offered by authors in this special issue is that 'it does not go far enough to connect how place ... has been inexorably linked to the genocide of Indigenous peoples and continued settler colonialism' (Calderon, 25; see also Bang et al.; Engel-Di Mauro and Carroll; and Paperson). 'While settler colonial violence and oppression is not an explicit aspect of place-based education,' Calderon continues, 'it nonetheless fails to meaningfully address colonial legacies in education and particularly how conceptions of place have been involved in their continuance' (25). In our view, the specific interventions that land education offers to place-based and environmental educators and researchers are (1) the refusal of emplacement and replacement discourses in place-based education and (2) the refusal of settler futurity as the referent of purpose or justice. We discuss each of these interventions in turn.

### *The refusal of emplacement and replacement discourses in place-based education*

Gruenewald and Smith's influential edited volume, *Place-Based Education in the Global Age* (2008), locates a book by Wes Jackson, called *Becoming Native to this Place* (1996), as providing questions that get at the core themes of place-based education (Gruenewald and Smith 2008, xix). These questions are indeed important, including 'What educational forms promote care for places?' and 'What does it take to conserve, restore, and create ways of being that serve people and places?'

Yet to answer them, Jackson, a settler, problematically advocates adopting a 'national goal' of 'becoming native to this place, this continent' (1996, 3). With no lexiconical self-consciousness, Jackson appropriates a generalized version of Indigenous cultures, invoking the need to form an expanded *tribe,* the need to be *native* in a *modern world.* Mention of the 'first natives here' is entirely contained in the past – 'they' (the Indigenous peoples) were not burdened with the 'exercise of technology assessment' (evaluating uses of fossil fuels and other industrial impacts on the environment), as 'we' (the settlers) must be (3).

Gruenwald's later chapter in the same edited volume employs Jackson's focus on 'becoming native' to aid his introduction to the concept of *reinhabitation* (Gruenewald 2008; see also Greenwood 2013; Greenwood and McKenzie 2009; Swayze 2009). In Gruenewald's words, 'Reinhabitation roughly equates with the deeper agenda of many environmental educators: to learn how to live well together in a place without doing damage to others, human and nonhuman' (2008, 143). In describing her approach to reinhabitation within an environmental education program, Swayze (2009) says it has included these aims, 'embracing the local; using a customized, participatory approach (to inquiry); reconsidering the role of formal curriculum; and, re-thinking what "success" is and how it is measured' (63).

Yet, because these definitions and approaches to reinhabitation do not recognize the settler colonial histories of and Indigenous claims to the land that is intended to be reinhabited, it is a concept that has been engaged and problematized by authors in this special issue (Bang et al.; Calderon; Paperson). Together, authors in this special issue ask, *how can a place be inhabited or reinhabited if it has already long been inhabited by Indigenous peoples without this functioning as another form of settler emplacement as colonization?* (see also Morgensen 2009). It is precisely at the juncture of concepts that have gained so much traction within place-based education discourses, like reinhabitation, that the epistemological and ontological differences between place-based education and land education may be readily observed, and where the need for a recognition and analysis of settler colonialism and settler emplacement and replacement are most evident.

More recent work on (re)inhabitation suggests it is necessarily coupled with decolonization (Greenwood 2013; Greenwood and McKenzie 2009; Gruenewald 2008; McKenzie 2008). But if theories of reinhabitation are reliant upon replacement discourses like Jackson's, or other discourses that attempt to relieve settler anxiety and dis-location, reinhabitation may actually thwart decolonization.[4]

### *The refusal of settler futurity as the referent of purpose or justice*

A second intervention needs less explanation, but can have far greater impact on place-based and environmental education and research; understanding and fostering sustainable relationships to land and the environment cannot happen when those activities are accountable to a futurity in which settlers continue to dominate and occupy stolen Indigenous land. Maintaining settler futurity cannot be the purpose or side-effect of environmental education and research; this is not to say there is no future/ity for now-settlers, but that their relationships to Indigenous land and peoples must be informed by an unsettled imaginary. Environmental justice can only take place with Indigenous peoples and epistemologies at the center (see Calderon; Meyer; Sato, Silva and Jaber; Whitehouse et al. this issue). In addition, such theories of change cannot be expected to answer questions of what settlers' lives will look like in/after the process of decolonization (Morgensen 2009; Paperson this issue; Tuck and Yang 2012). Land education de-centers settlers and settler futurity as the primary referents for possibility. Land education seeks decolonization, not settler emplacement. Land education is accountable to an Indigenous futurity.

### *Modes and methods of land education research*

A final key consideration of the special issue that we want to highlight is the methodologies and methods of research mobilized across the articles; as well as how the articles work across various registers and the further research considerations entailed in these crossings. We end by discussing modes and methodologies of research in relation to the authors of the articles, the article reviewers, editors at *Environmental Education Research*, and the articles' anticipated readers.

As indicated already, a range of methodologies and methods of research are drawn upon in the articles included in the collection. These include historical analysis (McCoy), critical cartography (Paperson), ethnography (Paperson), social mapping (Sato, Silva, and Jaber), community-based design research (Bang et al.), document analysis (Calderon; Whitehouse et al.), film analysis (Korteweg and Oakley), photography (Meyer), and descriptive analyses of teaching practices (Engel-Di Mauro and Carroll). Though varied in shape and approach, we regard all of the contributions as research articles: some drawing on and sharing empirical data collected through qualitative data collection methods (e.g. interviews and participant observation in the articles of Bang et al.; Paperson; Sato, Silva and Jaber), others are based on the empirical and conceptual analysis of textual or visual forms (e.g. the curriculum document analysis and film analysis of articles by Calderon; Korteweg and Oakley). Approaches of argumentation also vary across articles, from visual approaches (Meyer), poetic approaches (Bang et al.), to partial stories (Paperson), and reconstructed histories (McCoy). Forms of research in environmental education have expanded beyond those that are modeled on scientific methods and modes of representation (Hart 2005; McKenzie 2009), and with growing numbers of scholarly works available on Indigenous research methodologies and considerations (e.g. Kovach 2010; Smith 1999/2013; Wilson 2008), there is a need for a continued expansion of understandings in what counts as research in the reviewing, editing, and reading practices within environmental education.

We also want to draw attention to the ways in which the methodologies and methods engaged in the issue gather and represent data on a variety of registers in considering land and land education. These include the temporal and spatial, as well as material and other aspects of land. This is most clearly evident in the mapping articles by Sato, Silva, and Jaber, and by Paperson, in which relationships with land are mapped temporally (in relation to history/future) and spatially (in relation to geography) through visual and oral mapping exercises. Other articles, such as those by Bang et al. and Whitehouse et al., similarly work across these multiple registers in representing Chicago or Sea Country as storied land and as sites of land education. These methodological dimensions of the articles ask us to consider not only what land education is or might be, but how can we effectively research it? In what ways can we or should we try to understand learning in relationship to land? On what registers can we or should we collect data? And what are the various ethical considerations and protocols implied in these potential methods and modes of research? (Smith 1999/2013; Wilson 2008).

Also important for environmental education researchers to consider are the challenges in expanding the field topically into new domains and priorities, such as those of land education. Many of the authors represented in this issue could be considered 'new' or early career scholars, in that they have completed doctorates within the last 10 years; and to some extent bring new experiences and topical concerns to educational research. In some cases, authors also are part of growing proportion of critical Indigenous educators and researchers contributing to rapidly expanding bodies of scholarly work on Indigenous education and research within and beyond the field of environmental education. These are dynamics that both support the possibilities raised through this issue, but also are challenges in bridging fields, in getting past reviewers and/or in finding appropriate reviewers, in publishing with impact. As Linda Tuhiwai Smith wrote 15 years ago: 'While researchers are trained to conform to the models provided for them, Indigenous researchers have to meet these criteria as well as Indigenous criteria which can judge research as not "useful," "not Indigenous," "not friendly," "not just." Reconciling such views can be difficult' (1999/2013, 140). As special issue editors, at times we questioned who we were writing and editing for, and the extent to which the politics and language of this introduction and of the issue should be addressed to readers familiar and/or unfamiliar with the issues and priorities raised herein. We envision and appreciate the possibilities and responsibilities of reading and writing environmental education research across paradigms, methods, and audiences (Reid 2013).

In closing this introduction to the issue, we hope the collection inspires more place-based and environmental education works that specifically engage settler colonialism. Further, we hope the special issue draws attention to the need to analyze the settler colonial histories of the places and ways in which we conduct environmental education research. Settler colonialism has not only violently interrupted Indigenous life, but it has resulted in 'quick and brutal' environmental degradation (Robinson and Tout 2012, 156, see also McCoy this issue).

> The mass extinctions; resource scarcity; reliance on damaging coal, mining and logging industries; public unpreparedness for seasonal drought, floods and bushfires; and rapid processes of urbanization, which together distinguish the contemporary Australian situation [and the situation of most other settler colonial nation-states], indicate that settler Australians have not yet managed to become grounded on this continent and do not yet possess adequate or appropriate knowledges – in either form or degree – concerning the management and maintenance of Australian lands. (Robinson and Tout 2012, 156, insertion ours)

We issued the call for this special issue in 2011, before the remarkable Indigenous movement *Idle No More* was founded in Canada; before it spread across North America and gained expressions of recognition and support from Indigenous and non-Indigenous peoples around the globe. *Idle No More* has already taught the world about what we hope a land education does and will do: that is, to remind people to place Indigenous understandings of land and life at the center of environmental issues and other (educational) issues; provide an explicit critique and rendering of settler colonialism, treaties, and sovereignty; invite and inspire acts of refusal, reclamation, regeneration, and reimagination; and theorize pathways to living as 'separate sovereignties on shared territory' (Simpson 2013). Structural antagonisms and incommensurabilities throb at the base of land education, but because land education is accountable to Indigenous resistance and futurity, the pathways are already making their own tracings.

## Acknowledgment

We extend our deeply felt thanks to Alan Reid and Claire Drake, to the editorial board, to all of the participating authors, to all of our reviewers, to all of those who spread word about this special issue, and to all of those who have taught us that *it's about the land, it's about the land, it's about the land.*

## Notes

1. Multicultural settler societies may consider Indigenous peoples to be just another ethnic or race group, which now successfully folded into the multicultural fabric, should expect no pre-existing or special rights at all.
2. To punctuate a prior point, one of the contributions of settler colonial studies is the interruption of the binary of 'settler' and 'Indigenous,' by also theorizing the perspectives and structural locations of (descendants of) chattel slaves (Tuck and Yang 2012; Wilderson 2010; Wolfe 2006), arrivants, and migrant workers (Byrd 2011; Patel 2012), and others living in settler colonial nation-states.
3. In contrast, Indigenous futurity forecloses settler colonialism and settler epistemologies. This does not mean that Indigenous futurity forecloses living on Indigenous land by non-Indigenous peoples. That is to say that Indigenous futurity does not require the erasure of now-settlers in the ways that settler futurity requires of Indigenous peoples (see also Tuck and Gaztambide-Fernández 2013).
4. Tuck and Yang (2012) have cautioned against deploying the term 'decolonization' without specific attention to the repatriation of Indigenous land, recognition of Indigenous sovereignty, and abolition of slavery in all forms in the US nation-state. Decolonization is not a metaphor that can be applied to social justice projects that do not result in changes in land distribution, use, and especially relationships. Following Fanon (1968), Tuck and Yang emphasize that decolonization is always a historical process, specific to land and place.

## References

Agrawal, Arun. 2002. "Indigenous Knowledge and the Politics of Classification." *International Social Science Journal* 54 (173): 287–297.

Baldwin, Andrew. 2012. "Whiteness and Futurity: Towards a Research Agenda." *Progress in Human Geography* 36 (2): 172–187.

Battiste, Marie. 2000. *Reclaiming Indigenous Voice and Vision*. Vancouver: UBC Press.

Bird, S. Elizabeth, ed. 1996. *Dressing in Feathers: The Construction of the Indian in American Popular Culture*. Boulder, CO: Westview Press.

Bowers, Chet A. 2003. *Mindful Conservatism: Rethinking the Ideological and Educational Basis of an Ecologically Sustainable Future*. New York: Rowman & Littlefield.

Brooks, Lisa. 2008. *The Common Pot: The Recovery of Native Space in the Northeast*. Minneapolis, MN: U of Minnesota Press.

Burkhart, Brian Y. 2004. "What Coyote and Thales can Teach Us: An Outline of American Indian Epistemology." In *American Indian Thought: Philosophical Essays*, edited by A. Waters, 15–26. Malden, MA: Blackwell.

Byrd, Jodi A. 2011. *The Transit of Empire: Indigenous Critiques of Colonialism*. Minneapolis, MN: U of Minnesota Press.

Cajete, Gregory. 1994. *Look to the Mountain: An Ecology of Indigenous Education*. Durango, CO: Kivaki Press.

Chambers, Cynthia. 2008. "Where are We? Finding Common Ground in a Curriculum of Place." *Journal of the Canadian Association for Curriculum Studies* 6 (2): 113–128.

Chilisa, Bagele. 2011. *Indigenous Research Methodologies*. London: Sage.

Cook-Lynn, Elizabeth. 1997. "Who stole Native American studies?" *Wicazo Sa Review* 12 (1): 9–28.
Coulthard, Glen S. 2007. "Subjects of Empire: Indigenous Peoples and the 'Politics of Recognition' in Canada." *Contemporary Political Theory* 6 (4): 437–460.
Deloria, Vine. 1969. *Custer Died for Your Sins: An Indian Manifesto*. Norman, OK: University of Oklahoma Press.
Donald, Dwane. 2012. "Forts, Curriculum, and Ethical Relationality." In *Reconsidering Canadian Curriculum Studies: Provoking Historical, Present, and Future Perspectives*, edited by N. Ng-A-Fook and J. Rottman, 39–46. New York: Palgrave MacMillan.
Fanon, Frantz. 1968. *The Wretched of the Earth*. New York: Grove Press.
Friedel, Tracy L. 2011. "Looking for Learning in all the Wrong Places: Urban Native Youths' Cultured Response to Western-oriented place-based Learning." *International Journal of Qualitative Studies in Education* 24 (5): 531–546.
Greenwood, David. 2013. "A Critical Theory of Place-conscious Education." In *International Handbook of Research on Environmental Education*, edited by Robert B. Stevenson, Michael Brody, Justin Dillon and Arjen Wals, 93–100. New York: Routledge.
Greenwood, David, and Marcia McKenzie. 2009. "Context, Experience, and the Socioecological: Inquiries into Practice." *Canadian Journal of Environmental Education* 14 (1): 5–14.
Gruenewald, David A. 2003. "The Best of Both Worlds: A Critical Pedagogy of Place." *Educational researcher* 32 (4): 3–12.
Gruenewald, David. 2008. "Place-based Education: Grounding Culturally Responsive Teaching in Geographical Diversity." In *Place-based Education in the Global Age: Local Diversity*, edited by David Gruenewald and Greg Smith, 137–154. Mahwah, NJ: Lawrence Erlbaum.
Gruenewald, David, and Gregory A. Smith. 2008. *Place-based Education in the Global Age: Local Diversity*. Mahwah, NJ: Lawrence Erlbaum Associates.
Hart, Paul. 2005. "Transitions in Thought and Practice: Links, Divergences and Contradictions in Post-critical Inquiry." *Environmental Education Research* 11 (4): 391–400.
Hinkson, John. 2012. "Why Settler Colonialism?" *Arena Journal* 37/38: 1–15.
Jackson, Wes. 1996. *Becoming Native to a Place*. Washington, DC: Counterpoint.
Kawagley, Angayuqaq Oscar. 2010a. "Foreword." In *Alaska Native Education: Views from Within*, edited by Ray Barnhardt and Angayuqaq Oscar Kawagley, xiii–xv. Fairbanks, AK: University of Alaska Fairbanks.
Kawagley, Angayuqaq Oscar. 2010b. "Alaska Native Education: History and Adaptation in the New Millenium." In *Alaska Native Education: Views from within*, edited by Ray Barnhardt and Angayuqaq Oscar Kawagley, 73–98. Fairbanks, AK: University of Alaska Fairbanks.
Knapp, Clifford. 2008. "Place-based Curricular and Pedagogical Models: My Adventures in Teaching Through Community Contexts." In *Place-based Education in the Global Age: Local Diversity*, edited by David Gruenewald and Greg Smith, 5–28. Mahwah, NJ: Lawrence Erlbaum.
Korteweg, Lisa, and Connie Russell. 2012. "Editorial: Decolonizing + Indigenizing = Moving Environmental Education Towards Reconciliation." *Canadian Journal of Environmental Education* 17: 5–14.
Kovach, Margaret Elizabeth. 2010. *Indigenous Methodologies: Characteristics, Conversations, and Contexts*. Toronto: University of Toronto Press.
Le Grange, Lesley. 2009. "Participation and Participatory Action Research (PAR) in Environmental Education Processes: For What are People Empowered?" *Australian Journal of Environmental Education* 25: 3–14.
Lowan, Greg. 2009. "Exploring Place from an Aboriginal Perspective: Considerations for Outdoor and Environmental Education." *Canadian Journal of Environmental Education* 12: 42–58.
MacLean, Edna Ahgeak. 2010. "Culture and Change for Inupiat and Yup'ik People of Alaska: Alaska Native Education: History and Adaptation in the New Millenium." In *Alaska Native Education: Views from Within*, edited by Ray Barnhardt and Angayuqaq Oscar Kawagley, 41–58. Fairbanks, AK: University of Alaska Fairbanks.

McKenzie, Marcia. 2008. "The Places of Pedagogy: Or, What we can do with Culture through Intersubjective Experiences." *Environmental Education Research* 14 (3): 361–373.

McKenzie, Marcia. 2009. "Scholarship as Intervention: Critique, Collaboration and the Research Imagination." *Environmental Education Research* 15 (2): 217–226.

Meyer, Manulani Aluli. 2008. "Indigenous and Authentic: Hawaiian Epistemology and the Triangulation of Meaning." In *Handbook of Critical and Indigenous Methodologies*, edited by Norman K. Denzin, Yvonna S. Lincoln and Linda Tuhiwai Smith, 217–232. London: Sage.

Mignolo, Walter. 2003. *The Darker Side of the Renaissance: Literacy, Territoriality, and Colonization*. Ann Arbor, MI: University of Michigan Press.

Morgensen, Scott Lauria. 2009. "Un-settling Settler Desires." In *Reflections and Resources for Deconstructing Colonial Mentality*, edited by Unsettling Minnesota Collective, 157–158. Minneapolis, MN: Self published source book. Accessed May 13, 2013. http://unsettlingminnesota.files.wordpress.com/2009/11/um_sourcebook_jan10_revision.pdf

Morgensen, Scott Lauria. 2011. "The Biopolitics of Settler Colonialism: Right Here, Right Now." *Settler Colonial Studies* 1: 52–76.

O'Riley, Pat, and Peter Cole. 2009. "Coyote and Raven Talk about the Land/Scapes." In *Fields of Green: Restorying Culture, Environment, and Education*, edited by Marcia McKenzie, Paul Hart, Heesoon Bai and Bob Jickling, 125–134. Cresskill, NJ: Hampton Press.

Patel, Lisa. 2012. *Youth Held at the Border: Immigration, Education, and the Politics of Inclusion*. New York: Teachers College Press.

Rasmussen, Derek, and Tommy Akulukjuk. 2009. "My Father was Told to Talk to the Environment First Before Anything Else: Arctic Environmental Education in the Language of the Land." In *Fields of Green: Restorying Culture, Environment, and Education*, edited by Marcia McKenzie, Paul Hart, Heesoon Bai and Bob Jickling, 285–298. Creskill, NJ: Hampton Press.

Reid, Alan. 2013. "Environmental Education Research: Towards and Beyond Passionate, Scholarly Conversation." *Environmental Education Research* 19 (2): 147–153.

Robinson, Alice, and Dan Tout. 2012. Unsettling Conceptions of Wilderness and Nature. *Arena Journal* 37/38: 153–175.

Shava, Soul. 2013. "The Representation of Indigenous Knowledges." In *International Handbook of Research on Environmental Education*, edited by Robert B. Stevenson, Michael Brody, Justin Dillon and Arjen E. J. Wals, 384–393. New York: Routledge.

Simpson, Leanne. 2013. "Politics based on Justice, Diplomacy based on Love: What Indigenous Diplomatic Traditions Can Teach Us." *Briarpatch Magazine online*. Accessed May 13, 2013. http://briarpatchmagazine.com/articles/view/politics-based-on-justice-diplomacy-based-on-love

Smith, Linda Tuhiwai. 1999/2013. *Decolonizing Methodologies: Research and Indigenous Peoples*. London: Zed Books.

Smith, Jo. 2011. "Aotearoa/New Zealand: An Unsettled State in a Sea of Islands." *Settler Colonial Studies* 1 (1): 111–131.

Spillers, Hortense J. 2003. *Black, White, and in Color: Essays on American Literature and Culture*. Chicago, IL: University of Chicago Press.

Styres, Sandra, Celia Haig-Brown, and Melissa Blimkie. 2013. "Toward a Pedagogy of land: The Urban Context." *Canadian Journal of Education/Revue canadienne de l'éducation* 36 (2): 188–221.

Styres, Sandra, and Dawn Zinga. 2013. "The Community-first land-centered Theoretical Framework: Bringing a 'Good Mind' to Indigenous Education Research." *Canadian Journal of Education/Revue canadienne de l'éducation* 36 (2): 284–313.

Swayze, Natalie. 2009. "Engaging Indigenous Urban Youth in Environmental Learning: The Importance of Place Revisited." *Canadian Journal of Environmental Education* 14: 59–73.

Tuck, Eve, and Ruben Gaztambide-Fernández. 2013. "Curriculum, Replacement, and Settler Futurity." *Journal of Curriculum Theorizing* 29: 72–89.

Tuck, Eve, and K. Wayne Yang. 2012. "Decolonization is Not a Metaphor." *Decolonization: Indigeneity, Education & Society* 1 (1): 1–40.

Veracini, Lorenzo. 2011. "Introducing." *Settler Colonial Studies* 1 (1): 1–12.

Vizenor, Gerald, Eve Tuck, and K. Wayne Yang. 2014. "Resistance in the Blood." In *Youth Resistance Research and Theories of Change*, edited by Eve Tuck and K. Wayne Yang, 107–117. New York: Routledge.

Watson, Irene. 2007. "Settled and Unsettled Spaces: Are We Free to Roam." In *Sovereign Subjects: Indigenous Sovereignty Matter*, edited by Aileen Moreton-Robinson, 15–32. Sydney: Allen & Unwin.

Wilderson, Frank B., III. 2010. *Red, White, & Black: Cinema and the Structure of U.S. Antagonisms*. Durham, NH: Duke University Press.

Wilson, Shawn. 2008. *Research is Ceremony: Indigenous Research Methods*. Blackpoint, NS: Fernwood.

Wilson, Angela Cavender, and Eli Taylor. 2005. *Remember This!: Dakota Decolonization and the Eli Taylor Narratives*. Lincoln, NE: U of Nebraska Press.

Wolfe, Patrick. 2006. "Settler Colonialism and the Elimination of the Native." *Journal of Genocide Research* 8 (4): 387–409.

Wolfe, Patrick. 2011. "After the Frontier: Separation and Absorption in US Indian Policy." *Settler Colonial Studies* 1 (1): 13–51.

Eve Tuck
*Department of Educational Studies, State University of New York at New Paltz, New Paltz, NY, USA*

Marcia McKenzie
*Department of Educational Foundations, University of Saskatchewan, Saskatoon, SK, Canada*

Kate McCoy
*Department of Educational Studies, State University of New York at New Paltz, New Paltz, NY, USA*

# Speaking back to Manifest Destinies: a land education-based approach to critical curriculum inquiry

Dolores Calderon

*Department of Education, Culture and Society, University of Utah, Salt Lake City, USA*

This article examines the ways in which settler colonialism shapes place in the social studies curriculum, producing understandings of land and citizenship in educational settings. To do this, the author uses the emergent framework of land education to move forward the important projects of place-based education, especially its potential for centering indigeneity and confronting educational forms of settler colonialism in environmental education. To emphasize how place-based education can intersect with land education, the author outlines how a concept of place, informed by Indigenous knowledge, renders settler colonialism visible. The author then describes how current models of place-based education differ from land education in a number of ways. Finally, using a land education approach, the author demonstrates how schooling, through social studies curriculum, transmits a settler colonial land ethic that must be made explicit in order to decolonize settler colonial relations attached to current pedagogical models of place. The author insists land education – like environmental education – must take place across the curriculum (k-16). However, land education implies a commitment to begin to understand the process of decolonization that takes seriously the centrality of settler colonialism.

## Introduction

Place has been central in my examination of social studies curriculum as a vehicle for producing understandings of land and citizenship in educational settings (Calderon 2008, 2011). In this article, I contextualize place within a land education model. Specifically, I articulate how land education moves forward the important projects of place-based education, especially its potential for centering indigeneity and confronting educational forms of settler colonialism.

To emphasize how place-based education can intersect with land education, I first briefly outline how I use and understand the concept of place in this essay. Next, I describe how current models of place-based education differ from land education in a number of ways, illustrating how my own theorizing and understanding of place expands upon place-based education models to arrive at what is more appropriately understood as land education. Finally, using a land education approach, I demonstrate how schooling, through examples from a social studies curriculum, transmits a settler colonial land ethic that must be made explicit in order to decolonize settler colonial relations attached to current pedagogical models of place.

In developing a land education model, I draw upon Dolores Delgado Bernal's (1998) cultural intuition, Linda Tuhiwai Smith's (2012) decolonizing methodologies, and Deloria's (1979, 1992, 2006) seminal work on western metaphysics and his (Deloria and Wildcat 2001) notion of power of place. I draw from these theorists' respective works in formulating my own framework for understanding place that centers Indigenous notions of place and specifically articulate how my own subjectivity is integral to conceptualizing place as both an embodiment and practice of place. This interdisciplinary approach provides me with the necessary tools for interrogating dominant understandings of place rendered through schooling, which I highlight through decolonizing readings of social studies curriculum. Indeed, as Pendleton Jiménez's (2006) articulation of 'Chicana pedagogies of the land' – which center Chicana bodies within the framework of colonial interactions – points out, one's identity is caught up in both the historical and current colonial processes of the places we are from. This settler colonial identity (Calderon 2008, 2011) manifests itself in myriad ways and involves a complex relationship between peoples, geographies, natural landscapes, settler laws, and the resulting violence of this longstanding globalization project (Calderon 2008). Ultimately, such an understanding, I argue, allows me to see and name realities and corresponding ideologies that are missing from mainstream educational research and current place-based education models.

My examination of social studies curriculum textbooks thus attempts to show how settler identities are produced through schooling processes associated with settler legacies that underlie the diversity of land relations in the US. An important starting place for understanding how educational models produce colonial understandings of place is to focus on how settler ideologies in educational tools such as textbooks construct and make sense of the world in ways that maintain settler colonialism. In such a context, I argue that dominant settler ideologies of land leave little room for Indigenous-informed frameworks and little to no possibility for decolonizing work in education. To truly commit to decolonizing work concerning place we must first understand the US and its educational institutions as products of settler colonialism.

## Place-based education and settler identities

One of the major limitations of critical place-based education as it is generally theorized is that it does not go far enough to connect how place in the US has been inexorably linked to the genocide of Indigenous peoples and continued settler colonialism. While settler colonial violence and oppression is not an explicit aspect of place-based education, it nonetheless fails to meaningfully engage colonial legacies in education and particularly how conceptions of place have been involved in their continuance. For example, Smith and Sobel's (2010) latest work provides a description of the aims and goals of place-based education as well as a springboard for how one might envision land education in relation to current place based models. At the most general level, place-based education centers learning (and teaching) within local communities (Rural School and Community Trust 2005; Smith and Sobel 2010) and has been traditionally associated with rural endeavors. Place-based education also incorporates hands-on approaches (Sobel 2004), coupling learning with real world significance (Rural School and Community Trust 2005) by promoting active ideas of citizenship in places students inhabit (Rural School and Community Trust 2005; Sobel 2004). Place-based models can focus on a variety of topics, including critical political perspectives in communities, entrepreneurialism, and environmentally centered approaches that take into account the biosphere of the local, culture, citizenship, and community (Smith and Sobel 2010; Sobel 2004), to name a few.

While place-based education models emphasize community needs and engagement, they do not go far enough to promote decolonizing goals that should be included in any place-based education model interested in cultural and ecological sustainability. In this regard, Gruenewald's (2003a, 2003b) work, pairing critical pedagogy with place-based education and promoting place-conscious education, is a step in the right direction.

Gruenewald's introduction of a decolonizing agenda is important in the development of place-based education. A critical engagement with place demands an examination of taken for granted, unconscious attitudes about social place (Gruenewald 2003b). However, such a taken-for-granted attitude, I suggest, is not a mistake. Rather, it is a product of deliberate miseducation (Calderon 2011). If as place-based education models purport, we are to teach through schooling how to promote models of sustainability and community, we also need to understand how sustainability and community cannot be achieved if the communities Indigenous to place are not central in this formulation. Moreover, the concept of territoriality must be a central component of such work. For this reason, land education is better suited to take on such commitments. Yet how does a land education approach differ from place-based, eco-justice models of education? In what follows, I suggest the following elements of land education to be integral to place-based education models and practices and as so framed can be considered part of its foundation:

- Land education centers the relationship between land and settler colonialism. Thus, it is informed by theories and studies on settler colonialism. Such a positioning is important, particularly from an Indigenous perspective, because it makes ideologies and structures of settler colonialism explicit. It demands that in articulating place-based models for forming relationships with place, the legal landscapes (Delaney 1998) of settler colonialism be delineated and deconstructed.
- Land education challenges us to consider the politics of naming. Similar to Pendleton Jiménez's (2006) work that explores how Chicana pedagogy must start with one's relationship to the land in order to understand how 'colonial curriculum[s]' function 'in tandem with the renaming of lands and physical removal of Indigenous people from them' (222), land education demands an explicit political analysis. Specifically, it situates settler land policies and ethics targeting Indigenous peoples at the forefront of understanding how most people come to be in a given place through displacements that continue at the expense of Indigenous peoples.
- Pedagogically, land education requires one to move towards a decolonizing reinhabitation of place (Brandt 2009; Gruenewald 2003a; Peña 1998). Reinhabitation must be characterized as more than simply promoting neoliberal sustainable, environmental practices (Peña 1998). It must first explore the notion of territoriality – how settlers' access to territory and the resulting

elimination and removal of Indigenous peoples, enabled by both legal and ideological mechanisms of removal (Wolfe 2006), is the dominant land ethic of a settler society. Brandt (2009), drawing from Peña (1998), states that to be truly decolonizing, reinhabitation 'occurs when local, democratic self-management of degraded homelands becomes possible and stakeholders come to understand the colonizing effects of past historical practices' (97). Indeed, land education requires decolonization be more than a metaphor that reifies settler emplacement (Morgensen 2009) and actively address settler/Indigenous relations (Tuck and Yang 2012).

- Land education requires us to consider Indigenous agency and resistance tied to Indigenous cosmologies. Concurrently, reinhabitation, on the part of settlers, demands the absence/removal of settlers/settlerism from place, in order to afford Indigenous peoples the opportunity to maintain and heal spiritual relationships with the land (Bang et al., forthcoming). This responds to Deloria's (2006) warning against the misuse and abuse of ceremony and the 'erosion of the old [Indigenous spiritual] ways' (xvii) in many tribal communities, and it builds upon his (2001) urgent work to infuse Indian education with Indigenous metaphysics – 'the realization that the world, and all its possible experiences, constituted a social reality, a fabric of life in which everything had the possibility of intimate knowing relationships, because ultimately, everything was related' (2).
- Finally, land education destabilizes the local, turning towards how ethics of land are informed by dominant ideologies that shape the relationship with the local that place-based models do not engage.

As a way to more clearly define aspects of land education, I advance an analysis of how a land education approach to a social studies curriculum excavates the ways settler colonialism in US history textbooks is normalized. Before I do that, however, I provide further context for a land education approach and in particular, how it illuminates the ways settler colonialism shapes pedagogies of place.

## Land education

What then might a land education that is built upon Indigenous scholarship and community work look like, as an alternative to current expressions of place-based education? Simply put, such a land education must start from the supposition that all places were once Indigenous lands and continue to be. While many Indigenous peoples are removed from their home territories, this does not sever the relationships that Indigenous groups have with their places of origin and their sacred sites. If environmental educators are to pursue the work of consciousness raising through education connected to place, there has to be an acknowledgement of this reality to critically examine what it means to inhabit lands that were once (and continue to be) the homelands of Indigenous nations.

One important way land education does this is by centering Indigenous realities as the appropriate starting place for educational inquiry regarding place. Land education, in other words, acknowledges that Indigenous knowledge(s)/cosmologies are many times the most viable knowledge systems related to place-based goals of critical sustainability, community building (Brandt 2009; Cajete 1994; Peña 1998), and addressing issues of territoriality. As such, a land education model must embrace protocols that are mindful of how Indigenous knowledge has been co-opted and omitted especially through processes of schooling. Land education models, alternatively, require that Indigenous peoples lead discussions regarding land education in communities (Aikenhead 1997), expanding upon place-based education's emphasis and mandate of incorporating community in schooling by privileging the standpoint of the Indigenous (Kawagley and Barnhardt 1999). Such a focus on Indigenous realities necessitates the development of relationships between schools and local Indigenous peoples. While this description of land education may seem straight forward enough, the application of it cannot be simply checking off a to-do list. There is deeper work that must accompany land education.

It is not an easy task acknowledging that the place we find ourselves is Indigenous land and that is why it is essential to form relationships with Indigenous peoples to relearn about the place we live. Indeed, as the analysis of social studies research I conclude with below shows, because an entire ideological and institutional project has been put in place that has effectively erased Indigenous realities in the present and reconstructed Indigenous peoples as relics of the past (Calderon 2008, 2011; Kirkness 1977; Mallam 1973; O'Neill 1984; Swanson 1977; Vogel 1968, 1974), it follows that students must be first guided through a process of decolonization. By decolonization I mean uncovering how settler colonial projects are maintained and reproduced, with understandings of land being one of the primary ways such identities are formed. Without such exercises in decolonization, it is impossible to achieve goals of sustainability and the wedded notion of a community building that rejects anthropocentric and Eurocentric understandings of land and citizenship. This is because, I conceive land education as one that uses both western and non-western forms of knowledge to achieve decolonizing understandings of land or place. For instance, to begin the work of decolonizing, students must be pedagogically led through an understanding of colonial identities relative to land (Pendleton Jiménez 2006) similar to place-based education's emphasis on starting learning with the 'local'. However, a land education model demands we decolonize the 'local' in order to understand how settler colonialism is currently enacted and taught. This means, for example, assessing how different colonial processes impacted a place and subsequently shaped it, informing the notions of territoriality present in that space today.

Understanding that the chief impetus of historical wrongs was, for example, territorial acquisition, allows students to understand that the place or land they inhabit was illegally and violently taken. By working back, students and teachers can begin moving towards decolonizing understandings of community and to think about what non-colonial relations[1] might look like both in theory and practice. Here we can see that a land education approach requires that students understand themselves fully within the context of place. This means not only understanding themselves in the present and future of place, but also the past and how all three shape who they are today and where they dwell (Pendleton Jiménez 2006).

However, such theoretical groundwork must also include a critical understanding of the US and other nation-states as settler societies. To enumerate how decolonial perspectives are integral to land education, in what follows I sketch a framework for understanding settler colonialism that draws on a transdisciplinary literature recently developed and applied to my research on social studies textbooks. For environmental educators, social studies curriculum is particularly important because it is one of the primary ways a land ethic is created, especially through dominant paradigms related to how national identity and citizenship help construct damaging and unsustainable relations to land.

## Centering settler colonialism in land education

What then is meant by settler society, and how might we theorize settler colonialism as a point of departure for land education, given the possible implication of education in maintaining settler ideologies? Weitzer's (1990) definition of settler societies is a good place to begin. He notes that 'Settler societies are founded by migrant groups who assume a superordinate position vis-à-vis native inhabitants and build self-sustaining states that are de jure or de facto independent from the mother country and organized around the settlers' political domination over the Indigenous population' (25). Weitzer insists, however, that societies that displaced, eliminated, or assimilated Indigenous peoples are no longer settler states. In this fashion, he argues that the US is no longer a settler society for the reason that the 'original divisions between settlers and natives no longer shape the sociopolitical order' (26) of the US, and because Indigenous peoples were displaced or eliminated. Weitzer's argument is important to highlight because unlike other settler societies, such as Australia and New Zealand, there is relatively little work (outside the scope of Indigenous scholarship) that acknowledges the US as a settler society.

Thus, while I contend that the US continues to be a settler state, I differ from Weitzer in arguing that this division between Indigenous peoples and settlers continues to shape the sociopolitical order within the US in multiple ways. In other words, Weitzer's characterization of the US as a non-settler society promotes instead what some theorists have termed epistemological 'ignorance' (Calderon 2011; Margonis 2007; Mills 2007; Tuana 2004, 2006) regarding Indigenous peoples. This ignorance is actually a product of how gaps in knowledge are actively produced in order to protect power, in this case settler colonialism in the US. It is not surprising that Weitzer makes such a claim, because the US has successfully promoted epistemological ignorance concerning Indigenous peoples (Calderon 2011).

In fact, in asserting that the US is no longer a settler state, Weitzer (1990) enacts an *ideological erasure of Indigenous populations*. Indeed, his narrative represents the *success* of the US in promoting ideological erasure of Indigenous peoples (Veracini 2011). As I shown below, the original division between settlers and Indigenous peoples in the US continues to shape the sociopolitical order as evidenced in discourses concerning American identity (Ahluwalia 2001; Calderon 2008) and territoriality (Wolfe 1999, 2006). The notion of territoriality is indeed central to settler colonialism and land education, and arguably, countering this ideological erasure must be a key goal and foundational to the decolonizing land education sketched above.

Territoriality is most simply characterized as settlers' access to territory and the resulting elimination and removal of Indigenous peoples enabled by both legal and ideological mechanisms of removal (Wolfe 2006). In settler colonialism – unlike colonialism where resources and labor are extracted from a colony, Wolfe (2006) explains, because settlers come to stay, '… invasion is a structure not an event' (388). This structure operates according to what Wolfe (2006) refers to as a 'logic of elimination,' which includes, for instance, '… officially encouraged miscegenation, the breaking-down of native title into alienable individual freeholds, native citizenship, child abduction, religious conversion, resocialization in total institutions such as missions or boarding schools, and a whole range of cognate biocultural assimilations' (388). Thus, it is clear that the institutionalization of territoriality in settler colonialism is inexorably linked to other characteristics of settler colonialism, and as Wolfe (2006) contends, territoriality is at the heart of settler colonialism.

## Key categories of settler identity construction in social studies textbooks

While my work on settler colonialism and social studies is multilayered and discussed in full elsewhere (Calderon 2008, 2011), I offer a snapshot of two important characteristics of settler colonialism related to territorialism. These are (1) the role of settler nationalism in reproducing settler territoriality, and (2) the role of White supremacy in enabling settler territoriality. In short, the concept of territoriality outlined above that functions within a selection of social studies textbooks can be shown as maintaining a settler land ethic that supports mindsets that enable environmentally bankrupt land use practices.

### *Settler nationalism*

The first feature to note in constructing settler identities in a range of social studies textbooks concern narratives of immigration and how these shape ideologies and structures of settler nationalism (Moran 1999, 2002). Territoriality is central to the project of settler nationalism within these textbooks, where settler nationalism can be shown to operate through practices of settler colonialism, as this relates to the problem of what to do with the people who are already there. This 'problem' is narrated in these texts as remedied primarily by the attempted elimination and displacement of Indigenous peoples in order to open up lands for Europeans to settle on (Moran 2002; Weitzer 1990; Wolfe 1999, 2006). Often wedded to this removal has been the symbolic move on the part of settlers to, as Wolfe (2006) describes, 'recuperate indigeneity in order to express its [immigrants'] difference – and, accordingly, its independence – from the mother country' (389), resulting in a project of settler nationalism (Moran 1999, 2002).

As my discussion of social studies curriculum reveals below, this symbolic co-optation of indigeneity, reproduced in schooling, informs a particular type of settler nationalism. For instance, US history curricula have tended to frame Indigenous peoples as immigrants in order to co-opt Indigenous presence as an extension of settler nationalism. Additionally, history texts that rely on the triumph of 'science'-based explanations as a key narrative device, reframe American Indians as a part of a larger immigrant-nation identity. For example the *American Odyssey: The United States in the 20th Century* (1997) frames Indigenous peoples as immigrants, providing 'scientific' evidence for this narrative of immigration:

> Archaeological evidence indicates that across the wide, grassy land bridge that once connected Asia and North America trekked the first people to settle in North America … The first settlers stalked big game such as mammoths and bison … Scientists disagree on when people first came to the Americas and on how many waves of settlement they rode. (22)

Another text, *The American Vision* (2005), more directly affirms this view of Indigenous peoples as migrants:

> No one can say for certain when the first people arrived in America. … Presently, scientific speculation points to a period between 15,000 and 30,000 years ago … How long ago the first Americans appeared remains a hotly debated question. Scientists can state much more confidently, however, who these earliest people were, how they arrived in America, and what their lives were like. (13)

A land education approach, guided by Indigenous knowledge, shows that these 'scientific' origin stories directly contradict many Indigenous cosmologies, particularly creation stories that assert origins directly related to specific geographies in the US, such as the Hopi and the diverse Pueblo creation stories that describe the emergence of their peoples from places in the southwest.

### *White supremacy and territoriality*

The second feature of settler colonialism to note is the role of White supremacy as central to the development of an ideology of settler colonialism through the project of settler nationalism. The main characteristic of settler nationalism, as described above, is constructed vis-à-vis an Other. Settler nationalism incorporates aspects of territoriality that rely on ideas of cultural and biological settler superiority. As a White supremacist ideology perpetuated within settler societies, it was (and continues to be) used to affirm the idea that the new settler societies were superior to the 'old societies' settlers left behind in Europe (Moran 2002; Wolfe 1999). This racialized ideology informs the belief that settler expansion is thus, in some sense, 'inevitable' and 'necessary', in order for the flourishing of this newly created morally, culturally, politically, and economically superior society (Moran 2002).

The discourse of inevitability in settler colonialism manifests itself in related ideological and institutional assertions. The history books show these have included the legal *doctrine of discovery*, invented by American courts in 1823 to justify the taking of Indigenous lands based on notions of European conquest and superiority over Indigenous peoples (Williams 1990), promotion of popular ideologies such as 'Manifest Destiny' that promoted settler expansion, and continuous taking of Indigenous lands through policies such as the Dawes Act. These examples of territoriality typically resulted in an adversarial relationship between tribes and the emerging sense of a 'United States of America.'

One of the popular ideologies representative of settler nationalism discussed at length in social studies textbooks is *Manifest Destiny*. At its core is the nineteenth century idea that European immigrants were destined to lands in the US. While many US history textbooks treat settler expansion into the western territories of the US as a dark time in its history, they nevertheless promote narratives that present this clash between settlers and tribes, and the displacement of tribes by settlers as inevitable, in order to give way to the superior Western civilization of settlers. Indeed, textbooks follow a settler colonial logic of territorialism.

The text *The Americans: Reconstruction to the 21st Century* (2006), beginning with early nineteenth century settler expansion into the west describes:

> … in the 1840s, expansion fever gripped the country. Many Americans began to believe that their movement westward was predestined by God. The phrase 'manifest destiny' expressed the belief that the US was ordained to expand to the Pacific Ocean and into Mexican and Native American territory. Many Americans also believed that this destiny was manifest, or obvious and inevitable. (130–131)

Another textbook, *America: Pathways to the present* (2002), describes how beliefs of settler superiority enabled removal of Indigenous peoples:

> For generations, many Americans viewed the West as a wild, empty expanse, freely available to those brave enough to tame it. But the West was not empty. Others had been living there for centuries … Following the Civil War, the railroad companies began pushing their way deeper into the West … The Plains soon swarmed with settlers, many of whom felt justified in taking Native American lands. Settlers believed they had a greater right to the land because they improved it by producing more food and wealth than did the Native Americans. (180)

Textbooks also use this historical period to dramatize the cultural differences between settlers and tribes, with special emphasis paid to land use. For example, *The Americans* (2006) describes Indigenous culture in relation to land use in the following terms:

> Native Americans on the plains usually lived in small extended family groups with ties to other bands that spoke the same language … The Plains Indian tribes believed that powerful spirits controlled events in the natural world …. Despite their communal way of life, however, no individual was allowed to dominate the group. The leaders of a tribe ruled by counsel rather than by force, and land was held in common for the use of the whole tribe. (203)

The text distinguishes Native American land usage from that of White settlers, explaining that White settlers were instead driven by economic incentives:

> The culture of the white settlers differed in many ways from that of the Native Americans on the plains. Unlike Native Americans, who believed that land could not be owned, the settlers believed that owning land, making a mining claim, or starting a business would give them a stake in the country. They argued that Native Americans had forfeited their rights to the land because they hadn't settled down to 'improve' it. Concluding that the plains were 'unsettled,' migrants streamed westward along railroad and wagon trails to claim the land. (203)

While these textbooks do not make a value judgment concerning these cultural differences, from a land education framework they do not need to be the dominant ethic related to land and use, even as in a classroom the uncritical use of such texts would belie the view that Indians had to be displaced in order to make room for the more efficient, more appropriate use of land. This is because the thematic of 'improvement of land use' signals an inevitability of settler expansion as well as a particular set of utilitarian and extractive ethics with the land. The following excerpt from *The American Vision* is a textual example of this:

> Unit 5: The birth of Modern America 1865–1900, Section 3 Native Americans – An American Story: In the end, Ten Bears and the other chiefs had little choice but to sign the treaty. The army's main representative at the council, General William Tecumseh Sherman, told them bluntly that they would have to accept the deal: 'You can no more stop this than you can stop the sun or moon' you must submit and do the best you can' – adapted from Tribes of the Southern Plains. (425)

While US history textbooks vary in detail regarding the impacts of westward expansion they do articulate the reality that Native Americans were displaced, many times violently. This displacement was encouraged by ideologies and policies that facilitated expansionism. The narrative of westward expansion is typically told from a Eurocentric perspective, with a limited attempt to include native viewpoints (however hegemonic). In addition, while the textbooks point out that settlers and Indians had differing views regarding land, they fail to explore the reasons for these differing cultural attitudes. They also fail to critically engage how settler cultural attitudes shaped policies that were detrimental for Indian peoples.

However, before these viewpoints are included, work must be done to disrupt settler identity. Without the implementation of a rigorous land education, the inclusion of Indigenous viewpoints will continue to be marginalized because current trends of multiculturalism simply integrate material into existing curriculum frameworks. It must also be emphasized that tribes have produced extensive culturally relevant curriculums. Yet without first adopting a rigorous land education framework, including these materials as part of existent curriculum frameworks for non-Indigenous peoples may do little to disrupt settler identities. In fact, I argue these powerful curriculums would simply be territorialized – that is, understood within the context of settler ideology.

## Land education as unlearning settler identities

By way of a conclusion, it is important to reiterate why land education takes up what place-based education fails to consider – the ways in which place is foundational to settler colonialism. Land education is important for environmental educators and students because it asks them to rethink their relation to land as a dynamic ecological *and* cultural project of recovery and rehabilitation. Moreover, land education forces educators to engage the question of sustainability but not solely in ecological terms. Land education also requires educators and students to ask how their identities with place have been constructed and whose have been omitted in settler curricula. In this sense, the land education framework argued for here, recasts the question of sustainability in terms of the possibility of making extinct settler informed understandings of place.

These insights are not new. Indigenous communities, scholars, activists, and allies have been articulating these insights for a very long time. Global Indigenous movements, coming together most recently under the banner of *Idle No More* – a grassroots response to legislation in Canada that undermines environmental protections of that settler nation's water systems and diminishes First Nations' sovereignty and ability to protect their homelands – demand such dialogue. It demands environmental education make visible and begin to address the inherent contradictions of settler colonialism within its project of education, as well as that of wider educational systems, priorities and processes.

## Acknowledgement

The author would like to thank Dr Clayton Pierce for his invaluable feedback on the article.

## Note

1. In order to imagine non-colonial relations, one must first understand the production of colonial ontologies within settler states (Byrd 2012; Calderon 2008, 2011). I define colonial ontology 'as a project that promotes a hierarchy of being in which white settler state

citizenship is defined as the dominant form, and the racialized "minority" other is defined as the subordinate. This hierarchy of being is mediated by a number of corollary rights defining the parameters of access to this ontology (such as integration, diversity, and equity), and promoting settler dominance over Indigenous groups (doctrine of discovery, federal supremacy, and limited sovereignty)' (2011, 74). Moreover, within the US, Indigenous peoples are constructed as a monolithic (Byrd 2012) racial minority (Calderon 2008, 2011), which subordinates and erases the multiple tribal claims to territory that directly contest settler ownership (Wolfe 2006). Thus, colonial ontologies are intimately tied to land (See for instance Gomez's (2005) work, which explores the construction and reproduction of colonial ontologies in the southwest).

## References

Ahluwalia, Pal. 2001. "When Does a Settler Become a Native? Citizenship and Identity in a Settler Society." *Pretexts: Literary and Cultural Studies* 20 (1): 63–73.

Aikenhead, Glen S. 1997. "Toward a First Nations Cross-cultural Science and Technology Curriculum." *Science Education* 81 (2): 217–238.

Appleby, Joyce, Alan Brinkley, Albert S. Broussard, James M. McPherson, and Donald A. Richie. 2005. *The American Vision*. New York: The McGraw-Hill.

Bang, Megan, Lawrence Curley, Adam Kessel, Ananda Marin, Eli Suzukovich, and George Strack. 2014. "Muskrat Theories, Tobacco in the Streets, and Living Chicago as Indigenous Land." *Environmental Education Research* 20 (1): 37–55.

Brandt, Carol B. 2009. "A Thirst for Justice in the Arid Southwest: The Role of Epistemology and Place in Higher Education." *Educational Studies* 36 (1): 93–107.

Byrd, Jodi. 2012. *The Transit of Empire: Indigenous Critiques of Colonialism*. Minneapolis, MN: University of Minnesota Press.

Cajete, Gregory. 1994. *Look to the Mountain: An Ecology of Indigenous Education*. Skyland, NC: Kivaki Press.

Calderon, Dolores. 2008. "Indigenous Metaphysics: Challenging Western Knowledge Organization in Social Studies Curriculum." PhD diss., University of California.

Calderon, Dolores. 2011. "Locating the Foundations of Epistemologies of Ignorance in Normative Multicultural Education." In *Epistemologies of Ignorance and Studies of Limits in Education*, edited by Nathalia Jaramillo and Eric Malewski, 105–127. Charlotte, NC: Information Age.

Cayton, Andrew R. L., Elizabeth I. Perry, Linda Reed, and Alan M. Winkler. 2002. *America: Pathways to the Present, Modern American History*. Needham, MA: Prentice Hall.

Danzer, Gerald, Jorge Klor de Alva, Larry S. Krieger, Louis E. Wilson, and Nancy Woloch. 2006. *The Americans: Reconstruction to the 21st Century*. California ed. Evanston, IL: McDougal Littell.

Delaney, David. 1998. *Race, Place, and the Law, 1836–1948*. Austin: University of Texas Press.

Delgado Bernal, Dolores. 1998. "Using a Chicana Feminist Epistemology in Educational Research." *Harvard Educational Review* 68 (4): 555–579.

Deloria, Vine. 1979. *Metaphysics of Modern Existence*. San Francisco, CA: Harper's.

Deloria, Vine. 1992. *God is Red: A Native View of Religion*. Golden, CO: Fulcrum Publishing.

Deloria, Vine. 2006. *The World we Used to Live in: Remembering the Powers of the Medicine Men*. Golden, CO: Fulcrum Publishing.

Deloria, Vine, and Daniel Wildcat. 2001. *Power and Place: Indian Education in America*. Golden, CO: Fulcrum Resources.

Gomez, Laura E. 2005. "Off-white in an Age of White Supremacy: Mexican Elites and the Rights of Indians and Blacks in Nineteenth-century New Mexico." *Chicano–Latino Law Review* 25: 9–59.

Gruenewald, David A. 2003a. "The Best of Both Worlds: A Critical Pedagogy of Place." *Educational Researcher* 32 (4): 3–12.

Gruenewald, David A. 2003b. "Foundations of Place: A Multidisciplinary Framework for Place-conscious Education." *American Educational Research Journal* 40 (3): 619–654.

Kawagley, Angayuqaq Oscar, and Ray Barnhardt. 1999. "Education Indigenous to Place: Western Science Meets Native Reality." In *Ecological Education in Action: On Weaving Education, Culture, and the Environment*, edited by Gregory A. Smith and Dilafurz R. Williams, 117–133. Albany: State University of New York Press.

Kirkness, Verna J. 1977. "Prejudice about Indians in Textbooks." *Journal of Reading* 20 (7): 595–600.

Mallam, R. Clark. 1973. "Academic Treatment of the Indian in Public School Texts and Literature." *Journal of American Indian Education* 13 (1): 1–6.

Margonis, Frank. 2007. "W.E.B. Du Boise and Alain Locke: A Case Study in White Ignorance and Intellectual Segregation." In *Race and Epistemologies of Ignorance*, edited by Shannon Sullivan and Nancy Tuana, 173–196. Albany: State University of New York Press.

Mills, Charles W. 2007. "White Ignorance." In *Race and Epistemologies of Ignorance*, edited by Shannon Sullivan and Nancy Tuana, 11–38. Albany: SUNY Press.

Moran, Anthony. 1999. "Imagining the Australian Nation: Settler Nationalism and Aboriginality." PhD diss., University of Melbourne.

Moran, Anthony. 2002. "As Australia Decolonizes: Indigenizing Settler Nationalism and the Challenges of Settler/Indigenous Relations." *Ethnic and Racial Studies* 25 (6): 1013–1042.

Morgensen, Scott Lauria. 2009. "Un-settling Settler Desires." In *Reflections and Resources for Deconstructing Colonial Mentality*, edited by Unsettling Minnesota Collective, 157–158. Minneapolis, MN: Self Published Source Book. Accessed May 13, 2013. http://unsettling-minnesota.files.wordpress.com/2009/11/um_sourcebook_jan10_revision.pdf

Nash, Gary B. 1997. *American Odyssey: The United States in the Twentieth Century*. New York: Glencoe/McGraw-Hill.

O'Neill, Patrick G. 1984. "Prejudice towards Indians in History Textbooks: A 1984 Profile." *The History and Social Science Teacher* 20 (1): 33–39.

Peña, Devon G. 1998. "Los Animalitos: Culture, Ecology, and the Politics of Place in the Upper Rio Grande." In *Chicano Culture, Ecology, and Politics: Subversive Kin*, edited by Devon G. Peña, 25–57. Tucson: University of Arizona Press.

Pendleton Jiménez, Karleen. 2006. "'Start with the Land' Groundwork for Chicana Pedagogy." In *Chicana/Latina Education in Everyday Life: Feminista Perspectives on Pedagogy and Epistemology*, edited by Dolores Delgado Bernal, C. Alejandra Elenes, Francixa E. Godinez, and Sofia Villenas, 219–230. Albany: State University of New York Press.

Rural School and Community Trust. 2005. *Addressing the Crucial Relationship between Good Schools and Thriving Rural Communities. Annual Report 2005*. Arlington, VA: Rural School and Community Trust.

Smith, Linda Tuhiwai. 2012. *Decolonizing Methodologies: Research and Indigenous Peoples*. 2nd ed. London: Zed Books.

Smith, Gregory A., and David Sobel. 2010. *Place-and-community-based Education in Schools*. New York: Routledge.

Sobel, David. 2004. *Place-based Education: Connecting Classrooms and Communities*. Great Barrington, MA: The Orion Society.

Swanson, Charles H. 1977. "The Treatment of the American Indian in High School History Texts." *The Indian Historian* 10 (2): 28–37.

Tuana, Nancy. 2004. "Coming to Understand: Orgasm and the Epistemology of Ignorance." *Hypatia* 19 (1): 194–232.

Tuana, Nancy. 2006. "The Speculum of Ignorance: The Women's Health Movement and Epistemologies of Ignorance." *Hypatia* 21 (3): 1–19.

Tuck, Eve, and K. Wayne Yang. 2012. "Decolonization is Not a Metaphor." *Decolonization: Indigeneity, Education and Society* 1 (1): 1–40.

Veracini, Lorenzo. 2011. "Introducing Settler Colonial Studies." *Settler Colonial Studies* 1 (1): 1–12.

Vogel, Virgil. 1968. "The Indian in American History Textbooks." *Equity and Excellence in Education* 6 (3): 16–32.

Vogel, Virgil. 1974. *The Indian in American History*. 4th ed. Evanston, IL: Integrated Education Associates.

Weitzer, Ronald. 1990. *Transforming Settler State: Communal Conflict and Internal Security in Northern Ireland and Zimbabwe*. Berkeley: University of California Press.

Williams, Richard A. 1990. *The American Indian in Western Legal Thought: The Discourses of Conquest*. New York: Oxford University Press.

Wolfe, Patrick. 1999. *Settler Colonialism and the Transformation of Anthropology: The Politics and Poetics of an Ethnographic Event*. London: Cassell.

Wolfe, Patrick. 2006. "Settler Colonialism and the Elimination of the Native." *Journal of Genocide Research* 8 (4): 387–409.

# Muskrat theories, tobacco in the streets, and living Chicago as Indigenous land

Megan Bang[a], Lawrence Curley[a], Adam Kessel[b], Ananda Marin[c], Eli S. Suzukovich III[b,c] and George Strack[d]

[a]*Learning Sciences and Human Development, University of Washington, Seattle, USA;* [b]*Education Department, American Indian Center of Chicago, Chicago, USA;* [c]*Psychology, Northwestern University, Evanston, USA;* [d]*Miami Tribe of Oklahoma*

In this paper, we aim to contribute to ongoing work to uncover the ways in which settler colonialism is entrenched and reified in educational environments and explore lessons learned from an urban Indigenous land-based education project. In this project, we worked to re-center our perceptual habits in Indigenous cosmologies, or land-based perspectives, and came to see land re-becoming itself. Through this recentering, we unearthed some ways in which settler colonialism quietly operates in teaching and learning environments and implicitly and explicitly undermines Indigenous agency and futurity by maintaining and reifying core dimensions of settler colonial relations to land. We describe examples in which teachers and community members explicitly re-engaged land-based perspectives in the design and implementation of a land-based environmental science education that enabled epistemological and ontological centering that significantly impacted learning, agency, and resilience for urban Indigenous youth and families. In this paper, we explore the significance of naming and the ways in which knowledge systems are mobilized in teaching and learning environments in the service of settler futurity. However, we suggest working through these layers of teaching and learning by engaging in land-based pedagogies is necessary to extend and transform the possibilities and impacts of environmental education.

## Muskrat theories

Muskrat is an earth diver (Vizenor 1981).

> He finds home in shadowy wetlands – relational dynamisms between land and water – amongst the plant medicines that grow here.

Our elders know the story of why this is (Archibald 2008). Wetlands are places of continual birth, death, and rebirth.

> Scientists have said that wetlands are 'on the front lines' of globalization and climate change. They name wetlands as critical environmental niches, which are correlated with significant human survival and development. Ironically, in more recent human

> history, the depraved view of land as material has led to their filling or drainage without regard by nation states across the earth.

After annihilation, manipulation and removal of Indigenous peoples from particular lands, major cities were founded and expanded by filling wetlands, for example Chicago, formerly known as Shikaakwa, among others names of this land (Stryes and Zinga 2013). The filling in of wetlands – their intended erasure – can be viewed as perhaps a climatic move of settler colonialism – the attempted replacement of original lands with new land structures.

> Chicago is a wetland that becomes part prairie and part oak savannah. It's hard to see with the *layers of colonial fill*, but actually it's hiding in plain sight (Brayboy 2004). The wetlands are (re)becoming themselves. Despite the centuries of attempts of erasure, remaking, and geographical violence (Said 1994), the emergence of land and water in dynamic relationships and the life it supports, emerges.

Rebirthing of Land is not new, if we remember, as we find our way in becoming.
Indigenous people live *in* the wetlands of Chicago and Shikaakwa.

> Generations of Indigenous nations have been in relations – ancestral, medicinal, migrational, and economic – with these wetlands. An elder in the Chicago Native community took us for a walk through the alleys of Chicago and pointed out our plant relatives. Literally, asema (tobacco, and not the genetically altered form bred for colonial agriculture) grows in the cracks of pavement here, and grows in contested lands, normatively known as forest preserves. Asema – sprinkled throughout the city, in emergent unforeseen places, because Land is always re-becoming itself.
>
> *This is true for us*
>
> even if current practices and politics of recognition, territory, and morality don't concede, yet.
>
> After all muskrat lives in and between land and water.

## Tobacco in the streets

Almost 15 years ago, Indigenous elders began walking the perimeter of the Great Lakes to bring awareness to the declining health of the lakes and the earth at large (see www.motherearthwaterwalk.com). The Great Lakes ecosystems are the home to many Indigenous nations and are the largest body of freshwater in the world. They are also experiencing significant decline and said to be facing ecological collapse. These walks continue to occur to raise awareness and seed change for the Great Lakes. Members of the Chicago[1] inter-tribal American Indian community[2] participated in one of these walks nearly a decade ago. Compelled by the message of the walks, along with several other serendipitous affordances and enduring efforts to ensure cultural and sovereign continuity, a research project involving over a hundred community members came together to develop innovative science learning environments for Native youth, families, and community living in Chicago. As some of our readers will know and others will not, the opening of this article emerges from the stories of the people from these Lands. This paper is intended to voice some of what we have learned and the tensions we encounter as we continue to work our 'willful contradictions' (McKenzie 2004) toward 'decolonial imaginaries' of 'viable futures of survivance' (Grande 2004; Richardson and Villenas 2000; Vizenor 1994). For us, viable futures of survivance means working to move our practice beyond historicized us/them dichotomies and willfully contradicting common narratives of assimilated and landless urban Indians toward longer views of our communities and our homelands not enclosed by colonial timeframes.

Our authorship reflects the core teachers and one of the principal investigators of the research project. We come from six different nations (Ojibwe, Lakota, Choctaw, Little Shell Band of Chippewa-Cree, Miami, and Navajo), and each of us has various histories embedded in typified experiences of Indigenous peoples of North America. For some of us, Chicago is part of our original homelands and has figured centrally in the unfolding of our communities from ancestral time. Some of us have more recent relationships with this land set in motion by European contact and dispossession – relocation, removals, dispersals. Some of our parents or grandparents survived boarding schools, some were relocated here by federal policy, and some 'chose' to migrate here. Some of us are enrolled tribal members and some of us have 'descendant' status. Most of us are young and we have an elder among us. All of us have learned to live, be members of families, and make community in Chicago/Shikaakwa, consciously together.

Indigenous scholars have suggested that moving toward educational self-determination[3] requires the reclaiming, uncovering, and reinventing of our theoretical understandings and pedagogical best practices (e.g. Battiste 2002; Smith et al. 1999; Tippeconnic 1999). Trying to work within a methodological paradigm of decolonization (Smith 1999) we used several methodological tools to develop both theory and practice that empowered our community. We collectively worked to center Indigenous epistemologies and ontologies by (re)storying our relationships to Chicago as altered, impacted, yet still, always, Indigenous lands-whether we are in *currently* ceded urban territory or not. A critical dimension of the work was making visible the impacts of settler colonial constructions of urban lands as ceded and no longer Indigenous and concomitant views of naturalized settler futures (Tuck and Yang 2012) on our community and especially our youth. In this paper we will argue that the constructions of land, implicitly or explicitly as no longer Indigenous, are foundationally implicated in teaching and learning about the natural world, whether that be in science education, place-based education or environmental education. Learning about the natural world is a critical necessity given the socio-scientific realities (e.g. climate change) that are currently and will continue to, shape the lands and life that land supports, more specifically for present purposes the lives of both Indigenous and non-Indigenous peoples. For us science education, place-based education, and environmental education are critical sites of struggle because they typically reify the epistemic, ontological, and axiological issues that have shaped Indigenous histories (Brayboy and Castagno 2008). From a more hopeful perspective, we also see them as sites of potential transformings – forming a nexus between epistemologies and ontologies of land and Indigenous futurity. In our view, realizing this transformative potential will require engaging with land-based perspectives and desettling (Bang et al. 2012) dynamics of settler colonialism that remain quietly buried in educational environments that engage learning about, with and in the land and all of its dwellers.

In our experience, explicitly reengaging land-based perspectives in the design and implementation of a place-based science learning environment, what we call an emergent form of urban Indigenous land-based pedagogies, enabled epistemological and ontological balancing that significantly impacted learning for urban Indigenous youth and families (Bang and Medin 2010; Bang et al. 2010). In the remainder of this paper, we aim to contribute to uncovering the ways in which settler colonialism is entrenched and reified in educational environments. To do this, we provide a critical reading of educational environments that position place and nature as central to their approaches and learning objectives (e.g. place-based, environmental, and science education broadly construed). We include these three broad areas of scholarship because the learning environments that we developed were informed by and make contact with each in various ways. Further, while we do not intend to equate these three forms of education, we suggest that each, to some degree, utilize knowledge about the natural world derived from western scientific systems and settler-colonial relations to land and Indigenous peoples. Our critique is at a grain size that we believe either holds across these bodies of work and does not require the flattening or equating of them or that there are commonalities across them we hope makes visible the still entrenched settler-colonial dynamics that are endemic to education more broadly.

### *Settler-colonial informed readings of place in education*

Both place-based education and critical pedagogy have been bounded by dichotomous and some might say competing discourses. On the one hand, place-based education seems to focus on the environments and ecologies of outdoor rural spaces, and on the other, critical pedagogies often focus on the urban, multicultural context (Gruenewald 2008). To broadly elevate the importance of place and to bridge these two approaches, Gruenewald (2003) proposed a critical pedagogy of place. Critical place-based education and eco-justice work have amplified voices resisting destructive forms of globalization and neo-liberalism and have helped to create an intellectual space connected to Indigenous realities as well (Sutherland and Swayze 2012). However, we continue to wonder about the liberatory possibilities for Indigenous people in current forms of place-based education. As Bowers (2003) argues, there are reifications of western intellectual traditions in place-based pedagogies that further silence some cultural communities. The reification of western intellectual traditions is often made possible by the denial or erasure of 'Indigenous points of reference,' which, as Marker (2006) points out, is a form of epistemic violence. While the denial or erasure of Indigenous points of reference may not be intentional, educational environments that uncritically mobilize them and leave settler-colonial interpretations silenced are complicit in this erasure.

In order to understand the effects of settler colonialism on place focused learning environments, we trace the ontology of settler colonialism and its subsequent impacts. Just as colonialism employs a grammar of race and inferiority; settler colonialism employs this grammar of race and inferiority but toward a logic of elimination (Veracini 2011). In settler-colonial societies, settler normativity is constructed through a set of dialectic relationships based upon circles of inclusion and exclusion in which the settler constructs himself as normative and superior vis-à-vis Indigenous and non-Indigenous others. This positioning of settlers is structurally maintained by employing a set of rules that are situated in and reify the circles of inclusion and exclusion (e.g. hypodescent and blood quantum).

The core of the settler-Indigenous dialectical structure is defined by the desire to erase or assimilate Indigenous people alongside a continued symbolic Indigenous presence (Wolfe 2006). Scholars of settler colonialism have argued that the conceptual construction of uninhabited land, a form of Indigenous absence, opens the space for settler majorities to establish their ways of knowing, doing and being as normative and morally superior and begin attempts to indigenize settler majority identities (Veracini 2011). In short, settler majorities simultaneously develop identities defined by manifest destiny and genesis amnesia (Bourdieu 1977). The process of erasure and sustained symbolic presence codifies a binary logic often taking the form of 'virtuous settler' and 'dysfunctional native' (Wolfe 2006) or the historicized 'Ecological Indian' (Friedel 2011) which underpins the structure of settler identity and is often encoded in learning environments.

In our view, pathways and pedagogies that make explicit and resist the epistemic and ontological consequences of settler colonialism (i.e. suppression and denial of Indigenous peoples' lifeways or encoding settler identities in learning environments) will be necessary for viable, just, and sustainable change. Land education does just that, and, in our view, at minimum, demands attention to two critical and oscillating issues born of settler colonialism: (1) the reification of what Mignolo calls the 'zero point epistemology' (2007), upon which western knowledge of the natural world is predicated, its anthropocentric consequences, and its continued devaluing and/or attacks on Indigenous ways of knowing (e.g. Semali and Kincheloe 1999) and (2) the absence or presence of indigeneity and the subsequent effects.

### *Indigenous presence and disruptions of the 'zero point epistemology'*

Some scholars have suggested that the middle ages set in motion the creation of a 'zero point of observation and of knowledge,' or the 'zero point epistemology' (ZPE): a perspective that denied all other perspectives defined through forms of theo-politics and ego-politics of knowledge' (Castro-Gómez 2002; Mignolo 2007). The varying forms of absence (complete or partial) and the presence of Indigenous people in place-focused work is an example of the ZPE and teaches conceptions of place in the service of settler colonial legitimacy. This legitimacy rests on the need to 'disavow Indigenous presence' and to construct meanings of land as vast, uninhabited spaces ripe for discovery (Deloria et al. 1999; Veracini 2011); typically either fertile for human cultivation or endangered and in need of paternalistic protection. Mignolo (2007) argues that engagement with 'critical border thinking' is a necessary condition for change and is grounded in the experience of the colonies and subalterns. Engaging in critical border thinking, according to Mignolo (2007), is a shift to the geo- and body-politics of knowledge and a fracture of ZPE because borders are not just geographic; they are also epistemic and in our view ontogenetic. Many learning environments facilitate engagement with concepts and constructs developed within the ZPE, teaching and knowledge exchange, as well as understandings of human learning itself. For example, an analogous development of place-devoid constructions of knowledge has the been the development of locating learning in the mind as opposed to in or connected to one's body and to lands. However, there has been increasing work in the understandings of embodied cognition (Hall and Nemorovsky 2012), in theorizing relationships between mind and brain, physical health and mental health, and the relationships between culture and learning (e.g. Nasir et al. 2006).

Much of the place-based literature acknowledges the relationship between land and culture (e.g. Greenwood 2009; Gruenewald 2003; Gruenewald and Smith 2008) and calls for deep consideration of these relations, because, as Gruenewald (2003) points out, 'when we fail to consider place as products of human decisions, we accept their existence as noncontroversial or inevitable, like the falling of rain or the fact of the sunrise' (627). If we are to disrupt relationships to land that are constructed from the ZPE, then critical considerations of the ontological and epistemological foundations of much of the content being taken up and normalized in learning environments (see Bang et al. 2012 for concrete examples) is necessary. The challenge for place conscious educators is to create learning environments for new generations of young people that do not facilitate and cultivate conceptual developments and experiences of land that are aligned with 'discover(y)/(ing)' frameworks which elevate settlers' rationales for their right to land.

From a critical settler-colonial reading, place-based education, in which there is an Indigenous absence, even when relational pedagogies are prescribed, enables 'indigenizing settler majority' identities (Pearson 2002; Veracini 2011). For example, some place-based work theorizes that in order to counter the ways in which language use and institutions deny peoples' connections to place (Bowers 2002; Gruenewald 2003; Sobel 1996), innovative pedagogies that focus on the need to build personal relationships to place – to specific locals to 'rejuvenate carnal, sensory empathy with the living land that sustains us' (Abram 1996, 69) – must be developed. Gruenewald (2003) notes these types of arguments shift an emphasis from a discourse of change to a discourse of 'rooted, empathetic experience' (8). In an attempt to expand what rootedness might mean and opening a space for Indigenous presence, Gruenewald and Smith (2008), suggest that 'place consciousness must also include consciousness of the historical memory of a place, and the tradition that emerged there, whether these have been disrupted or conserved' (xxi). Importantly, however, just any form of Indigenous presence does not resist settler colonial paradigms, as many are reflective of the settler-Indigenous dialectical structure previously discussed.

Often the Indigenous 'presence' in this dialectical relationship that is found in learning environments is shaped and anchored in historicized victory narratives of conquest and assimilative narratives that place the discourse of indigeneity within colonial realms of race – not in discourses of territory and sovereignty.[4] Engagement with historicized and assimilative narratives contributes to the logic of elimination by making the primary issue of land and the continued struggles of Indigenous peoples invisible. Further, even appropriate stories of colonial histories, can be an example of what Tuck and Yang (2012), suggest is a move to white innocence (or the alleviation of white guilt, Simpson 2011) and metaphorization of decolonization because though they may not engage in the erasure of Indigenous past, they presume settler stability and the absence of decolonized sovereign Indigenous futures. Thus, the challenge to place-based work is in articulating the difference between residing and dwelling in a place. The recognition of the difference in kind (residing and dwelling) can easily get applied as a difference in degree[5] and thus enables settler majorities indigenizing themselves, or as Deloria and Lytle (1998) calls it 'playing indian,' and claiming settler sovereignty as the normative and moral/intellectual authority.

Deficit narratives of urban Indigenous communities often claim there are limitations to the living of Indigenous lives in urban places because they are supposedly disconnected to Indigenous homelands and sacred places is intimately intertwined with issues of residing and dwelling. The urban Indian narrative reinscribes the settler-indigenous dialectic by framing Indigenous land (i.e. urban places) through postcontact dispossessions and reemploying a logic of elimination (i.e. urban lands are not Indigenous lands, therefore urban Indians are not Indigenous). Marking urban land as invisible, or not authentic lands, and non-Indigenous, reinscribes the settler-indigenous dialectic that services the logic of elimination for territorial acquisition (Wolfe 2006). This dialectic is complicit in the domestication of decolonization and the denial of repatriation of Indigenous lands (Tuck and Yang 2012), urban and rural; further, it limits imaginative creations of indigenous futurity that are not bound by colonial conceptions of land.

Interestingly, there are quiet and loud revolutions within normative disciplines to rupture the concept of the ZPE (e.g. Helmreich 2011; Ingold 2000; Kirksey and Helmreich 2010), though it remains to be seen whether this work can stand in solidarity with settler colonial consciousness. Regardless, these emergent transformations have had little influence on the ways in which learning about the 'natural world' across science, place-based, and environmental education are conceptualized broadly. Although we think place-focused education scholarship could provide critical leadership in constructing different trajectories of knowing, being, and becoming, significant work remains to be done. This work involves tracing and transforming the ways that some of the core constructs in education, as well as the fields of cognition and human development, conceptualize culture, and nature (see Bang et al. 2012).

The development of liberatory learning environments, we believe, will hinge on the ways in which constructs of culture and land, as well as the epistemic and ontological stances embedded therein, are conceptualized, encoded and facilitated. Land education requires many things including: critical border thinking and the rupturing of the ZPE through the spatial turn (Kitchens 2009), solidarity with consciousness of land and settler colonialism, constant resistance to land perpetually becoming a resource for global markets and negating presumptions about the absence of sovereign Indigenous futures. In our view, one of the most critical, elusive and perhaps contradictory aspects of learning environments are those that elevate anthropocentric relationships and consequently 'other' both place-based and land education. While place-focused work has opened critical spaces of scholarship and taken the laudable stance to explicitly reject anthropocentricism, a central need for land education in relation to anthropocentricism, as distinct from place-based education still remains because it makes visible the ways in which anthropocentricism is destructive to Indigenous cosmologies.

### *Place, nature, culture, and anthropocentrism*

Place-based education actively works toward being nonanthropocentric (e.g. for overview see Gruenewald 2003); however, we believe accomplishing this transformative stance in lived practice, requires deeper consideration of the intersections between settler colonialism, the content derived from normative scientific paradigms that has been constructed around the division of nature and culture and is routinely taken up in learning environments (see Bang et al. 2012; Ingold 2011), and theories of learning and development implicitly embedded throughout. Being in the world gives form to children's learning and development – that is, people are continually coming into being through experiences. Individuals that have experiences or engage in practices in which place is a backdrop tend to reason anthropocentrically and view humans as separate or as different from the rest of the world (Bang, Medin, and Atran 2007; Medin and Bang, forthcoming). Anthropocentricism in reasoning and 'world as the backdrop to human activity' has been theorized as a human universal rather than a socially or ideologically constructed phenomenon, particularly in learning and developmental work (e.g. Carey 1985). Increasingly, however, there is work demonstrating that patterns of human thinking and development, which were once thought of as universal in these disciplines, differ across place and culture (e.g. Medin et al. 2010; Herrmann, Medin, and Waxman 2011; Herrmann, Waxman, and Medin 2010).

We suggest that taking anthropocentrism as a universal developmental pathway privileges settler colonial relationships to land, reinscribes anthropocentrism by constructing land as an inconsequential or inanimate material backdrop for human privileged activity and enables human dislocation from land. One way that the phenomenon of dislocation occurs is through the construction of places as objects or sites, which Bowers (2001) names as fundamentally a problem of anthropocentricism and Gruenewald (2003) suggests is deeply pedagogical. Corbett (2007) explores the ways in which mobile modernity extends the disembedding of peoples from places, a process that Griffiths (2007) has called 'the deforestation of the mind' (25).

For Indigenous learners, this conceptual and developmental pathway functions as a form of dispossession and epistemic (and in our view ontological) violence (e.g. Marker 2006; Wildcat 2009). Indigenous scholars have focused much attention on relationships between land, epistemology and, importantly, ontology (e.g. Cajete 2000; Deloria 1979; Meyer 1998). Places produce and teach particular ways of thinking about and being in the world. They tell us the way things are, even when they operate pedagogically beneath a conscious level (Cajete 2000; Kawagley 1995). Richardson (2011) makes the observation that much of contemporary learning theory is object focused and runs 'roughshod' over Indigenous theories of learning and development, which we feel at a bare minimum are focused on the development and maintenance of respectful reciprocal subject-subject relations. The intersection between object focused learning theory and constructions of places as human-shaped objects reifies settler colonial relationship to knowledge and power.

As an example, in another study, we looked at the representations of ecosystems in curricula and human presence or absence. Nearly all of the curricular materials we looked at had no human represented in ecosystems (Bang, Medin, and Atran 2007) – this absence is emblematic of the nature/culture epistemic divide in western ways of knowing. Further, if you go to the internet and search for images of ecosystems you will reproduce this phenomenon (Medin and Bang, forthcoming). Indeed, Casey (1997) (as cited in Gruenewald 2003) suggests 'that there is a fundamental paradox of place – it is everywhere, yet it recedes from consciousness as we become engrossed in our routines in space and time'(25). In our view, the recession of place from consciousness depends on the ways in which we understand and routinize our relationships to other beings. The receding of place is only the case if we maintain anthropocentric forms of being in which all other forms of life are relegated to the backdrops of human existence or as resource (Ingold 2011).

The implicit and explicit narratives and representations of human/land relations in learning environments is a specific example of the way in which Indigenous epistemologies and ontologies are denied. Burkhart (2004), in an effort to clearly articulate the difference in ontology between western and Indigenous knowledges, made a revision of the famous Descartes adage 'I think, therefore I am' to express something closer to an Indigenous ontology to 'We are, therefore I am.' Extending this, we might imagine that the ontology of place-based paradigms is something like 'I am, therefore place is,' in contrast, the ontology of land-based pedagogies might be summarized as 'Land is, therefore we are.' This reframing in our view carries considerable weight in relation to the way we think about, study, and live culture, learning and development with land. In the next section we aim to concretize the dimensions we have been exploring and describe the ways in which we worked to live 'land is, therefore we are' through specific examples of our project and the subsequent emergent urban land-based pedagogies.

## Learning to (re)story Chicago as Indigenous lands

Drawing from a six-year community-based design research project, a modified methodological tool used to create and study learning environments (see Bang et al. 2013; Brown 1992; Penuel et al. 2011), we came to simultaneously theorize or conscientize, resist, and develop transformative praxis (Smith 2004) in moments of teaching and learning and developed our version of land education. We pause for a moment to explain what design-based research is and why we choose it as a tool.

Design-based research (DBR) is a methodology that was developed from the recognition of the inadequacy of many educational research traditions to understand the complexities of learning and the development and implementation of learning environments. DBR scholars are typically committed to developing transformative solutions to pressing educational problems immediately, and thus, design research is driven by goals of progressive refinement of both theory and practice (Brown 1992; Collins, Joseph, and Bielaczyc 2004) that enables researchers to contextualize theoretical questions about learning in lived lives and involves 'a sequence of decisions made to balance goals and constraints' (Edelson 2002, 108). Unfortunately, the development of learning environments (i.e. schools) rarely engages decision makers that are drawn from students' communities and has been noted to be an important factor in reinscribing current power paradigms (Sawyer 2006). As an initial step in retooling design research in our context, we engaged a broad range of community members as the decisions makers in the design and enactment of a place-based science-learning environment. We refer to this process as *community-based design research* (CBDR) (See Bang et al. 2010 for more details) and view it as aligned with what Gutiérrez and Vossoughi (2010) have named social design experiments.

The choice of a methodology that carefully examines the development and implementation of a learning environment in our view was also aligned with needs in our community produced by federal Indian education policies (e.g. boarding schools or generation of foster children) that claimed the rights and practices of teaching and parenting as their domains and were enacted toward the settler-colonial logic of elimination (literally). In our view, this now seemingly settled structure has continued to keep Indigenous peoples out of classrooms in the role of teacher as evidenced by the low number of Native teachers (e.g. Moran and Rampey 2008). The intent of using CBDR as a tool was to support community members in reframing, revisioning, and restoring (see Smith 1999) the classroom level of teaching and learning for Indigenous children to instantiate educational self-determination. In our experience, community-based design work afforded communities critical space to work through the historical traumas of settler colonialism (Duran, Duran, and Yellow Horse Brave Heart 1998; Walters et al. 2011) that has produced our experiences with formal education and helps us to better see the 'complexity, contradiction and the self-determination of lived lives' (Tuck 2009, 416) in order to create better teaching and learning with our children and youth. Further, we see the iterative nature of design research aligned with Indigenous epistemologies because it elevates creation, processes, and practices of knowing in nonlinear and specific contexts in ways that in our opinion few other research tools in the study of learning environments do. In short, for us, CBDR allowed us to generate forms of land education.

Following our design process was the creation and implementation of youth and family programs held at the American Indian Center of Chicago, a local community organization. These learning environments, originally described as 'informal' place-based science learning environments, were initially held during the summer and then expanded to year-round programming for youth and Saturday programming for youth and their families. During our design work we contemplated many, many ideas but continually returned to three compelling themes: (1) knowing Chicago as the lands of our ancestors and specifically visiting old village sites, (2) knowing Chicago as wet*lands* where many medicinal and edible plants grew and continue to grow, and (3) understanding the impacts of invasive species on these lands. We organized our pedagogy around knowing and coming to know through building relationships with land. Specifically, designers decided in order to know ourselves and our ancestors better, we should remake relationships with our plant relatives and we named our units 'Remaking Relatives.' Exemplifying how *knowing* and *coming to know* was articulated we look to Sarah, an elder in our group. During a design meeting she said:

> I think we have to keep in mind … we need to express these concepts that we're putting together for the kids in Indian thought because what you see … is we're really fishing around for the correct English words to express the Indian thought. In creating this curriculum we also have to use our Indian thought to create our own language of how we're going to express these concepts and what we want our kids to learn and understand as well as to help us to be able to become familiar with that language … because we, as Native people, we have that connection, that non Indian people are searching for. They say recycling and all of these terms whereas we say we're living in harmony and we recognize our relatives, stuff like that. But they're not to that point of recognizing any relatives. They're at the point of knowing that you have to recycle in order to help the environment and to stop the, what is that, the global warming. They're not talking about helping the earth heal. They're not talking about helping our relatives to survive. Those kinds of concepts are what we talk about and the people who study about the birds and all of that, they come from a different concept also but they still don't recognize the birds as being relatives. They look at the birds as being a very important part of the cycle of life that keeps the earth in balance. But we have that missing piece that we need to find words, how to put our thoughts down and create that language that we need in our curriculum.

Sarah highlights differences between western and Indigenous ways of knowing (e.g. recycling/global warming, harmony/healing/relatives). Echoing Veracini, we suggest that Sarah is saying the group needs to both recognize and move beyond the ZPE and is voicing the core distinction between Indigenous peoples (relations to land) and settler colonial societies (relations to property). In other words, she is telling us that we need to uphold land as our relative, not as a material object to protect for perpetual use or conservation. Further, Sarah here connects these to issues of language. Throughout our design process, elders and community members explored these issues and we constructed, adapted, and improvised materials for use in our programs (see Bang et al. 2010 for details). However, once we moved past the planning stage to the implementation phase many previously unseen dynamics became apparent and we became particularly focused on the micro-practices of teaching.

One particularly important dimension that became visible is the role of naming in learning and the ways in which naming is the site at which issues with references between Western and Indigenous epistemologies unfold. During teacher meetings, we often found ourselves in recursive conversations around conceptual terminology and naming (see Marin and Bang, forthcoming). This began, in part, by our awareness about the function and profound impact of language extermination on our communities and knowledge systems (e.g. Hermes 2012). While this carries significant epistemological implications, it became increasingly clear to us how scientific terminology and English obscured the ontological differences we were trying to navigate in moments of 'instructional' practice.

A particular content focus we took up was the importing of plants from other places and specifically common Buckthorn, a native species in Europe that was brought to North America in the early 1800s. This plant is particularly destructive to woodlands and oak savannahs and is considered a deeply problematic invasive species. The act of naming became particularly important as we continued to develop curricula around 'invasive species' (see Bang and Medin 2010; LaDuke 2005). We, the teachers in the program, recognized our use of the term invasive species signaled a particular epistemic and ontological stance to youth – a western science one specifically – and not one that we intended. Thus, the term invasive species placed buckthorn, and other plants that were forcibly migrated to Chicago, outside our design principle around naming our plant relatives because while they may not have been *our* relatives, the term disposed them as relatives to any humans. Further, the term failed to make visible the motivation of settlers that brought flora and fauna from their homelands to make these new lands like home – or what has been termed ecological imperialism (Crosby 2004; McKinley 2007). While supporting 'border crossing' (Aikenhead 2001), meaning helping students to learn in western scientific paradigms in addition to Indigenous, did become an important focus for us, it was not where we were yet in the process, and thus, this insight became another specific example of the ways in which Indigenous erasure can happen in a learning environment – even when we are working hard to be mindful of settler colonialism.

Following Sarah's advice to find words to express Indian thought, 'we fished around' to find a name centered in our own epistemic and ontological centers. In what we view as an form of critical border thinking, we began referring to these plants formerly named 'invasive species' to 'plants that people lost their relationships with.' Further, we delved into knowing the migrations of these plants and their relationship with contact and colonialism in the Americas. While at that time we were not closely examining Sarah's words in the way we are now, we think our pedagogical transformations (renaming of invasive species and as we will see weaving the history and current presence of land restructuring into our practice) reflect our learning on her meanings in pedagogically specific ways. In the specific case of naming our plant relatives, it marked an intentional type of relationship, as well as an intentional pedagogical focus on relationships. Mignolo and Tlostanova (2006) suggest we need a 'relentless critical awareness of what guiding principles are structuring engagement in moments' (458). The teachers 'awareness' of the embedded nature of language we think of as a classroom level example of Mignolo's point. Using pedagogical language like 'plants that people have lost their relationship with,' ruptures the epistemology of the zero point, because it begins to always see ontology and epistemology[6] and refuses a settler colonial narrative of and relationship to land.

Learning about our relationship with our plant relatives in this way opened the space for old perceptual ways to lead and we experienced a cascading effect on how our work continued to unfold. For example, we increasingly engaged in reading the land (see Marin and Bang, forthcoming) and expanded our learning of their (plant relatives) relationships to land and water. Just as we worked to see our plant relatives from a long view, we also began to see the waters they grew in the same way. While this may seem simple, increasingly scholars are investigating the deep socio-cultural nature of attentional habits, the semitotic resources mobilized in such attentional habits and the shaping of knowledge construction (see Correa-Chavez, Rogoff, and Mejia Arauz 2005; Eberbach and Crowley 2009; Goodwin and Goodwin 2012; Marin 2013; Tulbert and Goodwin 2011). While we did this during our program with youth and families even our planning took this turn. We no longer sat in rooms to plan our activities, we went for walks through our neighborhoods to plan our activities, or we visited other specific locations within the city.

We began to articulate a pedagogical vision for ourselves in which land was our teacher and our job as teachers was to support our youth in developing right relations with land. As we continued to make sense of our plant relatives' relationships to land and water, four wetlands became our core places of learning. In turn, we began working toward understanding land's and water's relationships to time and history. Two wetlands we frequently visited were historically known village sites and officially part of the Cook County Forest Preserve system. The two others we visited, were places of restoring wetlands – one by human design and one because humans left it alone. While it is likely that place based or environmental education could easily take up the study of these two wetlands, we suggest that in a land-based pedagogy we took up these wetlands in unique ways.

In our project, the juxtapositions of these wetlands made explicit the ways in which the altering and restructuring of land in North America was and is a foundational practice in settler colonial paradigms in a variety of ways. For our purposes, here, we highlight two key dimensions made visible through the engagement of different wetlands. The first was the recognition of how the filling of wetlands factored greatly in the settlement of the Chicago areas and establishing Chicago as a national transportation hub and why some forest preserves or parks in which the wetlands were located were there (some are still connected to land claim issues and cannot be transferred to individual property ownership legally). The second was the difference between land altering toward erasure and land altering for aiding. The restoring wetland via human 'neglect,' or the places in which settler colonial structures (practice of filling) were no longer being closely imposed, made visible the ways in plant relatives and water were remerging and eroding the fill. In intentionally restored spaces, uses of techniques like burning (a technique used historically by Indigenous peoples) were developed with knowledge of and supported plant relatives of these lands (prairie plants have deep root systems that can survive burning whereas non-indigenous plants in these places tend not to and do not survive). As teachers, we began to track and weave into our thinking, and in the moment-to-moment interactions in teaching and learning, the waves of ecological restructuring that has occurred in Chicago; from the filling of wetlands, to the reengineering of the direction of the Chicago river, the mass destruction of prairie lands for agriculture, to the importing of plants from other places. Relentless efforts to story land from long views of time and experience, and elevating the importance of and reclaiming naming practices we see as critical dimensions in urban land based pedagogies. In short, as a matter of pedagogical principle, we worked to make always visible the history and change of the lands we live in, in short, land became our first teacher and our learning environments emerge from there.

For Indigenous scholars, relational pedagogies of land are not new (Cajete 2000; Kawagley 1995) even in Shikaakwa. Burkhart (2004) writes that 'a native philosophical understanding must include as experience, not simply my own … If I am to gain a right understanding I must account for all that I see, but also all that you see and all that has been seen by others.' Re-remembering to 'see' Chicago as Indigenous lands enabled the development of urban land-based pedagogies. We see the shift to land and water as an example of what he is talking about and of what land-based pedagogies recreate; making sense of what plants 'see.' Critically important, however, this move is a non-anthropocentric stance that ruptures normative paradigms of plants. Berthold-Bond (2000) calls for a change in perceptual habits and suggests that places must be experienced differently – that place-conscious education must develop pedagogies that learn to listen to what places are telling us. In effect, re-centering our perceptual habits in Indigenous ontologies and epistemologies, we came to see land re-becoming itself and reclaim our continuing presence or 'stories-so-far' (Massey 2005) in Chicago and Shikaakwa from narratives of deficit and disposed urban Indians.

## Discussion

Re-storying Chicago required journeying through those layers of colonial fill, which quietly operate in teaching and learning environments to make visible dynamics of settler colonialism. In this paper, we have described various examples of these dynamics including: (1) the broad constructions Indigenous absence and various forms of Indigenous presence, (2) the constructions of lands as uninhabited or that make invisible the waves of land restructuring over time, and (3) specific examples from an urban land based education project that centered Indigenous epistemologies and ontologies. As Indigenous people, we do not need to re-inhabit or learn to dwell in the places in which we have always dwelt (see Bowers 2009). For the teachers involved in this project, the process was not about re-inhabitation – it was learning from land to restore(y) it and ourselves as original inhabitants – that is living our stories in contested lands (Somerville 2007) and restoring land as the first teacher even in 'urban' lands. Narratives in which Indigenous people are absent, or relegated to a liberal multiculturalism that subsumes Indigenous dominion to occupancy, and narratives and positionings of land as backdrop for anthropocentric life, will only help to produce new narratives of territorial acquisition and fail to bring about needed social change (Tuck and Yang 2012; see related point in Greenwood 2009).

In part, what we are suggesting is that although we may have ceded territory in the current era, something we will continue to learn hard lessons about, a long view of humans' histories suggests that what would be worse is if we continue to cede our ontologies and epistemologies with territory by becoming blind to land. Land is here and so are new generations of Indigenous youth – if we raise them. Alfred (2005) says that what we need to do is rethink how we reference ourselves and 'to cause mental awakening and to give people knowledge of the selves and of the world thereby restoring the memory of who we truly are as Onkwehonwe' (282). Our project helped to expand the mental awakenings in our community and to build possibilities toward young people not being forced into genesis amnesia (Bourdieu 1977) in the service of settler futurity. The (re)storying of these ontologies and epistemologies meant we could move towards Indigenous identity and possibility living in our ceded lands not defined by current power paradigms of simultaneous dispossession and containment and able to resist and act on dimensions of political, sociological, and ideological prescriptions that produce them and ensure settler futures. Urban land-based education helped us build toward viable futures of robust indigeneities (Simpson 2011) of survivance and sovereignty of lived lives and Land reclamation.

## Muskrat theories

Muskrat dives to retrieve lands that live beneath the waters.

> Sometimes to necssarily till the relations between water and land in order to support the unique plants that thrive in these wetlands.

And sometimes muskrat dives for remaking home lands.

> Diving through the settler colonial fill, we have started to retrieve the good lands that still flow. Relearning to see and story our relational dynamisms with land and water, is making way for decolonizing projects in land currently named urban and ceded.

As we continue our stories-so-far (Massey 2005), we believe Muskrat will dive and help re-story our lands again as we continue our paths of becoming.

## Acknowledgements

We are grateful to all of the Chicago American Indian community members, teachers, designers, and research assistants who participated in this work and taught us so much. Special thanks to Cynthia Soto and Douglas Medin for their leadership and insight. Thanks to Lori Faber and Jasmine Alfonso who have supported us in the work and in producing this manuscript.

## Funding

This material is based upon work supported by the National Science Foundation [1205758 and 1208209].

## Notes

1. Chicago was one of the original cities the US government relocated Native peoples to by force, choice, and in effort to assimilate us into the American mainstream during what is known as the Termination and Relocation era of the 1940–1960's.
2. There are more than 150 tribes from across North America represented in the Chicago community.
3. Self-determination refers to the legal, political, social, and cultural beliefs in which tribes in the United States exercise self-governance and decision-making on issues that affect our own people.
4. Gruenwald (2008) explores the dynamics of this issue (not named as an issue of settler colonialism) through the ways in which 'diversity' in American institutions is

constructed about racial representation, not about diverse ways of knowing and engaging the world.

5. See the Exxon-Valdez decision, 1994 WL 182, 856 and 104 F.3d 1196, in which the judge did not find Native Alaskan fishing practices as different in kind from other Alaskans thus denying their claim as a prime and significantly consequential example of a kind-degree slippage.
6. While we make no definitive claim here, we do want to point out that this phrase mirrors the types of translations of heritage language meanings.

## References

Abram, D. 1996. *The Spell of the Sensuous*. New York: Pantheon.

Aikenhead, G. 2001. "Students' Ease in Crossing Cultural Borders into School Science." *Science Education* 85 (2): 180–188.

Alfred, T. 2005. *Wasáse: Indigenous Pathways of Action and Freedom*. Ontario: Broadview Press.

Archibald, J. 2008. *Indigenous Storywork*. Vancouver: UBC Press.

Bang, M., and D. Medin. 2010. "Cultural Processes in Science Education: Supporting the Navigation of Multiple Epistemologies." *Science Education* 94 (6): 1008–1026.

Bang, M., D. L. Medin, and S. Atran. 2007. "Cultural Mosaics and Mental Models of Nature." *Proceedings of the National Academy of Sciences* 104 (35): 13868–13874.

Bang, M., D. Medin, K. Washinawatok, and S. Chapman. 2010. "Innovations in Culturally-based Science Education through Partnerships and Community." In *New Science of Learning: Cognition, Computers and Collaboration in Education*, edited by Myint Swe Khine and Issa M Saleh, 569–592. New York: Springer.

Bang, M., B. Warren, A. S. Rosebery, and D. Medin. 2012. "Desettling Expectations in Science Education." *Human Development* 55 (5–6): 302–318.

Bang, M., A. Marin, L. Faber, and E. S. Suzukovich. 2013. "Repatriating Indigenous Technologies in an Urban Indian Community." *Urban Education* 48 (5): 705–733.

Battiste, M. 2002. *Indigenous Knowledge and Pedagogy in First Nations Education: A Literature Review with Recommendations*. Ottawa, ON: Apamuwek Institute.

Berthold-Bond, D. 2000. "The Ethics of 'place'." *Environmental Ethics* 22 (1): 5–24.

Bourdieu, P. 1977. *Outline of a Theory of Practice*. Translated by R. Nice. Cambridge: Cambridge University Press.

Bowers, C. A. 2001. *Educating for Eco-justice and Community*. Athens, GA: The University of Georgia Press.

Bowers, C. A. 2002. "Toward an Eco-Justice Pedagogy." *Environmental Education Research* 8 (1): 21–34.

Bowers, C. A. 2003. "Can Critical Pedagogy Be Greened?" *Educational Studies* 34: 11–20.

Bowers, C. A. 2009. "Why the George Lakoff and Mark Johnson theory of Metaphor is Inadequate for Addressing Cultural Issues Related to the Ecological Crises." *Language & Ecology* 2 (4): 1–16.

Brayboy, B. M. 2004. "Hiding in the Ivy: American Indian Students and Visibility in Elite Educational Settings." *Harvard Educational Review* 74 (2): 125–152.

Brayboy, B. M. J., and A. E. Castagno. 2008. "How Might Native Science Inform Informal Science Learning?" *Cultural Studies of Science Education* 3 (3): 731–750.

Brown, A. L. 1992. "Design Experiments: Theoretical and Methodological Challenges in Creating Complex Interventions in Classroom Settings." *The Journal of the Learning Sciences* 2 (2): 141–178.

Burkhart, B. Y. 2004. "What Coyote and Thales Can Teach Us: An Outline of American Indian Epistemology." In *American Indian Thought: Philosophical Essays*, edited by A. Waters, 15–26. Malden, MA: Blackwell.

Cajete, G. 2000. *Native Science: Natural Laws of Interdependence*. Santa Fe: Clear Light.

Carey, S. 1985. *Conceptual Change in Childhood*. Cambridge: Bradford Books.

Casey, E. 1997. *The Fate of Place: A Philosophical History*. Berkeley: University of California Press.

Castro-Gómez, S. 2002. "The Social Sciences, Epistemic Violence and the Problem of the Invention of the Other." *Napantla: Views from the South* 3 (2): 269–285.

Collins, A., D. Joseph, and K. Bielaczyc. 2004. "Design Research: Theoretical and Methodological Issues." *Journal of the Learning Sciences* 13 (1): 15–42.

Corbett, M. 2007. "Travels in Space and Place: Identity and Rural Schooling." *Canadian Journal of Education* 30 (3): 771–792.

Correa-Chavez, M., B. Rogoff, and R. Mejia Arauz. 2005. "Cultural Patterns in Attending to Two Events at Once." *Child Development* 76 (3): 664–678.

Crosby, A. W. 2004. *Ecological Imperialism: The Biological Expansion of Europe, 900–1900*. Cambridge: Cambridge University Press.

Deloria, V. 1979. *The Metaphysics of Modern Existence*. 1st ed. San Francisco, NC: Harper & Row.

Deloria, V., B. Deloria, K. Foehner, and S. Scinta. 1999. *Spirit & Reason: The Vine Deloria, Jr. Reader*. Golden, CO: Fulcrum.

Deloria, V., and C. M. Lytle. 1998. *The Nations Within: The Past and Future of American Indian Sovereignty*. Austin, TX: University of Texas Press.

Duran, B., E. Duran, and M. Yellow Horse Brave Heart. 1998. "Native Americans and the Trauma of History." In *Studying Native America: Problems and Prospects*, 60–76. Madison: University of Wisconsin Press.

Eberbach, C., and K. Crowley. 2009. "From Everyday to Scientific Observation: How Children Learn to Observe the Biologist's World." *Review of Educational Research* 79 (1): 39–68.

Edelson, D. C. 2002. "Design Research: What We Learn When We Engage in Design." *The Journal of the Learning Sciences* 11 (1): 105–121.

Friedel, T. L. 2011. "Looking for Learning in all the Wrong Places: Urban Native Youths' Cultured Response to Western-Oriented Place-Based Learning." *International Journal of Qualitative Studies in Education* 24 (5): 531–546.

Goodwin, M. H., and C. Goodwin. 2012. "Car Talk: Integrating Texts, Bodies and Changing Landscapes*." *Semiotica* 191 (1/4): 257–286.

Grande, S. 2004. *Red Pedagogy: Native American Social and Political Thought*. Lanham, MD: Rowman & Littlefield.

Greenwood, D. A. 2009. "Place, Survivance, and White Remembrance: A Decolonizing Challenge to Rural Education in Mobile Modernity." *Journal of Research in Rural Education* 24 (10): 1–6.

Griffiths, J. 2007. *Wild: An Elemental Journey*. New York, NY: Penguin.

Gruenewald, D. A. 2003. "The Best of Both Worlds: A Critical Pedagogy of Place." *Educational Researcher* 32 (4): 3–12.

Gruenewald, D. A. 2008. "The Best of Both Worlds: A Critical Pedagogy of Place*." *Environmental Education Research* 14 (3): 308–324.

Gruenewald, D., and D. Smith. 2008. *Place-based Education in the Global Age: Local Diversity*. Mahwah, NJ: Lawrence Erlbaum.

Gutiérrez, K. D., and S. Vossoughi. 2010. "Lifting off the Ground to Return Anew: Mediated Praxis, Transformative Learning, and Social Design Experiments." *Journal of Teacher Education* 61 (1–2): 100–117.

Hall, R., and R. Nemirovsky. 2012. "Introduction to the Special Issue: Modalities of Body Engagement in Mathematical Activity and Learning." *Journal of the Learning Sciences* 21 (2): 207–215.

Helmreich, S. 2011. "Nature/Culture/Seawater." *American Anthropologist* 113 (1): 132–144.

Herrmann, P. A., D. L. Medin, and S. R. Waxman. 2011. "When Humans Become Animals: Development of the Animal Category in Early Childhood." *Cognition* 107 (22): 9979–9984.

Herrmann, P., S. R. Waxman, and D. L. Medin. 2010. "Anthropocentrism is not the First Step in Children's Reasoning about the Natural World." *Proceedings of the National Academy of Sciences* 107 (22): 9979–9984.

Hermes, M. 2012. "Indigenous Language Revitalization and Documentation in the United States: Collaboration Despite Colonialism." *Language and Linguistics Compass* 6 (3): 131–142.

Ingold, T. 2000. *The Perception of the Environment: Essays on Livelihood, Dwelling and Skill*. London: Psychology Press.

Ingold, T. 2011. *Being Alive: Essays on Movement, Knowledge and Description*. New York: Routledge.

Kawagley, O. 1995. *A Yupiaq Worldview*. Prospect Heights, IL: Waveland Press.

Kirksey, S., and S. Helmreich. 2010. "The Emergence of Multispecies Ethnography." *Cultural Anthropology* 25 (4): 545–576.

Kitchens, J. 2009. "Situated Pedagogy and the Situationist International: Countering a Pedagogy of Placelessness." *Educational Studies* 45 (3): 240–261.

LaDuke, W. 2005. *Recovering the Sacred: The Power of Naming and Claiming*. Cambridge: South End Press.

Marin, A. 2013. *Learning to Attend and Observe: Parent-Child Meaning Making in the Natural World*. PhD diss.: Northwestern University.

Marin, A., and B. Bang. Forthcoming. *Repatriating Science Teaching and Learning: Finding Our Way to Storywork*.

Marker, M. 2006. "After the Makah Whale Hunt." *Urban Education* 41 (5): 482–505.

Massey, D. 2005. *For Space*. London: Sage.

McKenzie, M. 2004. "The 'Willful contradiction' of Poststructural Socio-ecological Education." *Canadian Journal of Environmental Education (CJEE)* 9 (1): 164–177.

McKinley, E. 2007. "Postcolonialism, Indigenous Students, and Science Education." In *Handbook of Research on Science Education*, edited by S. K. Abell and N. G. Lederman, 199–226. Mahwah, NJ: Lawrence Erlbaum.

Medin, D., and M. Bang. Forthcoming. The Cultural Side of Science Communication. Proceedings of the National Academies of Science.

Medin, D., S. Waxman, J. Woodring, and K. Washinawatok. 2010. "Human-centered Reasoning is Not a Universal Feature of Young children's Reasoning: Culture and Experience Matter When Reasoning about Biological Entities." *Cognitive Development* 25 (3): 197–207.

Meyer, M. A. 1998. "Native Hawaiian Epistemology: Sites of Empowerment and Resistance." *Equity & Excellence in Education* 31 (1): 22–28.

Mignolo, W. 2007. "Delinking: The Rhetoric of Modernity, the Logic of Coloniality and the Grammar of De-coloniality." *Cultural Studies* 21 (2–3): 449–514.

Mignolo, W. D., and M. V. Tlostanova. 2006. "Theorizing from the Borders." *European Journal of Social Theory* 9 (2): 205–230.

Moran, R., and B. Rampey. 2008. *National Indian Education Study—Part II: The Educational Experiences of American Indian and Alaska Native Students in Grades 4 and 8 (NCES 2008–458).* Washington, DC: National Center for Education Statistics, Institute of Education Sciences, U.S. Department of Education.

Nasir, N., A. Rosebery, B. Warren, and C. Lee. 2006. "Learning as a Cultural Process: Achieving Equity Through Diversity." In *Cambridge Handbook of the Learning Sciences*, edited by R. K. Sawyer, 489–504. Cambridge: Cambridge University Press.

Penuel, W. R., B. J. Fishman, B. H. Cheng, and N. Sabelli. 2011. "Organizing Research and Development at the Intersection of Learning, Implementation, and Design." *Educational Researcher* 40 (7): 331–337.

Pearson, D. 2002. "Theorizing Citizenship in British Settler Societies." *Ethnic and Racial Studies* 25(6): 989–1012.

Richardson, T. 2011. "Navigating the Problem of Inclusion as Enclosure in Native Culture-based Education: Theorizing Shadow Curriculum." *Curriculum Inquiry* 41 (3): 332–349.

Richardson, T., and S. Villenas. 2000. "'Other' Encounters: Dances with Whiteness in Multicultural Education." *Educational Theory* 50 (2): 255–273.

Said, E. 1994. *Culture and Imperialism*. New York: Vintage Books.

Sawyer, R. K. ed. 2006. *The Cambridge Handbook of the Learning Sciences*. New York: Cambridge University Press.

Semali, L. M., and J. L. Kincheloe, eds. 1999. *What is Indigenous Knowledge? Voices from the Academy*. New York: Falmer Press.

Simpson, A. 2011. "Settlement's Secret." *Cultural Anthropology* 26 (2): 205–217.

Sobel, D. 1996. *Beyond Ecophobia: Reclaiming the Heart in Nature Education*. Vol. 1. Great Barrington, MA: Orion Society.

Smith, L. T 1999. *Decolonizing Methodologies: Research and Indigenous Peoples*. London: Zed Books.

Smith, G. H. 2004. "Mai i Te Maramatanga, Ki Te Putanga Mai o Te Tahuritanga: From Conscientization to Transformation." *Educational Perspectives* 37 (1): 46–52.

Somerville, M. 2007. "Place literacies." *Australian Journal of Language and Literacy* 30 (2): 149–164.

Styres, S. D., and D. M. Zinga. 2013. "The Community-First Land-Centred Theoretical Framework: Bringing a 'Good Mind' to Indigenous Education Research?" *Canadian Journal of Education/Revue Canadienne de L'éducation* 36 (2): 284–313.

Sutherland, D., and N. Swayze. 2012. "The Importance of Place in Indigenous Science Education." *Cultural Studies of Science Education* 7 (1): 83–92.

Tippeconnic III, J. W. 1999. "Tribal Control of American Indian Education: Observations Since the 1960s with Implications for the Future." In *Next steps: Research and Practice to Advance Indian Education*, edited by K. G. Swisher and J. W. Tippeconnic III, 33–52. Charleston, WV: ERIC/CRESS (ED 427 904).

Tuck, E. 2009. "Suspending Damage: A Letter to Communities." *Harvard Educational Review* 79 (3): 409–427.

Tuck, E., and W. K. Yang. 2012. "Decolonization is not a Metaphor." *Decolonization: Indigeneity, Education & Society* 1 (1): 1–40.

Tulbert, E., and M. H. Goodwin. 2011. "Choreographies of Attention: Multimodality in a Routine Family Activity." In *Embodied Interaction. Language and Body in the Material World*, edited by J. Streeck, C. Goodwin, and C. LeBaron, 79–92. Cambridge: Cambridge University Press.

Veraci, L. 2011. "On Settlerness." *Borderlands E-Journal* 10 (1): 1–17.

Vizenor, G. R. 1981. *Earthdivers: Tribal Narratives on Mixed Descent*. Minneapolis, MN: University of Minnesota Press.

Vizenor, G. 1994. *Manifest Manners: Postindian Warriors of Survivance*. Hanover, NH: Weslyan University Press.

Walters, K. L., R. Beltrán, D. Huh, and T. Evans-Campbell. 2011. "Dis-placement and Dis-ease: Land, Place, and Health among American Indians and Alaska Natives." In *Neighborhoods, Communities, and Health: Expanding the Boundaries of Place*, edited by

L. M. Burton, S. P. Kemp, M. Leung, S. A. Matthews, and D. T. Takeuchi, 163–199. New York: Springer.

Wildcat, D. R. 2009. *Red Alert. Saving the Planet with Indigenous Knowledge*. Golden, CO: Fulcrum Press.

Wolfe, P. 2006. “Settler-colonialism and the Elimination of the Native.” *Journal of Genocide Research* 8 (4): 387–409.

# Sea Country: navigating Indigenous and colonial ontologies in Australian environmental education

Hilary Whitehouse[a], Felecia Watkin Lui[b], Juanita Sellwood[c], M.J. Barrett[d] and Philemon Chigeza[c]

*[a]School of Education and Centre for Research and Innovation in Sustainability Education, James Cook University, Cairns, Australia; [b]School of Indigenous Australian Studies and The Cairns Institute, James Cook University, Cairns, Australia; [c]School of Education, James Cook University, Cairns, Australia; [d]College of Education, University of Saskatchewan, Saskatoon, Canada*

In this paper, we contribute to land education research by focusing on the Torres Strait Islands in the Coral Sea at the far north of tip of Cape York, Australia. We describe the Torres Strait Islander concept of Sea Country and Torres Strait *Ailan Kastom* (translated as 'Island Custom'). We then analyse some of the ways in which settler colonisation has challenged these ways of knowing and being. Our inquiry looks at how Sea Country is positioned within two contemporary Australian examples of environmental education: firstly, within the new Australian Curriculum cross-curriculum priorities that mandate that special attention be given to Aboriginal and Torres Strait Islander histories and cultures and also to the concept of sustainability; and secondly, within the Great Barrier Reef Marine Park Authority's *Sea Country Guardians* programme This analysis of environmental education curriculum and practice identifies the ways in which the concept of Sea Country and the Indigenous cosmology it represents are simultaneously supported and ignored in the current Australian environmental education context.

## Introduction

From Australian Aboriginal and Torres Strait Islander perspectives, land is alive. So is the sea (Council for Aboriginal Reconciliation 1994). In this paper, we apply the framework of land education research to the tropical sea, in this case, the Coral Sea at the northernmost part of eastern Australia. We analyse how Torres Strait Islander relational ontologies and understandings of Sea Country are being engaged in contemporary environmental education contexts. We first provide a brief overview of the emergent field of land education, and define Sea Country. We then describe the area of the Torres Strait Islands and provide a historical description and analysis of some of the methods by which settler colonisation actively disrupted the traditional concept of Sea Country. Next, we provide a brief analysis of the new Australian Curriculum 5.1 cross-curriculum priorities that mandate that special attention be given to both Aboriginal and Torres Strait Islander histories and cultures, and to the concept of sustainability (Australian Curriculum Assessment and Reporting Authority [ACARA] 2013a, 2013b). This analysis identifies the ways in which the ancient concept of Country is tentatively supported and yet simultaneously ignored in the Australian Curriculum. Finally, we discuss a current example of a Sea Country educational programme specific to the Cape York and Torres Strait region that may be analysed as supporting a move towards decolonised educational practice, but only within remote regions of Australia.

We write as five authors from different educational disciplines and differing national and cultural perspectives. Two authors are Torres Strait Islander scholars, one is Shona (African) Australian, one is an American Australian and one a Canadian animist scholar. We find common ground in our commitment to environmental education and sustainability practices that are respectful of people and the ancient, intricately beautiful concept of Country.

## Land education

One of the tasks for contemporary environmental education research is to realistically consider the complex colonial past as a means for shaping a more equitable future. There are many ways of doing this work; one of those ways is known as land education. Land education research specifically sets out to disrupt colonialist epistemologies that have acted to deny other perspectives within environmental education, calling attention in particular to Indigenous relations to land, where epistemology is integral to being and knowing – and thus being known – in the world (Meyer 2008). In their introduction Tuck, McKenzie and McCoy (2013) argue one purpose of land education is to centre the historical and contemporary contexts of colonisation and colonialism within environmental education practice and research. Land education pays attention to geographies and histories together; in Australia, contemporary environmental learning cannot be severed from our difficult past. Any place in the Australian continent is a place with a colonist story. Much place-based education situates learning in the local (Gruenewald and Smith 2008) and the notion of place challenges the frequently – inscribed dualism of culture and environment (Greenwood 2008; McKenzie 2008). Yet, for Australian Aboriginal and Torres Strait Islander peoples, for whom culture and land management practices are one and the same, recent, popular, and Westernised, approaches to place-based education do not, and perhaps cannot, adequately capture the range and nuances of possible understandings and relations.

The field of land education offers possibility for decolonising human relations with land and water, flora and fauna as well as theoretical opportunities to erase dualisms between nature and culture. Land education proposes a valuable theoretical framework for reconsidering what it means to engage in environmental education. In giving explicit emphasis to decolonisation as well as acknowledgement and recognition to the epistemological, ontological and cosmological relations different peoples have with lands and waters, approaches to land education have the potential to provide a welcoming and useful space for many peoples and their educational practices. As Indigenous scholar Meyer (2008) writes, ‘One does not simply learn about land, we learn best *from* land’ (219). In this paper, we aspire to open dialogue on the importance of the concept of land education, by bringing attention to the old, extant practice of Sea Country education, with the purpose of considering how land and sea can be included together in this new and growing field of research.

## Sea Country

The Council for Aboriginal Reconciliation (1994) explains Country as a 'place of origin, literally, culturally or spiritually'. Country is 'a shorthand for all the values, places, resources, stories, and cultural obligations associated with … [a] geographical area. For coastal Aboriginal peoples and Torres Strait Islanders, "country" includes both land and sea areas which are regarded as inseparable from each other'. Country, as the term is taken up in Australia, does not mean 'the environment'. Country is better understood as a vital interconnected web of social, ecological and spiritual relationships; it epitomises the way of existing in and viewing the world that might be termed the 'relational ontology' of Indigenous Australians. Torres Strait Islanders deem Sea Country to be where 'island, reef and ocean comprise a cultural and experiential continuum' (Scott and Mulrennan 1999, 146). 'Sea Country', also known as 'Saltwater Country', is an imperfect English translation of very old, extant and now flourishing Torres Strait Islander concepts and practices concerning care for saltwater 'land' that extends beyond littoral boundaries to the continental shelf and oceanic horizons. The terms refer to coastal, island and marine environments that together constitute the traditional estates of the coastal and maritime peoples in Australia (Smyth 1997).

The Torres Strait islands lie off the northernmost tip of Cape York, Queensland, on the eastern side of continental Australia. The islands were formed after the last sea level rise at the end of the last ice age. The Torres Strait totals an area of over 35,000 square kilometres, which consists of 2.6% terrestrial land, 6.2% tidally inundated reef flats and 91.2% open seas with mainly shallow water. The whole of this area is considered by all groups of Torres Strait Islanders to be Sea Country. As the Torres Strait is positioned on one of the world's largest continental shelves, known for its biodiversity and complex ecosystems (Torres Strait Regional Authority [TSRA] 2013), Sea Country is being increasingly recognised as essential for biodiversity conservation and environmental sustainability in northern Australia (see Hoffmann et al. 2012). Indeed, Torres Strait Islanders engage in the sustainable management of their marine resources in keeping with their cultural beliefs and customary practices. Environmental sustainability has long equalled cultural sustainability for the people of the Torres Strait, who, traditionally, have been both agriculturalists and seafarers (Torres Strait Island Regional Council [TSIRC] 2013).

It is important to emphasise just how central the sea is to the lives and mentalities of Torres Strait Islanders. Singe (1979, xi) considers the Torres Strait Islander lifestyle to be 'totally integrated with the sea'. As 11-year-old Torres Strait Islander Abigail Mooka wrote:

> Today I went fishing, in a little boat with a big machine. Row! Row! Went the big machine. Rock! Rock! We went rocking out to sea. Swap! Came a little school of fish. Tick! Tick! I felt one. Romp! Romp! I roll the line. At the end of my line is a big one. In it comes. It's a big snapper. I go back home. Torres Strait is the place I love. (Mooka 1990)

Sea Country is a way of making meaning that long precedes the colonisation of Australia by Europeans in the eighteenth century, 'anchoring understanding of place and time as continuing on from the past into the here and now' (Nakata 2010, 54). Whap (2001, 22–23) explains that Torres Strait Island knowledge is a 'living knowledge':

> It is knowledge 'passed on' by my ancestors to my grandparents, to my parents then to me, about the importance of life, surrounding nature, sea, land, wind, and sky, and how they interact in my life. This knowledge entails the concept that people 'belong' and are part of the land, sea and sky; these spheres are not set apart, but rather are kept balanced and in tune.

Both within Australia and internationally, theorising of Indigenous peoples' relationships explores knowledge-based relationships between ecology and social identity (see Meyer 2008; Scott and Mulrennan 1999). Land, water and sky become animate through relationships – to ancestors, to plants and animals, and to clouds, hills, rocks and mineral forms. In the Torres Strait, researchers Cordell and Fitzpatrick (1987, 1) were able to articulate a sense of relational place for the Mabuiag people of the Torres Strait as follows:

> What first appear to be undifferentiated patches of coral and salt water are Islanders' exclusive marine domains – a vast, intricate water library where history dwells in places, not in time, and all the sea is named. Islands, reefs, channels and the resources they contain belong to Badu and Mabuiag people because mythical ancestors like Sesere, Zigin, and Wad caught turtles, dugong, or fish there. These things belong to a time of unwritten language not taught in any textbook. Nearly all folk-tales start with this special sense of place. Islander history survives through the continued occupation and use of islands and reefs and the crisscrossing of home seas.

For Torres Strait Islanders, entities within a social-ecological system are not categorised into a binary opposition of 'people' and 'the environment'. Relationships, not things, are fundamental to Torres Strait Islander epistemology and ontology and it is the totality of these complex relationships that are captured within the terminology of Country. In educational terms, Country is also tens of thousands of years of accumulated knowledge. According to Rose (1996), the Australian situation is unique for there may be nowhere else in the world where such a body of knowledge has been built up 'so consistently' and for so long and with such stability through time. In Torres Strait Creole language, this knowledge is known as *long taim* (long time) knowledge, which is passed on by community elders, who are, traditionally, guardians of knowledge (Whap 2001).

Strong cultural, social, economic and spiritual links are forged between Torres Strait Islanders and their Sea Country through the distinct governing principle of *Ailan Kastom*, translated as 'Island Custom' (TSRA 2013). *Ailan Kastom* has universal acceptance amongst Torres Strait Islanders for describing and maintaining ways of knowing and being (Watkin Lui 2012). *Ailan Kastom* underpins relationships to Sea Country and also connections to family and community, as explained here by Loban (2008):

> As I got older I was taught the importance of the sea, never to underestimate it and to show appreciation when the occasion was appropriate. An example of appreciation is when we catch a lot of fish, we would throw some fish back or "chuck e talk" to thank

> our ancestors and the sea for being generous. Also I must share my catch equally among the Mabaygal (people) who caught the catch and from my share give a share to family members who were in a less fortunate state.

On a metaphysical level, the relationship between customary practices – *Ailan Kastom* – and Sea Country is one of the heart; it is what one privately feels and deeply knows in terms of a spiritual connection to Saltwater Country, particularly to coral reefs and to totemic sea animals such as dugong and turtle and crocodile. Torres Strait Islanders describe themselves as Saltwater People in recognition of their heartfelt connection to Sea Country. And whether a Torres Strait Islander resides within or outside the Torres Strait, s/he will always feel that affiliation to the sea and will have and maintain a specified kin relationship to important marine animals, plants, tides and currents (Smyth 1997). Sea Country and *Ailan Kastom* have recently been officially acknowledged in government legislation, marine management plans and other environmental initiatives, including environmental education, as we will discuss further. But despite this recognition, these old concepts have had to survive severe disturbances from British colonisation that persist to this day.

## Historical settler colonisation of Sea Country

It is important to understand that Australia is both a long-settled country and a federated settler nation just over 112 years old. Throughout the history of the British Empire and well into the twentieth century, Aboriginal and Torres Strait Islander knowledge, languages, understandings and rights were ruthlessly eradicated from political, economic and consequently educational practices. The concept of Sea Country, as we have described above, was deeply challenged by waves of immigration and colonising legislative practices. In pre-colonial Australia, all Saltwater Country was owned and managed within strictly delineated boundaries by many different peoples from many different language groups. In the Torres Strait, *Ailan Kastom* prescribed conditions and practices of ownership. But with Australian Federation in 1901, every beach was declared public space, with the Federal law excluding private property rights between high and low tide zones. While this legal manoeuvre manifested Australian ideals of freedom (the beach as open, with free passage for all), this move contradicted much older laws, lores and customs. In other words, the concept of the sea as a public commons or open access 'was imported to Australia at the time of colonisation' (Northern Land Council 2003).

Wolfe (2006) has argued that settler colonialism is not simply colonialism. Colonialism typically ends, whereas settler colonialism lasts forever, except in the rare event of complete evacuation. Settler colonialism is a project that wishes Indigenous people to vanish, and sometimes makes use of their labour before they are made to disappear. This notion is illustrated well by the mentality of the Christian missionaries in the Torres Strait in the early to mid-twentieth century, who felt it was their job to 'soothe the pillow of a dying race' (see Reynolds 1972). In terms of Australia's social, political and economic history (which is, of course, intimately bound with its environmental history), the intent of European settler colonialism was to replace an ancient, settled and known continent with new narratives of colonisation; that is Australia as a 'young" nation and Australia as a 'white' nation (Australian Broadcasting Corporation 2001).

The replacement of Sea Country as lived, known, loved, understood, mapped and cared for with the notion that it was empty land, or *terra nullius*, is mind-boggling to contemporary scholastic sensibilities. But, British colonisation of Australia (from 1788) was predicated on the legal fiction of *terra nullius* that 'allowed the European community of nations to expand their colonial horizons with minimal concern for Indigenous peoples' (Stephenson and Ratnapala 1993, 25). Indeed, inequity and contaminating prejudice run deep in Australia precisely because the colonial project was essentially a land grab for 'the biggest estate on Earth' (Gammage 2011). The effect of colonisation was that vast numbers of people were physically, politically, economically and socially alienated from their own country.

On the basis of colonial settlement, the Queensland government acquired 'absolute beneficial ownership' of all land and sea in the Torres Strait, and this was implemented by an annexation in 1878. A century later, however, Eddie Koiki Mabo, a Torres Strait Islander from Mer Island, successfully challenged the idea of Crown land ownership in the High Court of Australia. Mabo declared that traditional land and sea rights did exist because the Torres Strait Islands 'had been continuously inhabited and exclusively possessed by their people who lived in permanent settled communities with their own social political organisation' (Stephenson and Ratnapala 1993, 24).

What has come to be known as the 1992 landmark 'Mabo Decision' recognised that the common law of state tenure could *co-exist* with the 'native title' derived from customary laws and traditions; that is, coexist with *Ailan Kastom*. There have been many ripple effects throughout the polity in Australia since this watershed decision in the High Court. In the Torres Strait, formal recognition of Islanders' unique and holistic relationship with their Sea Country has been achieved both through the official awarding of native title and within the Torres Strait Treaty between Australia and Papua New Guinea.

Even though some of the legal structures have changed, many of the colonial assumptions that undermine a deeper recognition of Sea Country have not. It is important to understand that European colonisation in Australia was, and is, a structure, bound within a particular set of power relations, and not an event that only existed in the past. The powerful structure of colonisation still continues to have hegemonic effects and has had a significant impact on the ways in which Sea Country is taken up in Australian education in general and in the national curriculum. In a contemporary and socially changing nation, the (re)conciliatory projects taking place across the continent within education are providing important contexts where less colonised notions of 'sea' and 'Country' can be partially recovered, and hopefully maintained, in contemporary Australia.

There are many complexities and tensions faced when attempting to make space for Sea Country within formal (i.e. state-sanctioned) education practice. Non-Indigenous (immigrant) Australians are increasingly coming to understand a relational ontology of place wherein not only people, but also 'Country', hold and share knowledge with those who are able, and willing, to listen. However, the educational and political moves towards respecting this ontology are constantly challenged. Changing any part of the whole colonialist structure does not come easily. Until very recently, Sea Country was not sanctioned discourse within Australian state curriculum – and given that it has only just been included, it is not possible for us to definitively comment on how accepted it is and will be. However, we can discuss two current examples of curriculum programming to exemplify at least two ways in which understandings of Sea Country are tentatively supported. First, we look at the cross-curriculum priorities within the new Australian Curriculum (which at the time of writing is in its fifth published iteration). Then, we discuss a distinctive reef education and care programme in Cape York and the Torres Strait sponsored by the Great Barrier Reef Marine Park Authority (GBRMPA).

## The Australian Curriculum

There are three overarching cross-curriculum priorities in the Australian Curriculum (Version 5.1) that apply to the first 11 years of schooling, from the Foundation year to Year 10 (ACARA 2013b). These are: (1) Aboriginal and Torres Strait Islander histories and culture; (2) Asia and Australia's engagement with Asia; and (3) Sustainability. These priorities were decided by all state, territory and Commonwealth Ministers of Education in 2008 and published in the *Melbourne Declaration on Educational Goals for Young Australians* (2008). The ACARA, established by Commonwealth legislation in 2008, manages implementation of the Australian Curriculum. According to ACARA (2013a), the cross-curriculum priorities 'provide [school] students with the tools and language to engage with and better understand their world at a range of levels' and their integration into school curricula is intended to 'encourage conversations between learning areas and between students, teachers and the wider community'. Given their relevance to the topic of Sea Country education, we will discuss the first and third cross-curriculum priorities here.

The first priority, Aboriginal and Torres Strait Islander histories and culture, is introduced as 'a conceptual framework' and 'structural tool' and is illustrated by the following diagram and text, Figure 1 (ACARA 2013b).

The text reads as follows:

In the original journal special issue, this space contained a conceptual framework from the Australian Curriculum Assessment and Reporting Authority, showing the interconnected aspects of country, place, people, and culture. An explanation of this framework is given below, and the original version can be seen in the online version of the journal special issue.

> Aboriginal and Torres Strait Islander communities are strong, rich and diverse. Aboriginal and Torres Strait Islander Identity is central to this priority and is intrinsically linked to living, learning Aboriginal and Torres Strait Islander communities, deep knowledge traditions and holistic world view [*sic*].
>
> A conceptual framework based on Aboriginal and Torres Strait Islander Peoples' unique sense of Identity has been developed as a structural tool for the embedding of Aboriginal and Torres Strait Islander histories and cultures within the Australian curriculum. This sense of Identity is approached through the interconnected aspects of Country/Place, People and Culture. Embracing these elements enhances all areas of the curriculum. (ACARA 2013b)

In this overview text, Country and Place are located together in a weird hybrid where the ancient concept of Country bumps up against the contemporary notion of Place to become this conglomerate Country/Place. It is significant that Country is recognised here in the new curriculum, but also significant that Country is not permitted to stand on its own epistemological merits. The hybrid repeats itself in the description of the organising ideas (OIs), which reflect the essential knowledge, understandings and skills developed for each cross-curriculum priority. Statements such as 'Aboriginal and Torres Strait Islander communities maintain a special connection to and responsibility for Country/Place throughout all of Australia' (OI2) and 'Aboriginal and Torres Strait Islander Peoples have unique belief systems and are spiritually connected to the land, sea, sky and waterways' (OI3) (ACARA 2013b) do recognise pre-European customary relations, though how these are to be enacted in the lived curriculum is not addressed in the national document.

The Australian Curriculum reflects a desire to recognise the concept of Country, (though the term Sea Country does not emerge from the sea or the 'waterways'). However, the inclusion of /Place strongly suggests the terms are interchangeable, which they are not. This manoeuvre on the part of curriculum writers indicates a lack of understanding of the full meanings of Country, which are not replaceable by Place. We asked the question: Does this hybrid Country/ Place act as a form of ongoing settler colonialism? Or should we regard Country/ Place as at least one step forward towards an eventual full recognition of Country? To us, it appears that forcing Country and Place together (as if Place is an explanation for Country – again, which it is not) represents curriculum writers' discomfort with the vast, elusive, metaphysical nature of Country – a desire to tether the concept to a category (equivalent to the other categories of People and Culture), a classification definable and comprehensible to Western colonial sensibilities – not to let it exist, in all its ancient and powerful complexity, beyond the limits of a Western ontology.

Lowe and Yunkaporta's (2013, 5) detailed analysis of the Aboriginal and Torres Strait Islander content currently in the Australian Curriculum leads them to remark that 'public education is still a long way from engaging with Aboriginal and Torres Strait Islander epistemologies'. They note that what content is included is 'weak, often tokenistic and overwhelmingly unresponsive to historical and contemporary realities' (Lowe and Yunkaporta 2013, 12). The inability of the ACARA to sanction Country as the ancient and respectable entity it is, also means the Australian Curriculum 'does not provide students with an informed understanding of the effects of colonisation, or the similarities between the colonial power's justification for annexation, loss of sovereignty, and the forced removal of Indigenous peoples from their Country' (Lowe and Yunkaporta 2013, 11). Country gets a mention in the national cross – curriculum, priority but as it is not permitted to stand alone, the long, tracing effects of colonisation remain extant.

Further evidence for this emerges when we consider the Sustainability cross-curriculum priority. Aboriginal and Torres Strait Islanders' relational ontology and their animate spiritual connections with land, sky, winds and water do not appear in the descriptions of sustainability education. In this cross-curriculum priority, the language changes abruptly. Any sensitive recognition of Country – or even its colonial hybrid, Country/Place – gets subsumed by the systematised, scientific language of 'environments'. The Sustainability priority is set out as follows:

> Education for sustainability develops the knowledge, skills, values and world views necessary for people to act in ways that contribute to more sustainable patterns of living. It enables individuals and communities to reflect on ways of interpreting and engaging with the world. Sustainability education is futures-oriented, focusing on protecting environments and creating a more ecologically and socially just world through informed action. (ACARA 2013c)

There is no looking to the past or to old ways of being. Country is erased by 'sustainable patterns of living' and disappears beneath a flood of worthy 'futures-oriented' sentiments. The corresponding OIs boldly declare that, 'Sustainable patterns of living rely on the interdependence of healthy social, economic and ecological systems' (OI3) and that, 'Designing action for sustainability requires an evaluation of past practices, the assessment of scientific and technological developments, and balanced judgments based on projected future economic, social and environmental impacts' (OI8) (ACARA 2013c). Spirituality, connectedness, identities, histories and cultures simply fail to appear. It is not Country which is to be cared for, it is 'environments' (OI7).

While the first cross-curriculum priority reflects a desire to be inclusive of Aboriginal and Torres Strait Islander perspectives, the language employed to constitute the Sustainability priority simply ignores such perspectives. Here is a precise point where environmental and sustainability education fails to genuinely make visible the assumptions of settler colonialism. While the Sustainability cross curriculum priority acknowledges the 'interdependence' of what might be called natural and cultural processes, that very same language reveals the fundamental assumption that these are different and separately – identifiable concepts, reflecting the exclusive influence of deeply ingrained settler thinking. Furthermore, even though *Ailan Kastom* represents *long taim* sustainability practices and successfully learning for sustainability, no customary practice is reproduced in the Australian Curriculum statements on sustainability; no mention is even made of the long, continent-wide Indigenous history of caring for Country. The relational, storied, spiritual nature of Country, and its relevance to contemporary concerns about sustainability, still sits outside the limits of settler ontologies and understandings.

The language of the OIs and sustainability cross-curriculum priority statements acts as a reminder that settler colonisation is a structure that not only impacts thinking, but also decides the *content* of curriculum (see Somerville 2010). The concept of Country (and thus Sea Country) in the Australian Curriculum is at worst, ignored, and at best, extant but only as attached to the settler concept of Place. While there is good intention to include Indigenous relational cosmologies within current curricula, these aims are clearly compromised by the pervasive effects of (almost) unconscious colonist thinking. Beyond curriculum, specifically designated as Aboriginal and/or Torres Strait Islander, writers and educators fail to acknowledge the full, relational, sentient nature of Country.

## The GBRMPA *Sea Country Guardians* Programme

In contrast, we turn now to a geographically localised educational example where Sea Country is genuinely recognised and valued. The reef education programme developed by the GBRMPA provides a particular instance of environmental education curriculum that fully acknowledges Sea Country. This acknowledgement occurred because education staff at the GBRMPA consulted with the Traditional Owners in eastern Cape York and the Torres Strait and listened to and acted on their advice in the development of the *Sea Country Guardians* programme *Sea Country Guardians* is an adaptation of the highly successful *Reef Guardians* programme developed in 2003 by the GBRMPA for implementation in primary and secondary schools located in Great Barrier Reef catchments along the eastern seaboard. *The Reef Guardians* programme is offered to all Australian schools who wish 'to commit to the protection and conservation of Australia's World Heritage listed Great Barrier Reef' (ReefED 2011). The *Sea Country Guardians* programme which is much more regionally localised, explicitly draws on traditional Aboriginal cultural knowledge (in Cape York) and *Ailan Kastom* (in the Torres Strait) linked to established scientific environmental knowledge to enable children and young people to care and take responsibility for local onshore and offshore reefs. The *Sea Country Guardians* programme takes a community approach to fostering a community culture of custodianship for the Great Barrier Reef.

The *Sea Country Guardians* programme educates young people to become community leaders with support from community schools. The most ambitious programme aim is to have the concept of Sea Country guardianship become established, over time, as a way of thinking and acting in these regional and remote coastal communities. The pedagogies employed are sensitive to the employment and celebration of local language, and involve learning, developing respect for, and practicing tradition, law, and lore. They also include outdoor education practice, known as 'learning on country', in which children gain knowledge through a 'Look, Listen and Learn' process (Digital Learning Futures 2010). Being 'on country' is seen as central to children's and young people's learning, so the programme is designed to enable the young to walk their country, ideally with their elders, in order to come to know and respect all the interconnections of their Country.

The *Sea Country Guardians* programme engages with environmental education at what Nakata (2002, 2006, 2007, 2010) calls 'the cultural interface'. It is at this interface that epistemological meanings are negotiated and learning takes place. Nakata (2006, 272) argues that Australian educators need 'a different conceptualisation of cross cultural space, not a clash of opposites and differences, but … a layered entanglement of concepts, theories and sets of meaning' in order to renegotiate the colonised-coloniser space in the twenty-first century. However, while the cultural interface forged in the *Sea Country Guardians* programme succeeds in creating this multilayered 'entanglement', it remains imperfect. The programme is confined to the remote areas of Queensland – that is to Cape York and the Torres Strait. Settler society is far more comfortable with the term and the programme 'Reef Guardians', and most participating schools are reef guardians rather than Sea Country guardians. It is important that the GBRMPA recognised the concept of Sea Country within its landmark reef education programme but the acceptance of this educational move is presently geographically confined to the very remote communities of Queensland.

This example shows that educational programmes can disrupt the privileging of Eurocentric concepts (Barrett 2011). Country can (and should) be deciphered and understood through educational and academic study (see Nakata 2010; Somerville 2010; Whitehouse 2011). Although credit must go to the GBRMPA for actively rehabilitating Sea Country within a formalised education programme, given the strength and pervasiveness of the ideological premises of colonialism, there is still much work to be done at both the discursive and practical levels within this programme and across Australian environmental education.

## Conclusion

Our analysis of the cross-curriculum priorities in the Australian curriculum and the *Sea Country Guardians* programme demonstrates the fragility of Country (in general) and Sea Country (in particular) in Australian environmental education. National and international research increasingly shows that unless the difference between Indigenous people's priorities, values and spiritual orientations, and those of ecologists and government agencies, is acknowledged and dealt with seriously, it is likely that the Eurocentric and scientific approaches to knowing and being will continue to be privileged (e.g. Battiste 2008; Nakata 2007, 2010). If the pervasive structure of settler colonialism is ever to be substantially changed, significant reduction of epistemological and ontological biases within curriculum development and implementation is required.

Undoing colonising curriculum structures within environmental education will take much more than an occasional display of goodwill. At the very least, a sincere and sustained commitment by curriculum designers is necessary. Our analysis of two Australian cross-curriculum priorities surprised us. We thought that at least the national cross-curriculum priorities should speak to and with each other, but they do not. Given this lack of integration, it is unclear how teachers – and therefore their students – will be able to support a decolonised understanding of Country and Indigenous cultures generally within Australian national curriculum. The value of this land education discussion – which, of course, includes Sea Country – is in bringing to light these incongruities and in showing just how much more work needs to be done in promoting the project of decolonisation.

## Acknowledgements

The authors would like to thank the EER editors and reviewers for their significant feedback and responses to the original manuscript. The international peer review process was extremely helpful in enabling us to clarify our ideas and further develop this paper. We are most appreciative of these generous efforts. Thank you also to Noah Weisz for his editorial comments.

## References


[ACARA] Australian Curriculum, Assessment and Reporting Authority. 2013a. *Cross-curriculum Priorities*. http://www.acara.edu.au/curriculum/cross_curriculum_priorities.html.

[ACARA] Australian Curriculum, Assessment and Reporting Authority. 2013b. Aboriginal and Torres Strait Islander Histories and Cultures. http://www.australiancurriculum.edu.au/CrossCurriculumPriorities/Aboriginal-and-Torres-Strait-Islander-histories-and-cultures.

[ACARA] Australian Curriculum, Assessment and Reporting Authority. 2013c. *Sustainability*. http://www.australiancurriculum.edu.au/CrossCurriculumPriorities/Sustainability.

Australian Broadcasting Corporation. 2001. *Australia's Centenary of Federation: Birth of a Nation, Growth of the Commonwealth*. http://www.abc.net.au/federation/fedstory/home.htm.

Barrett, M. J. 2011. "Decentring Norms in Environmental Studies." *Collected Essays on Learning and Teaching* 9: 103–108.

Battiste, M. 2008. "The Struggle and Renaissance of Indigenous Knowledge in Eurocentric Education." In *Indigenous Knowledge and Education: Sites of Struggle, Strength, and Survivance*, edited by M. Villegas, S. Neugebauer, and K. Venegas, 85–91. Cambridge, MA: Harvard University Press.

Cordell, J. and J. Fitzpatrick. 1987. Torres Strait: Cultural Identity and the Sea. Cultural Survival Quarterly 11 (2): 15. http://www.culturalsurvival.org/publications/cultural-survival-quarterly/australia/torres-strait-cultural-identity-and-sea.

Council for Aboriginal Reconciliation. 1994. *Understanding Country. The Importance of Land and Sea in Aboriginal and Torres Strait Islander Societies*. Key Issue Paper No.1. Canberra: Council for Aboriginal Reconciliation, Commonwealth of Australia.

Digital Learning Futures. 2010. *Sea Country Guardians Messages*. http://www.learningfutures.com.au/sea-country-guardian-messages.

Gammage, B. 2011. *The Biggest Estate on Earth: How Aborigines Made Australia*. Sydney: Allen and Unwin.

Greenwood, D. A. 2008. "A Critical Pedagogy of Place: From Gridlock to Parallax." *Environmental Education Research* 14 (1): 336–348.

Gruenewald, D., and G. A. Smith. 2008. "Models for Place-Based Learning." In *Place-based Education in the Global Age: Local Diversity*, edited by David A. Gruenewald and Gregory A. Smith, 1–4. New York: Lawrence Erlbaum.

Hoffmann, B. D., S. Roeger, P. Wise, J. Dermer, B. Yunupingu, D. Lacey, D. Yunupingu, B. Marika, M. Marika, and B. Panton. 2012. "Achieving Highly Successful Multiple Agency Collaborations in a Cross-cultural Environment: Experiences and Lessons from Dhimurru Aboriginal Corporation and Partners." *Ecological Management & Restoration* 13 (1): 42–50.

Loban, F. 2008. *Ngalpun adhabath a goeygayil bangal (Our Sea, Our Future): An Examination of Torres Strait Protected Zone Joint Authority Principles and Torres Strait Islander Needs and Aspirations for Fisheries, from a Torres Strait Islander Perspective*. Unpublished masters thesis. Townsville: James Cook University.

Lowe, K., and T. Yunkaporta. 2013. "The Inclusion of Aboriginal and Torres Strait Islander Content in the Australian National Curriculum: A Cultural, Cognitive and Socio-political Evaluation." *Curriculum Perspectives* 33 (1): 1–14.

McKenzie, M. 2008. "The Places of Pedagogy: Or, What We Can Do with Culture Through Intersubjective Experiences." *Environmental Education Research* 14 (3): 361–373.

Meyer, M. A. 2008. "Indigenous and Authentic: Hawaiian Epistemology and the Triangulation of Meaning." In *Handbook of Critical and Indigenous Methodologies*, edited by N. K. Denzin, Y. S. Lincoln, and L. T. Smith, 217–232. Los Angeles, CA: Sage.

Ministerial Council on Education, Employment, Training and Youth Affairs. 2008. Melbourne Declaration on Educational Goals for Young Australians. Ministerial Council for Education, Early Childhood Development and Youth Affairs. http://www.mceecdya.edu.au/verve/_resources/national_declaration_on_the_educational_goals_for_young_australians.pdf.

Mooka, A. 1990. *In Poets of the Torres Strait: Year 7–1990 Our Lady of the Sacred Heart School, Thursday Island*, p. 32. Cairns: Priority Country Area Program Northern Region.

Nakata, M. 2002. "Indigenous Knowledge and the Cultural Interface: Underlying Issues at the Intersection of Knowledge and Information Systems." *IFLA Journal* 21: 280–290.

Nakata, M. 2006. "Australian Indigenous Studies: A Question of Discipline." *Australian Journal of Anthropology* 17 (3): 265–275.

Nakata, M. 2007. *Disciplining the Savages: Savaging the Disciplines*. Canberra: Aboriginal Studies Press.

Nakata, M. 2010. "The Cultural Interface of Islander and Scientific Knowledge." *Australian Journal of Indigenous Education* 39 (Supplement): 53–57.

Northern Land Council. 2003. *Caring for Country*. http://www.nlc.org.au/html/care_menu.html.

ReefED. 2011. *Reef Guardians Schools Overview: About the Program. Great Barrier Reef Marine Park Authority*. http://www.reefed.edu.au/home/guardians/about_the_program.

Reynolds, H. 1972. *Aborigines and Settlers: The Australian Experience*. North Melbourne: Cassell.

Rose, D. B. 1996. *Nourishing Terrains: Australian Aboriginal Views of Landscape and Wilderness*. Canberra: Australian Heritage Commission.

Scott, C., and M. Mulrennan. 1999. "Land and Sea Tenure at Erub, Torres Strait: Property, Sovereignty, and the Adjudication of Cultural Continuity." *Oceania* 70 (2): 146–176.

Singe, J. 1979. *The Torres Strait: People and History*. St. Lucia: University of Queensland Press.

Smyth, D. 1997. *Saltwater Country Aboriginal and Torres Strait Islander Interest in Ocean Policy Development and Implementation. Socio-cultural Considerations*. Australia's Ocean Policy Issues Paper 6. Canberra: Environment Australia.

Somerville, M. J. 2010. "A Place Pedagogy for 'Global Contemporaneity." *Educational philosophy and theory* 42 (3): 326–344.

Stephenson, M. A., and S. Ratnapala ed. 1993. *Mabo: A Judicial Revolution: The Aboriginal Land Rights Decision and its Impact on Australian Law*. St. Lucia: University of Queensland Press.

Torres Strait Island Regional Council (TSIRC). 2013. Culture. http://www.tsirc.qld.gov.au/our-region/culture.

Torres Strait Regional Authority (TSRA). 2013. *Environmental Management in the Torres Strait*. http://www.tsra.gov.au/land–sea-management-home.aspx.

Tuck, E., M. McKenzie and K. McCoy. 2014. Land Education: Indigenous, Postcolonial, and Decolonizing Perspectives on Place and Environmental Education Research. *Environmental Education Research* 20 (1): 1–23.

Watkin Lui, F. 2012. "The Politics of Divide: Representation and the Torres Strait Diaspora." *GSTF International Journal of Law and Social Sciences* 1 (1): 24–29.

Whap, G. 2001. "A Torres Strait Islander Perspective on the Concept of Indigenous Knowledge." *Australian Journal of Indigenous Education* 29 (2): 22–29.

Whitehouse, H. 2011. "Talking Up Country: Language, Natureculture and Interculture in Australian Environmental Education Research." *Australian Journal of Environmental Education* 27 (1): 56–67.

Wolfe, P. 2006. "Settler Colonialism and the Elimination of the Native." *Journal of Genocide Research* 8 (4): 387–409.

# An African-centred approach to land education

Salvatore Engel-Di Mauro and Karanja Keita Carroll

*Department of Geography and Department of Black Studies, State University of New York at New Paltz, New Paltz, USA*

Approaches to environmental education which are engaging with place and critical pedagogy have not yet broadly engaged with the African world and insights from Africana Studies and Geography. An African-centred approach facilitates people's reconnection to places and ecosystems in ways that do not reduce places to objects of conquest and things to be exploited for profitability and individual gain. Such an approach offers effective critiques of settler coloniser perspectives on the environment and deeper understandings of the relationship between worldview and ecologically sensitised education. Through examples from Africana Studies and Geography, this article provides an introduction to how an African-centred approach can contribute to the development of a Land Education perspective and improve college-level environmental education.

## Introduction

Place-based pedagogical approaches have turned attention to the importance of developing ecological understanding by connecting people to the actual places in which they live. Together with critical pedagogy, place-based alternatives can both call into question received views about how people relate to land and environments, and, more specifically, raise awareness and sensitivity to colonial relationships underlying people/environment relations. This at least is a thread common to even the most mutually antipathetic of approaches (Basole 2009; Bowers 2008; De Lissovoy 2010; Gruenewald 2008; McLaren, Macrine, and Hill 2010). However, perspectives centred in the African world (i.e. Africa and African Diasporas) remain largely outside the purview of these alternatives (e.g. Breidlid 2009, 2013; Glasson et al. 2006, 2010; Le Grange 2005; Mueller and Bentley 2009), and there has been little to no engagement with long-standing place-based and environment-focused perspectives developed in Africana Studies and Geography.

We aim herein to offer an African-centred perspective that further detects and unsettles colonisers' views promoted in much environmental education, even when guided by place-based approaches. We initiate this process in two ways. First, we explore how an African-centred perspective, as understood through Africana Studies, can be useful in reworking pedagogical materials that contribute to the making of a land-based approach. Unlike prevailing Eurocentric worldviews, an African-centred perspective can be particularly effective in facilitating people's reconnection to places and the ecosystems they inhabit in ways that do not reduce them, among other things, to objects of conquest, or things to be exploited for profitability and individual gain. Second, we attempt to show how ideas from an African-centred perspective can be implemented to improve college-level environmental education and thereby contribute to the development of a Land Education perspective in a North American context.

## Environmental education, place-based alternatives and settler colonialism

Tied to rising concerns over environmental degradation, the institutionalisation of environmental education in the West can be traced to the 1960s and in many cases, tries to offer holistic understandings of people's relationships to environments. Mainstream environmental education approaches have grounded their teaching in the non-human world, with the aim of living in it sustainably (e.g. Ernst and Theimer 2011; Hungerford 2009; Strife 2010). Regrettably, such approaches have often neglected to focus on lived experiences in society, the diversity of lived environments, and the ways in which environments are also products of social processes. In other words, what is often missing in such environmental education is the 'question of history, culture, politics and power' (Cole 2007, 36). There have been attempts to go beyond conceptions of nature as that which is not human or urban, but they remain limited because of the primary, if not sole, focus on the non-human at the expense of considering oppressive social structures.[1]

To some extent, the combination of critical pedagogy and place-based education (e.g. Gruenewald 2008) is an attempt to rectify neglect of the social underpinnings of what constitutes environment. Place-based education is rooted in efforts to raise the effectiveness of institutionalised schooling by integrating the curriculum with activities in the community in which students live. Such place-based approaches aim at both making institutionalised education relevant to students and sensitising students to the importance of the social and environmental aspects of the places in which they live. It puts the local (and local knowledge) at the centre of teaching about the world, both social and environmental, and so can serve as an entry point to raise awareness of and valorise systems of knowledge that are typically dismissed. At the same time, the emphasis on 'reinhabiting' the local seeks to avoid parochialism by involving students in examining linkages between places and by including Indigenous knowledge and multiple cultural perspectives regarding the making of a place (Gruenewald and Smith 2008; Sobel 2005).

What underlies these perspectives is a struggle against the reproduction of views that ignore relations of power in a capitalist system, whose main basis of existence has been and remains colonialism (Fenelon and Hall 2008). Colonialism is a structural condition whereby people are dichotomised into coloniser and colonised (Ladson-Billings and Donnor 2008, 67; Memmi 1991). Land is understood as a commodity, as something to control, own, and exploit for the coloniser's benefit. Both the colonised and the land in which they live are objectified, and often Indigenous peoples, including Africans in the case of colonisation in Africa, are regarded as part of nature, to also be conquered or forcibly assimilated into colonisers' ways.

Yet colonialism is context-dependent. In regions like the USA, settler colonialism is the foundation of current national states and pervades social relations. Its particularity lies in a combination of genocide-supported land conquest largely directed at Indigenous peoples and mass abduction-based slavery largely affecting

African people (Wolfe 2001). In settler colonialism, Indigenous peoples have been viewed by settlers as pests to be destroyed so as to enable sole use of their land. The world is ideologically fitted into a settler logic, whereby a superior coloniser – endowed with civilisation, science, rule of law, etc. – is considered as rightfully ruling over or extirpating an inferior colonised both physically and culturally. The colonised are viewed as people who are deemed not to possess the intrinsically higher qualities of the coloniser, including in their uses of land (Smith 2005).

These foundations yield a native–slave–settler triad that distinguishes the conditions of life and struggle among the peoples concerned, as well as their respective worldviews. Tuck and Yang (2012), following Wolfe (2001), argue that settler colonialism in North America is comprised of a triad of relations between Indigenous peoples who must be destroyed and be disappeared from the land, chattel slaves (mostly from Africa) who must be kept landless, and the settlers who make both Indigenous land and slave bodies into property. Tuck and Yang observe that

> Slavery in settler colonial contexts is distinct from other forms of indenture whereby *excess labor* is extracted from persons. First, chattels are commodities of labor and therefore it is the slave's *person* that is the excess. Second, unlike workers who may aspire to own land, the slave's very presence on the land is already an excess that must be dis-located. Thus, the slave is a desirable commodity but the person underneath is imprisonable, punishable, murderable. (2012, 6)

In the specific case of African Diasporas, one should additionally consider millennia-long differentiation of worldviews and centuries-long traumas meted out through European settler colonialism.

Many have attempted to overcome Eurocentrism by adopting analytical frameworks such as environmental racism, postcoloniality, and Indigenous peoples' knowledge. But these scarcely address settler colonialism. There is, for instance, little to no discussion about returning land to Indigenous peoples (Tuck and Yang 2012). By focusing on racism – what amounts to an outcome of settler colonialism – the framework of environmental racism evades these core issues. Similarly, postcolonial approaches are largely limited to showing the cultural mixing and mutual influences that colonisation also brought about, and to bringing out voices that continue to be suppressed as a result of continuities with colonial practices, such as in formal politics, economic policies, and education (Quigley 2009). Like much of postcolonial thought, recent work promoting Indigenous environmental knowledge exposes the exclusionary nature of western European knowledge systems, which treat Indigenous understandings as inferior, if they are at all considered. Efforts on this front typically concentrate on attaining mainstream status for Indigenous perspectives, on equal terms with the existing prevalent worldview (Beckford et al. 2010). As argued below, these alternative approaches remain partially mired in reproductions of settler colonial understandings by failing to consider land as a key issue. Instead, Eurocentrism must be exploded at its roots, which is what an African-centred approach can contribute.

## Problems with current environmental and place-based education

Despite laudable attempts otherwise, we suggest that much environmental and place-based education remains trapped in a culture-nature dichotomy typical of settler colonial ideologies and a condescending approach towards non-Europeans. To illustrate, the challenge for environmental education in cities is often defined as one of inadequate access to nature, as though cities were not ecosystems (e.g. Cook 2008; Ferreira 2012). Thus, one is forced to look for nature elsewhere or to find spots in a city that most resemble nature. For instance, the Young Achievers science programme relies upon a place-based, social justice-orientated kindergarten curriculum in Boston, featuring excursions to a cemetery to enable students to learn about flora and fauna. Connecting what is regarded by many as the best urban approximation of nature with human death (a cemetery) seems hardly to challenge the settler colonial perspective that people and nature are separable. Another curricular activity is centred on food production and takes children to a nearby orchard, rather than, say, an urban garden (Smith and Sobel 2010, 4–8). Even when local urban gardens or urban botanical gardens feature as part of the curriculum, as is increasingly done in environmental education (e.g. Blair 2009; Morgan et al. 2009), nature remains separated from people and human-impacted environments (see also Engel-Di Mauro 2008).

Such separation insinuates itself in other aspects of the curriculum, whereby the settler is neatly separated from the Indigenous, whose existence is erased, and histories of settler colonial social and environmental destructions are instead displaced to other countries, especially those formerly under direct colonial rule. In the 7th and 8th year of schooling for the Young Achievers science programme described in Smith and Sobel (2010), children are engaged in a study of deforestation in African and African Diaspora contexts (Sudan and Haiti) to learn about connecting human misery with environmental degradation and the ways in which social justice activism, exemplified by the Green Belt movement in Kenya, provides a solution. Then, students put concepts to practice by participating in tree planting in the Boston Nature Center (Smith and Sobel 2010, 12). However, such pedagogical practices reinforce settler colonial ideology by eliding Indigenous peoples' histories of forest–grassland ecotone creation and maintenance, the subsequent history of colonial destruction that created Boston and its largely deforested surroundings, the problem that European and European settler colonial cities in particular tend to be highly degrading of environments (local and worldwide, through massive resource consumption), and the current local struggles in cities like Boston itself for environmental justice. Instead, in a decontextualising move typical of a colonial lens on Africa (and other places), the focus is directed at contexts elsewhere without any explanation as to why deforestation has taken place in those places, without imparting to students the skills to connect colonial exploitation with environmental degradation, and without any questioning of the environmental devastation that is Boston itself, with its relative paucity of vegetation and its continuing heavy metal contamination problems, among other issues.

These ways of promoting place-based appreciation of environmental processes inadvertently, and ostensibly with the best of intentions, continue to instil a distancing of nature from one's community. They ironically reproduce the problem they try to surmount by starting with a presupposition that people are apart from nature, that environmental degradation is mainly elsewhere and involving non-Europeans, and that colonisation histories are irrelevant to learning about nature. Notably, parents cited in a report on the programme discussed earlier remarked on not just the importance of connecting people to nature, but also how in African communities, including in the USA, people view themselves as part of the environment. It appears that those engaged in running, writing about, and assessing the programme missed the contradiction between communities where people–nature dichotomies are absent and pedagogical techniques that reinforce colonisers' dichotomous understanding of place. Through such examples, settler colonialism thus continues to inform environmental education practice by privileging settlers' views and values (see also Swadener and Mutua 2008, 36–37). To resist this, we advocate an exposure of the fatal flaws of the settler colonial capitalist perspective, a culmination of a Northern Cradle ideology, so as to bring about the necessary cultural transformation in understandings of environments and a genuine appreciation for and adoption of multiple frameworks attuned to everyday ecological connections.

## Geography and Africana studies

It is surprising that such problems persist when there already exist outlets, even at the primary schooling level (mainly outside the USA), for the integrative approach called for by advocates of either environmental or place-based education (e.g. Gruenewald and Smith 2008). One of these outlets is in the teaching of Geography. Education, or the sharing/imparting of knowledge, is fundamentally spatial, in the sense of physical–spiritual and land-based understanding. As Meyer points out, space is crucial to shaping consciousness (Meyer 2008, 220). In this sense, Geography should be regarded as a source of insights, especially because place has always been a foundational component of geographical study and, over the past decades, critical and radical geographers have demonstrated the intrinsically multiple-scaled, interconnected, socio-natural, and contested aspects of places (Bauder and Engel-Di Mauro 2008; Castree 2003). It is regrettable that such work continues to be little known in many environmental education programmes. One consequence of this is illustrated by the above-critiqued Young Achievers science programme.

However, Geography as a whole retains, for the most part, an overwhelmingly Eurocentric understanding of the world (see e.g. Blaut 1999; Sheppard, Leitner, and Mariganti 2013), so perhaps it is fortunate that environmental and place-based educators have yet to draw from geographers, at least those geographers in the mainstream. A more promising avenue could be to combine the insights from critical and radical geographers and from scholars in Africana Studies. Africana Studies offers both a corrective and a potential for overcoming Eurocentric notions of the world as found within contemporary Geography departments. Africana Studies posits that culture and worldview are central components in understanding people's lived reality. Thus, to understand European propensities for the control, objectification, manipulation and exploitation of environments, an African-centred approach argues that it is essential to go to the root of western European thought. Cheikh Anta Diop, a foundational figure for African-centred perspectives, developed a framework to accomplish this task.

In Diop's Two-Cradle Theory, he posits that combinations of environmental conditions and social processes (familial systems, social customs and social values) contributed to the development of divergent worldviews, which are understood through what he calls the Southern Cradle, Northern Cradle and Zone of Confluence (Abdi 2008; Diop 1987, 1989, 1991). A cultural group's understanding of the universe (cosmology), nature of being (ontology), values (axiology) and knowledge (epistemology) contribute to the ways in which a people make sense of reality (i.e. their worldview). In the Northern Cradle worldview (currently northern and western Europe), generally harsher environments facilitated the development of a thought system where nature was viewed as an obstacle to basic survival and concern for others and close kin networks could be downplayed. The relatively limited amounts of natural resources and the difficulty in securing them provided a context whereby an instrumentalist view of nature, individualism, and aggressive behaviour could flourish. In contrast, in the Southern Cradle worldview, more favourable environmental conditions encouraged the development of an African thought system, based upon values of communalism, interconnectedness, spirituality and interrelationship, as well as centred on the interconnected nature of reality. A comparison between these conditions and responses to them has been suggested as responsible for the evolution of a xenophobic worldview within the Northern Cradle and a cooperative worldview within the Southern Cradle, with repercussions on the content and mode of knowledge transmission (education systems) (Diop 1987, 1989, 1991; Kamalu 1998).

A worldview is in part expressed through everyday environmental practices, ideas about the environment, and pedagogical approaches to imparting knowledge about the environment. Diop's analysis provides an explanation for the development of a western European (Northern Cradle) worldview by rooting it in the original environmental context in which it was forged. To understand the control of nature, one must see nature as an object, something outside of and unrelated to the self and that needs to be manipulated and exploited for personal gain. The approach to nature within the African world and throughout many Indigenous communities does not posit such relations. These approaches to nature recognise that nature provides for humanity just as humanity provides for nature (Kamalu 1998).

Arguably, the basis of current cultural differences lies in the formation of worldviews that emerged from relationships between peoples and the environments they inhabited over long periods and long ago. While these environments stayed consistent long enough to develop a particular consciousness, worldviews were also transported via cultural values, customs and mores. The movement and continuity of cultural consciousness allows for an understanding of both Africa and Europe beyond their presumed geographical boundaries. Thus, as we speak of Africa, African people and the African world, we speak to the reality of cultural continuity rooted in its historical origins. It does not follow, however, that a long-term cultural tendency necessarily makes for a predetermined outcome relative to environmental impact or social relations.

These insights provide the basis for the development of an alternative explanation for the relationship between humans and nature, especially in relation to African descended peoples. These perspectives not only provide cultural depth, but also offer a gateway for the development of future work using culture and worldview as part of an analytical framework.

## An African-centred approach to environmental education

Thus, for an African-centred approach to environmental education, it is imperative to return to Ancient Africa as a historical marker and exemplar. It was within the Nile Valley civilisation of Kemit (Egypt) that educational institutions were developed and predicated on an appreciation of interconnections between humans and nature. Rather than seeing nature as something to be studied, as an object detached from the self, Kemetians recognised that studying nature teaches one about both nature and self simultaneously. This interconnected relationship comes out of a worldview which says that all things are interrelated and interconnected, a worldview emanating from traditional African norms that are found in various ways throughout the African world (Carroll 2012; Hilliard 1986, 138).

As explained already, by advancing a focus on the African world, we posit that Africa does not just refer to a geographical location but also refers to a worldview. African people throughout their Diaspora then make up the African world. This Diaspora, though, originally rooted within a continent called Africa, has now spread the world over, bringing along a particular understanding of people/environment relationships. One pedagogical advance that we suggest is the recognition of the relationship between geographical Africa, African people and the African Diaspora. It provides a unique interpretive framework rooted within an African worldview that can make sense of human/nature relationships expressed among African descendants wherever they are.

There are many ways in which such an African-centred approach can be implemented in the college classroom. The examples that follow provide a glimpse into semester-long college-level courses that can fit departmental requirements for Africana Studies and Geography but also fulfil general education requirements and that are based on our own teaching experiences. Even if not part of a specific 'environmental education' curriculum, such Africana Studies and Geography courses offer insights for developing course content in land education.

One course we draw on here is *Introduction to Africa*, an Africana Studies course that focuses on the historical development of African civilisations from ancient Africa until prior to European contact with Western Africa. In this course, students are exposed to the intimate and long-term linkages between African peoples and the lands they have inhabited historically. For example, through the study of the ancient Egyptian civilisation, a focus is placed upon their cosmogony, which understood the origins of reality as based on humans, other living creatures and the physical environment working together in order to create life, harmony and mutual respect. Evidence of migration patterns is also discussed to show the movement of African people across space that allowed for the transmission of cultural values and beliefs that time has been unable to totally obliterate. The linkages expressed in this course demonstrate the importance of how worldview (Southern Cradle, in this instance) affects understandings of nature and connections to land as they relate to African historical realities, both ancient and current. An African-centred education approach thus integrates understandings of people/environment interactions with the development and continuities of an African worldview to explain, in part, the characteristics of African civilisations. By doing so, students gain an appreciation for the importance of considering worldviews in grasping the manner in which people relate to the environments in which they live.

Another course that provides examples of African-centred land education surveys African American history, engaging with African descendants' migration out of southern states into northern cities from the early to mid-1900s. The course confronts issues that propelled the mass migration, – racism, Jim Crow, employment and self-determination struggles among African Americans – and the ongoing process of return migration back to the south (Falk, Hunt, and Hunt 2004). While the southern USA can be connected to the brutal atrocities of enslavement, it still does not limit the manner and movement of African Americans to the south. This return migration can be interpreted as a relationship that these African descendants have with the southern USA as an African 'American' place of origin, involving long historical ties and spiritual linkages connected to local churches. Though current trends seem to locate economic factors as the primary reason for the new migration of African descendants in the USA, an African-centred perspective looks to provide more culturally relevant explanations for thought and action within the African world.

Students in this course are also exposed to the thinking of C. Tsehloane Keto (1994), who has advanced the notion of an 'Africa-centred perspective' of history. In doing so, Keto has engaged the relationship between geography and historical understanding. As knowledge of geography shapes knowledge of history, Keto has been extremely critical of the use of the Mercator cylindrical projection by geographers and educators. The Mercator map was devised for navigational purposes (and conquest by naval force) by keeping direction accurate. However, the effect is a distortion of area, and, in the case of the Mercator projection, areas in the northern hemisphere are disproportionately inflated, privileging Europe. Keto suggests using the Peters projection because it maintains greater accuracy for area (but not shape) and so shows a more balanced view of the northern and southern hemispheres.

This critical perspective on map reading is transferable to geography courses generally and exercises can be devised that point to Northern Cradle biases in coordinate systems as well, such as using relative location systems based on distance from sacred places or places of origins. Such pedagogical interventions raise awareness about the impossibility of a neutral map. They can also promote representations of the Earth's surface that are attuned to appreciating environments in meaningful ways, including through spiritual understandings, instead of reproducing abstraction and detachment from lands and oceans.

Another, more specific example of applying an African-centred approach as land education, is in *World Geography*. This course is an introduction to regional geography by studying what distinguishes the world's regions and countries and the interactions of peoples in the process of global integration. Unlike the previous two courses, environmental issues form an essential part of course content. In most offerings of the course, curricula are replete with Northern Cradle ideology that reproduces people's alienation from ecosystems by reinforcing culture-nature divides and that denies the contribution of non-European peoples in the making of places. African-centred perspectives help overcome such ideology by (1) pointing to the relative unity of African geography and the continuities in constructive relations between Africans and ecosystems, and (2) showing how places are not reducible to what Europeans do. These are two examples of the difference that an African-centred approach makes for students in learning about environments and places.

Furthermore, an example of culture–nature dichotomisation is in the segmentation of Africa into North and sub-Saharan regions and the treatment of Africa as limited to its continental extent. The construct of a sub-Saharan Africa is overwhelmingly common in geography textbooks and has repercussions for understanding ecosystems and how African life-ways have co-evolved with them in constructive ways. To show the falsity of this construct, following African-centred approaches to understanding the relative cultural unity of the African world, one can show how African spiritual understandings and environmental practices in the Americas, for example, are continuous with those in the African continent itself and how they have promoted sustainable ways of producing food, of recycling materials, and other such environmentally sustaining practices wherever African people live (e.g. Carney 2001; Kamalu 1998; Leach and Mearns 1996; Reij, Scoones, and

Toulmin 1996). The segmented Africa construct can also be undermined by pointing out the fictitious divide by showing the contrived nature of the boundaries between North and sub-Saharan Africa in terms of cultural traits (e.g. the distribution of languages and religions) and physical environments (the regional boundary does not coincide with ecosystem differences). One can then move to exploring ideological underpinnings, which involves settler colonial strategies of control by way of division, and long-standing Eurocentric imperialistic obsessions with the spread or presence of Islam and/or Arabs.

The importance of seeing places through an African-centred lens can also be brought home by using illustrations from nearby, as recommended by the above-cited place-based educators. Where we live, in the colony called 'New York State', almost every town bears a plaque stating when the place was 'settled' and bears little to no recognition of cultural influences other than European ones. Every now and then, there are attempts, for example, to signal the importance of the historical presence of African Diaspora communities, but typically this is by way of cemeteries or slave plantations, as if African people never taught 'whites' anything, never imparted cropping system knowledge, never contributed to the actual shaping of a landscape through such activities as farming, agricultural innovations and much else. Such ideological terms and silences buttress a view of the world that justifies the annihilation of other peoples and with it other ways and possibilities of relating to land, environment and place. Such a process of settler colonial indoctrination can be exposed by discussing these matters openly and by way of concrete examples from places with which students are familiar. Later in the semester in our *World Geography* course, readings and discussions link past and current African life ways, sustainable food production systems, and spirituality, including resistance to settler colonialism (slavery and plantation systems in particular, contrasted with environmentally sustainable Maroon communities). These links help reinforce the importance of African worldviews to the development of an ecologically sustainable society. Such an exercise goes a long way in conveying a sense of place that is not limited to that of privileged Northern Cradle perspectives and thereby students not only gain a fuller comprehension of Africa by exploring the African Diaspora experience in the USA but develop the means to question settler colonialism and comprehend its socially and environmentally devastating consequences.

## Conclusion

Using examples from Africana Studies and Geography, in this article, we offer a point of departure for the creation and implementation of college-level courses grounded in an African-centred approach to land education. Unlike prevailing Eurocentric perspectives, an African-centred perspective is particularly effective in facilitating people's reconnection to places and the environments/lands they inhabit in ways that do not reduce them, as in settler colonial perspectives, to separable objects of conquest or things to be exploited for profit. As the above illustrations show, African-centred approaches can thus contribute to undoing settler colonial assumptions in environmental education by stressing connectedness to place in ways that are attuned to local environments, social struggles and histories, and their interconnections. Meanings of place and environmental practices in the African Diaspora, for instance, are replete with long-lasting cultural continuities with potentials to develop constructive linkages to new surroundings as part of the reproduction of a Southern Cradle worldview. Such historical continuities defy settler colonial assumptions that impose breaks with the past and with other places. An example is the manner in which Boston's history is implicitly conceived in the Young Achievers science curriculum discussed above, as largely devoid of nature and without mention of the struggles and contributions of Indigenous peoples and Africans in making the urban ecosystem that is now Boston. That city is also treated as if its ecosystem characteristics were disconnected from the rest of the world (e.g. neo-colonial linkages at the global level) and, in particular, from cultural processes other than European ones. An African-centred understanding enables the development of sensitivity against such disconnections and imposed discontinuities, across time and space (e.g. African Diasporas to Africa), and to perspectives that tend to be ignored.

Land education through Africana Studies works to disrupt privileged conceptions of African life, history and culture pervading the basis of normative constructions of knowledge and orientations to environment. Given its interdisciplinary structure, geography can provide a more holistic interpretation of African world history if coupled with an African-centred conceptualisation of place. This conceptualisation promotes an integrative view of nature and people that stresses interrelation and interconnection with the land and its histories, histories that in the case of the African world span multiple continents. It is a conceptualisation founded on communalism, rather than individualism, so that environments are not only intrinsic to being human, but to the very existence of communities. In this, African-centred perspectives complement most Indigenous approaches by providing alternative means for the transmission of knowledge and understanding of land and one's place in it that brings to prominence diasporic connections to places erased by settler colonial approaches.

## Note

1. We recognize that exceptions to this exist, for example the work of Julian Agyeman and others who have written about environmental racism, environmental justice and other social justice issues as they relate to environment and environmental education. However, such works are not within the mainstream of environmental education yet.

## References


Abdi, A. 2008. "Europe and African Thought Systems and Philosophies of Education." *Cultural Studies* 22 (2): 309–327.

Basole, A. 2009. "Eurocentrism, the University, and Multiple Sites of Knowledge Production." In *Toward a Global Autonomous University*, edited by The Edu-Factory Collective, 32–38. New York: Autonomedia.

Bauder, H., and S. Engel-Di Mauro. 2008. *Critical Geographies: A Collection of Readings*. Praxis ePress. http://www.praxis-epress.org/CGR/contents.html.

Beckford, C. L., C. Jacobs, N. Williams, and R. Nahdee. 2010. "Aboriginal Environmental Wisdom, Stewardship, and Sustainability: Lessons from the Walpole Island First Nations, Ontario, Canada." *The Journal of Environmental Education* 41 (4): 239–248.

Blair, D. 2009. "The Child in the Garden: An Evaluative Review of the Benefits of School Gardening." *The Journal of Environmental Education* 40 (2): 15–38.

Blaut, J. 1999. "Environmentalism and Eurocentrism." *Geographical Review* 89 (3): 391–408.

Bowers, C. A. 2008. "Why a Critical Pedagogy of Place is an Oxymoron." *Environmental Education Research* 14 (3): 325–335.

Breidlid, A. 2009. "Culture, Indigenous Knowledge Systems and Sustainable Development: A Critical View of Education in an African Context." *International Journal of Educational Development* 29: 140–148.

Breidlid, A. 2013. *Education, Indigenous Knowledges, and Development in the Global South: Contesting Knowledges for a Sustainable Future*. New York: Routledge.

Carney, J. 2001. *Black Rice: The African Origins of Rice Cultivation in the Americas*. Boston, MA: Harvard University Press.

Carroll, K. K. 2012. "A Genealogical Review of the Worldview Concept and Framework in Africana Studies Related Theory and Research." In *African American Consciousness: Past and Present*, edited by J. L. Conyers Jr., 23–46. New Brunswick, NJ: Transaction.

Castree, N. 2003. "Place: Connections and Boundaries in an Interconnected World." In *Key Concepts in Geography*, edited by S. L. Holloway, S. R. Rice, and G. Valentine, 165–185. London: Sage.

Cole, A. G. 2007. "Expanding the Field: Revisiting Environmental Education Principles through Multidisciplinary Frameworks." *The Journal of Environmental Education* 38 (2): 35–45.

Cook, V. 2008. "The Field as a 'Pedagogical resource'? A Critical Analysis of Students' Affective Engagement with the Field Environment." *Environmental Education Research* 14 (5): 507–517.

De Lissovoy, N. 2010. "Decolonial Pedagogy and the Ethics of the Global." *Discourse: Studies in the Cultural Politics of Education* 31 (3): 279–293.

Diop, C. A. 1987. *Precolonial Black Africa*. New York: Lawrence Hill Books.

Diop, C. A. 1989. *The Cultural Unity of Black Africa: The Domains of Matriarchy & Patriarchy in Classical Antiquity*. London: Karnak House.

Diop, C. A. 1991. *Civilization or Barbarism: An Authentic Anthropology*. New York: Lawrence Hill Books.

Engel-Di Mauro, S. 2008. "Beyond the Bowers-McLaren Debate: The Importance of Studying the Rest of Nature in Forming Alternative Curricula." *Capitalism Nature Socialism* 19 (2): 88–95.

Ernst, J., and S. Theimer. 2011. "Evaluating the Effects of Environmental Education Programming on Connectedness to Nature." *Environmental Education Research* 17 (5): 577–598.

Falk, W. W., L. L. Hunt, and M. O. Hunt. 2004. "Return Migrations of African-Americans to the South: Reclaiming a Land of Promise, Going Home, or Both?" *Rural Sociology* 69 (4): 490–509.

Fenelon, J. V., and T. D. Hall. 2008. "Revitalization and Indigenous Resistance to Globalization and Neoliberalism." *American Behavioral Scientist* 51 (12): 1867–1901.

Ferreira, S. 2012. "Moulding Urban Children towards Environmental Stewardship: The Table Mountain National Park Experience." *Environmental Education Research* 18 (2): 251–270.

Glasson, G. E., J. A. Frykholm, N. A. Mhango, and A. D. Phiri. 2006. "Understanding the Earth Systems of Malawi: Ecological Sustainability, Culture, and Place-Based Education." *Science Education* 90 (4): 660–680.

Gruenewald, D. A. 2008. "The Best of Both Worlds: A Critical Pedagogy of Place." *Environmental Education Research* 14 (3): 308–324.

Gruenewald, D. A., and G. A. Smith. 2008. "Models for Place-Based Learning." In *Place-Based Education in the Global Age*, edited by D. A. Gruenewald and G. A. Smith, 1–4. New York: Routledge.

Hilliard, A. G. III. 1986. "Pedagogy in Ancient Kemet." In *Kemet and the African Worldview: Research, Rescue and Restoration*, edited by M. Karenga and J. H. Caruthers, 131–148. Los Angeles, CA: University of Sankore Press.

Hungerford, H. R. 2009. "Environmental Education (EE) for the 21st Century: Where Have We Been? Where Are We Now? Where Are We Headed?" *The Journal of Environmental Education* 41 (1): 1–6.

Kamalu, C. 1998. *Person, Divinity & Nature: A Modern View of the Person and the Cosmos in African Thought*. London: Karnak House.

Keto, C. T. 1994. *The Africa-Centered Perspective of History*. London: Research Associates/ Karnak House.

Ladson-Billings, G., and J. K. Donnor. 2008. "Waiting for the Call. the Moral Activist Role of Critical Race Theory Scholarship." In *Handbook of Critical and Indigenous Methodologies*, edited by N. K. Denzin, Y. S. Lincoln, and L. T. Smith, 61–83. Los Angeles, CA: Sage.

Le Grange, L. 2005. "Guattari's Philosophy of Education and Its Implications for Environmental Education in (Post)Colonial Africa." *Southern African Journal of Environmental Education* 22: 33–45.

Leach, M., and R. Mearns, eds. 1996. *The Lie of the Land: Challenging Received Wisdom on the African Environment*. Oxford: James Currey.

McLaren, P., S. Macrine, and D. Hill eds. 2010. *Revolutionizing Pedagogy: Educating for Social Justice within and beyond Global Neo-Liberalism*. London: Palgrave Macmillan.

Memmi, A. 1991. *The Colonizer and the Colonized*. New York: Beacon.

Meyer, M. A. 2008. "Indigenous and Authentic: Hawaiian Epistemology and the Triangulation of Meaning." In *Handbook of Critical and Indigenous Methodologies*, edited by N. K. Denzin, Y. S. Lincoln, and L. T. Smith, 217–232. Los Angeles, CA: Sage.

Morgan, S. C., S. L. Hamilton, M. L. Bentley, and S. Myrie. 2009. "Environmental Education in Botanic Gardens: Exploring Brooklyn Botanic Garden's Project Green Reach." *The Journal of Environmental Education* 40 (4): 35–52.

Mueller, M. P., and M. L. Bentley. 2009. "Environmental and Science Education in Developing Nations: A Ghanaian Approach to Renewing and Revitalizing the Local Community and Ecosystems." *Summer* 40 (4): 53–63.

Quigley, C. 2009. "Globalization and Science Education: The Implications for Indigenous Knowledge Systems." *International Education Studies* 2 (1): 76–88.

Reij, C., I. Scoones, and C. Toulmin, eds. 1996. *Sustaining the Soil: Indigenous Soil and Water Conservation in Africa*. London: Earthscan.

Sheppard, E., H. Leitner, and A. Mariganti. 2013. "Provincializing Global Urbanism: A Manifesto." *Urban Geography*. doi:10.1080/02723638.2013.807977.

Smith, A. 2005. *Conquest: Sexual Violence and American Indian Genocide*. Boston, MA: South End Press.

Smith, G. A., and D. Sobel. 2010. *Place- and Community-Based Education in Schools*. New York: Routledge.

Sobel, D. 2005. *Place-Based Education: Connecting Classrooms and Communities*. Great Barrington, MA: Orion Society.

Strife, Susan. 2010. "Reflecting on Environmental Education: Where is Our Place in the Green Movement?" *The Journal of Environmental Education* 41 (3): 179–191.

Swadener, B. B., and K. Mutua. 2008. "Decolonizing Performances: Deconstructing the Global Postcolonial." In *Handbook of Critical and Indigenous Methodologies*, edited by N. K. Denzin, Y. S. Lincoln, and L. T. Smith, 31–44. Los Angeles, CA: Sage.

Tuck, E., and K. W. Yang. 2012. "Decolonization is Not a Metaphor." *Decolonization: Indigeneity, Education & Society* 1 (1): 1–40.

Wolfe, P. 2001. "Land, Labor, and Difference: Elementary Structures of Race." *American Historical Review* 106 (3): 866–905.

# Manifesting Destiny: a land education analysis of settler colonialism in Jamestown, Virginia, USA

Kate McCoy

*Department of Educational Studies, State University of New York, New Paltz, USA*

Globally, colonization has been and continues to be enacted in the take-over of Indigenous land and the subsequent conversion of agriculture from diverse food and useful crops to large-scale monoculture and c ash crops. This article uses a land education analysis to map the rise of the ideology and practices of Manifest Destiny in Virginia. Manifest Destiny is the culmination (and continuation) of material and discursive relations that serve as a cover story for the formation (and maintenance) of the settler colonial triad of settlers, Indigenous peoples, and slaves. The article theorizes the settler colonial triad, an important construct of land education that provides a lens through which to investigate political-economic and epistemological links between agriculture, settler colonialism, and environment.

In Ghosh's (2008) novel *Sea of Poppies* set in nineteenth century India, Deeti worries over the shortage of thatch to maintain the roof of her hut and the coming shortage of 'wheat, dal, and vegetables' (27). There will not be enough to eat and the roof is likely to leak. The English colonizers demanded that the people in her part of India use their land to grow poppies for opium production and forced sale to China. Fields of opium poppies grown in monoculture had displaced subsistence family farming, prompting Deeti's worries about upcoming shortages and lack of food diversity.

Colonization has been and continues to be enacted in the takeover of Indigenous land and the subsequent conversion of agriculture from diverse food and useful crops to large-scale monoculture and cash crops and, notably, 'drug foods' (e.g. sugar, tea, coffee, tobacco, alcohol, and chocolate) and harder drugs (opium and coca and their derivatives)' (Jankowiak and Bradburd 2003). The impact of growing cash crops in monoculture for profit is considerable: It requires cheap labor or slave labor and large tracts of land. Although the example above is from India, in which a different form of colonialism prevailed (as discussed later in this article), this dynamic is also a defining feature of settler colonialism, wherein the colonizer does not merely take over land use, production, and labor – the colonizer as settler comes to stay.

In this process, ecological systems are decimated as monoculture crops deplete the soil of nutrients, attract pests and weeds, and require that forests and grasslands are turned into vast fields of tilled soil. Thus, food security is compromised when cash crops replace food crops. Lives and ways of life for Indigenous people are lost or, at the least, disrupted and undesirably altered. This was true of the sixteenth-century British colonial sugarcane plantations in the Caribbean (Angrosino 2003) as it is true of coffee colonialism in Laos today (Smith 2012).

Colonial Virginia was the first 'successful' English settler colony in what the English called the New World. There and in other settler colonies, 200 years before the term Manifest Destiny was first used, the machinery that enabled the ideological and material processes of its creation were set into motion. In this article, I use a land education approach to investigate this machinery that was forged in the complex inter-play between discourse, material phenomena, and practices–relays of what Barad (2007) calls 'intra-activity' (353). I position this inquiry as land education because it analyzes/considers a particular geographical location, attending to the significance of both that location and the confluence of people, discourse, and event in the transformation of Indigenous land into settler property. As such, this land education analysis involves both definition and critique of settler colonialism, its human and environmental impact, and its material and discursive legacy. It acknowledges Indigenous understandings of place and land, observing that at first, English understandings did not differ significantly from Indigenous understandings (Allen 2004; Banner 2007). Indeed, it was as England gained imperial power in its conquests and capitalist endeavors and, as a particular kind of ownership of land emerged, those similarities were ignored, with Indigenous cosmologies of land considered as developmentally or evolutionarily backward. It then became necessary to construct Indigenous peoples as savage, which is another key feature of settler colonial societies.

The intra-activity that I analyze reveals the mechanisms that created what Patrick Wolfe calls the settler colonial triad, a network of relations that includes settlers, chattel slaves, and Indigenous peoples.[1] In Jamestown, this triad is made up of English settlers, their indentured servants and slaves, and the Tsenacommacah – a name that refers to the Indigenous people and land of this region. To justify the emergence of this triad, the roots and shoots of the discourses and sets of practices that later became known as Manifest Destiny came into being. I call this paper 'Manifesting Destiny' because I wish to emphasize the processual nature of its formation. It did not spring ready-made from anywhere. It was built discursively and materially through the contingencies of history – the new interpretations of the Christian Bible with emerging modernity, the refusal of the land to yield up to English settlers the gold they were seeking, resistances of the Tsenacommacah to the desires of English settlers, and the necessities of the English leisure class for working-class poor and slave labor to work land when a viable economic opportunity presented itself in the mass production of tobacco as a cash crop.

Veracini (2011) points out that, unlike other forms of colonialism in which power imbalances remain visible in daily life, settler colonialism 'covers its tracks' (3); it aims to become invisible over time. The colonizer does not merely occupy and control the use of land as an overseer of a force of Indigenous labor in a system of exploitation and profit, as in external or exploitation colonialism, as, for example, with the English in India.[2] In settler colonialism, the colonizer comes to stay and to displace, decimate and may proclaim a desire to assimilate the Indigenous population (Wolfe 1999). Tuck and Yang (2012) argue that

> In the process of settler colonialism, land is remade into property and human relationships to land are restricted to the relationship of the owner to his property. Epistemological, ontological, and cosmological relationships to land are interred, indeed made pre-modern and backward. Made savage (5)

In the USA, Manifest Destiny provided an important rationale for the violence of settler colonialism, specifically the violences of dispossession of Indigenous peoples from their land and enslavement of Africans.

## History and environmental education research

The significance of this inquiry for environmental education research lies in its articulation of the historical and continuing production of Manifest Destiny as a settler colonial epistemology and political economy, in intra-action with particular lands, which have resulted and continues to result in environmental degradation and exploitation of peoples and resources. It demonstrates the usefulness of land education analyses in examining environmental practices, such as monocultural, drug cash-crop agriculture, practices that have become a feature of settler colonialism, for example. My aim is not to reconstruct how the Tsenacommacah lived – that story is more appropriately told or not told by Indigenous elders. Today's Virginia Indians note that '[h]istorical knowledge can be a sacred commodity,' 'not for general consumption' (Waugaman and Moretti-Langholtz 2006, 24). Nor do I wish to reproduce the myth of the Noble Savage or the 'ecological Indian' (Krech 1999). The significance here for environmental education and research is not to tout the ways the Tsenacommacah lived with the land as environmentally superior to settler colonial relations to land, though they may well have been. This is also not an attempt to articulate what Gruenewald and Smith (2008) have called 'place consciousness' (xxi), in which place seems presumed to exist before human intervention or in spite of human intervention.

My task is to provide an example of an historical approach to land education, in which I theorize how the case of Jamestown, Virginia establishes the settler colonial triad of 'settlers – Indigenous peoples – chattel' and recasts land as settler property and resource. This dynamic puts in motion a set of relations necessitated by the settler quest for identity linked with land, coupled with a vision that 'land must produce, and produce excessively, because "civilization" is defined as production in excess of the "natural" world' (Tuck and Yang 2012, 6).

## Producing Manifest Destiny: modernist interpretations of dominion

In this special issue, Calderon describes Manifest Destiny as a viral ideology that justifies white supremacy and territoriality by asserting that 'European immigrants were destined to lands in the USA' (2014). Brulle (1996) states that Manifest Destiny is the 'dominant discourse that [has] guided the USA relationship with the natural environment' from 1620 on. So Manifest Destiny is not just a justification for assimilating, displacing, and/or eradicating people and claiming land, it also makes 'exploitation of the natural environment into a duty' (67).

The birth of Manifest Destiny is almost unanimously located in time in the nineteenth century by scholars and historians. The term was introduced in 1845 in the popular press by journalist John O'Sullivan (though there is some dispute about who used the term first). Manifest Destiny is most often discussed as a situational and historically specific political doctrine that served to justify westward expansion in the nineteenth century USA. Deeper historical roots and more prominent contemporary relevance of the doctrine, however, are recognized by some scholars (e.g. Brulle 1996; Coles 2002). In this discussion, I am suggesting that the Virginia Company operated from a nascent, not-yet-named Manifest Destiny produced at the ideological crossroads of Protestant Religious and Enlightenment thought, spawning an epistemology of evolutionary anthropology in which the English came to know the Indigenous Other as an imaginary for England's more 'primitive' past (Wolfe 1999).

Prior to the seventeenth century, Christian Biblical scholars and theologians interpreted the origin story of Genesis as allegorical and metaphorical, specifically God's call for Adam and mankind to subdue the earth and have dominion over it and all its creatures:

> 26 And God said, Let us make man in our image, after our likeness: and let him have dominion over the fish of the sea, and over the fowl of the air, and over the cattle, and over all the earth, and over every creeping thing that creepeth upon the earth.
>
> 27 So God created man in his own image, in the image of God created he him; male and female created he them.
>
> 28 And God blessed them, and God said unto them, Be fruitful, and multiply, and replenish the earth, and subdue it: and have dominion over the fish of the sea, and over the fowl of the air, and over every living thing that moveth upon the earth. (Genesis 1:26–28)

In the allegorical readings of these verses, man was to control his baser passions and have dominion over the 'unruly impulses of the body' (Harrison 1999, 91), not absolutely rule over the earth and every living thing on it. It actually was not until the seventeenth century that these verses were interpreted to mean dominion over the natural world. Harrison suggests that these new readings came about due to an increasingly 'mechanical world view' in a 'religious landscape of this-worldly Protestantism,' and 'the new hermeneutics of modernity, which looks to the literal sense as the true meaning of a text' (1999, 96). These ideas were picked up by Francis Bacon, who described the task of the empirical sciences to expand 'the narrow limits of man's dominion over the universe' (quoted in Harrison 1999), and Rene Descartes, who posited that through scientific endeavor we 'thus make ourselves, as it were, the lords and masters of nature' (98). Harrison goes on to argue that seventeenth century discourse – religious and scientific – about 'human dominion is not an assertion of human tyranny over a hapless earth' (1999). It is a way for man to restore the earth to 'its prelapsarian order and perfection' (103) – its state before Adam's fall into sin. Nature, then, was viewed of the embodiment of sin in what was perceived as the world's wildness.

These discourses of dominion were set in intra-active relation (Barad 2007) to material practices of dominion, such as mapping/charting, exploration, and agriculture to prevent land from 'degenerate[ing] into a wilderness' (Harrison 1999, 100). John Locke maintained that the material processes of 'clearing, planting, cultivation, or stocking with animals' (101) made lands previously held in common into private property, which, he argued, was part of God's plan for dominion. Harrison points out: 'Logically, it followed that those who occupied lands, yet had done nothing to bring them under control, could legitimately be dispossessed of them' (1999, 101). They were evidence of the fall of man cast out from Eden, in a situation that must be corrected through Christian dominion.

### Tsenacommacah and dominion: Indigenous relations to land

The perception that the Tsenacommacah were mere occupiers of their land was not widely held among the first settlers. Instead, the first settlers saw the Tsenacommacah as skilled farmers, hunters, and stewards who understood well how their land could provide what was needed for their people to thrive. Firsthand accounts written by Gabriel Archer, William Strachey, and George Percy, for example, describe with admiration the sophisticated practices of land use, growing food, hunting, fishing, and foraging among the tribes in this area (collected primary writings in Haile (ed.) 1998). With land held in common (not privately owned by individuals) (Archer 1998b, 120), these practices fed everyone, even providing surplus that was sometimes shared with European settlers. Descriptions of gardens are common in many settler accounts. Percy describes traveling 'through the goodliest cornfields that ever was seen in any country' (1998, 93). Archer reports learning 'the growing of their corn' (1998a, 110), seeing 'low ground prepared for seed' (112), and visiting a 'plat of ground … bare without wood some 100 acres, where are set beans, wheat, peas, tobacco, gourds, pompions, and other things unknown to us in our tongue' (114). Strachey notes that '[a]bout their houses they have commonly square plots of cleared ground which serve them for gardens, some 100, some 200 foot square' (1998, 636). Indirect evidence suggests that the Tsenacommacah had enough land adjoining their villages to leave fields to return to forest when the soil was depleted from planting (Morgan 1975, 53, n.29). Strategic burning for clearing land and steering game for hunting (Percy 1998, 91; Strachey 1998, 640) created outdoor spaces that were open and park-like, including forests with large trees, but no underbrush, abundant with fruits, nuts, and berries (Archer 1998b, 120; Percy 1998, 96).

Growing different crops together in one field, rotating crops, and leaving lands fallow for long periods of time, combined with the burning practices employed in hunting and clearing land, made obtaining food less labor intensive for the Tsenacommacah than practices attempted by English colonizers. At the same time, Tsenacommacah practices encouraged the growth of fruit and nut trees for foraging and grasslands for game such as buffalo, deer, and elk. These practices of land use are set out in an Indigenous origin story – the story of First Woman – a story in which tobacco holds a significant part.

### First woman and the gift of agriculture[3]

Paula Gunn Allen, in her biography of Pocahontas (2004), recounts an origin story of agriculture and of tobacco. In her telling, First Woman and First Man had children and the numbers of family members increased so much that famine struck. Distraught by the rampant starvation of her children, First Woman instructs her husband: 'After I am dead,' she says,

> get two men to take me by the hair and draw my body all around the field I will point out to you beforehand. When they come to the center of the field, they should bury my

> bones there. Then, everyone should stay away from the place until seven months have passed. When it's time, let the people go again to the field and gather up everything they find there. Eat most of it. It's my flesh, and it will keep the people strong. Be sure to save some of it to put back in the ground so there will be more the next season. You can't eat my bones, of course

She continues, 'but they can be burned. The smoke will make your minds fresh and will bring peace to you and your descendants' (Allen 2004, 196–200, paraphrasing mine).

They follow her instructions and after seven months have gone by the men go to the field and discover it filled with tall, green plants. They taste some of the fruit, which tastes sweet. Her husband names it *skarmunal*, corn. In the center of the corn, he sees another plant. This one has broad leaves and no fruit, and it tastes bitter. This he calls *apook*, tobacco.

## Tobacco in the Tsenacommacah

*Apook* was the variety of tobacco grown by and in the Tsenacommacah (Allen 2004), classified by botanists as *Nicotania rustica* (Winter 2000a). *Apook* is a sacred plant and is used in rituals, ceremonies, and shamanistic practice (Allen 2004; von Gernet 2000). Archeological evidence suggests that *N. rustica* spread to eastern North America from Mexico with human migration (Wagner 2000). von Gernet (2000) hypothesizes that *N. rustica* initially 'underwent an artificial selection process by human foragers' (79), then later as population numbers increased and food-producing economies emerged it was cultivated in small, square plots near the houses in a village, along with other crops (von Gernet 2000). Another account suggests that '[m]ost groups raised it in small gardens,' which may have been separate from other crops (Winter 2000b, 14).

Tobacco for/in the Tsenacommacah was not a cash crop for trade or profit nor was it a recreational drug. It was grown in small batches for sacred, ritual use. Tobacco is mentioned in three contexts in nearly all early settler accounts – as a gift from the Tsenacommacah to the settlers, a crop in vegetable gardens or in separate plots, and an important element in rituals and ceremonies.

## Becoming Jamestown

The first and second Virginia Companies of England were formed in 1606. With charters from King James I to start a permanent colony and funding from private investments from wealthy nobles (Campbell 1959), the companies were to be money-making endeavors. The first settlers – mainly lesser nobility, knights, country gentry, and their indentured servants (Campbell 1959) – were looking for gold (Morgan 1975; Slivinski 2010) and 'whatever merchantable commodities come to hand' (Haile 1998, 19).

Along with the main goal of finding gold and other commodities, the King issued these charters 'in acknowledgment of the desire of both companies to propagate the Christian religion in America' (Haile 1998, 15). The English imagined themselves to be 'friends of God:' 'Claiming friendship with God embodied the English people's confidence and arrogance that God loved them more than others. It was [a] means of claiming superiority …' (Bond 2001, 15). The English believed that 'God wanted England to colonize North America' (18). As reward for this mission, for establishing strategic defense against the Spanish, who were competing for land in the New World, and for securing profits for the Virginia Company, settlers were offered 'full and exclusive rights to settle the land and enjoy its resources' (Haile 1998, 15). The land, however, was held by the company at first, not by individual settlers (Slivinski 2010). No mention is made in the first charter of 1606 of what to do about the inhabitants of the land, except to convert them to Christianity. This is not the case, however, with the 'instructions by way of advice' issued by the Council of Virginia, also in 1606. These instructions advised settlers not to 'offend the naturals,' to use them for food and for guides, but definitely not to trust them (Haile 1998, 21). The colonists were given specific suggestions for concealing their weaknesses so that they might keep the upper hand in their dealings. The second charter, issued in 1609, instructs the new governor to convert 'the Indians to Christianity by procuring their children for instruction, and getting them away from the "*iniocasokes*, or priest"' (23). Alliances were to be cultivated with enemies of the Powhatan Alliance, the name settlers gave the tribes of the Tsenacommacah. Powhatan was the name settlers called Wahunsenacawh, the leader of this alliance. These enemies, as well as Powhatan's allies, would be required to pay taxes and/or fees for passage through land settlers claimed: 'It [was] hoped the burden of tribute [would] force the Indians to fell the forest and become cashcrop farmers' (24).

Despite the fact that the great abundance of the land was admired and advertised in nearly all early settler accounts, few efforts were made for the colony to be self-sufficient. For sustenance, they relied on supplies from England and uneasy trade with the Tsenacommacah (Morgan 1975; Slivinski 2010). Neither source proved consistent. No gold was found, other efforts at making money failed, starvation was rampant, and mortality rates were shocking. And still, the Virginia Company 'never considered the problem of staying alive in Virginia to be a serious one' (Morgan 1975, 86). Though the settlers likely could have fed themselves, their efforts were focused on making money. They tried olives, silk, pitch, timber, tar, soap ashes, glass blowing, and cedar, but they could not capture an English market (Burns 2007; Morgan 1975). They compromised their relationship with the Tsenacommacah through senseless killings and torture, cutting off their only supply of food from the region. Had it not been for tobacco, settler colonialism may not have taken hold when it did. King James had grown tired of the Virginia Company's financial failures, its high mortality, and drain on the royal supplies (Burns 2007).

## Settler tobacco and chattel slavery: completing the settler colonial triad

*Apook*, the tobacco grown in and by the Tsenacommacah, did not appeal to European tastes. Settler William Strachey, writing between 1609 and 1612, says:

> There is here great store of tobacco, which the savages call *apooke*, howbeit it is not of the best kind. It is but poor and weak and of a biting taste; it grows not fully a yard above the ground, bearing a little yellow flower like to henbane; the leaves are short and thick, somewhat round at the upper end, whereas the best tobacco, of Trinidado and the Oronoque, is large, sharp, and growing 2 or 3 yards from the ground, bearing a flower of the breadth of our bellflowers in England. (1998, 680)

Europeans had become habituated to another strain of tobacco that had been brought back from Christopher Columbus's exploits in 1492. *Nicotania tabacum* was the strain Spanish soldiers and sailors and eventually the English smoked (Matthee 1995; Wagner 2000).

Any and all tobacco use had been condemned by King James I (1604) who considered it harmful and immoral and associated it with 'the barbarous Indians,' who he imagined used it to treat 'the Pokes, a filthy disease, whereunto these barbarous people are (as all men know) very much subject, what through the uncleanly and adust constitution of their bodies.' Despite his popular screed against it, tobacco in Europe went from being used for medicinal purposes to being used recreationally and fashionably in a very short time (Matthee 1995). It was the recreational use of tobacco that drove up its price and increased demand. Leaders of the Virginia Company, however, were reluctant at first to embrace it as the key to financial gain. Jamestown settlers eventually tried to export *N. rustica* to England, but the English – despite the fact that its own colony and its inhabitants were struggling and often failing to survive – continued to buy *N. tabacum* from their arch-rival Spain, who imported it from its colonies in the West Indies (Burns 2007).

It was not until 1612 that John Rolfe, and some argue with the assistance of Pocahontas, was able to perfect the cultivation of *N. tabacum* in the colony that tobacco became a viable commodity for the Virginia Company (Allen 2004; Burns 2007; Morgan 1975; Wagner 2000). Even so, some company members were not happy to make their fortunes in the production of a 'disreputable weed' (Morgan 1975, 93). Money talks, however, and even King James eventually quieted his discontent because he was powerless to refuse the tax revenues from tobacco sales that lined England's coffers (Burns 2007). Jamestown settlers responded to this market force by planting tobacco as though in a frenzy, 'bewitched by the affluence it brought' (Burns 2007, 62–63) and still neglecting to grow enough food. Most pertinent to this study is the fact that to really make money with tobacco requires a great deal of cheap labor and a great deal of land.

First, and fundamentally, to grow enough tobacco to sell it for profit required sufficiently large plots of land. Second, tobacco rapidly depleted the thin topsoil of the Tsenacommacah, sucking up the nitrogen, calcium, and potash, making it necessary to abandon fields for a time and to clear more and more land, displacing trees, other vegetation, animals, and the Indigenous inhabitants (Burns 2007). Third, growing tobacco on this scale required a large, cheap labor force. The response to this requirement created the need for even more land.

Indentured servants – poor people from the streets and jails of England – were brought to the Virginia colony to provide manual labor. Slivinski (2010) argues that they had little incentive to work. Their indentures were for a set time, not subject to measures of productivity. Hence, they 'work[ed] less and less efficiently' (28). Another disincentive was property policy. The Virginia Company owned the land collectively, so it made little difference to the workers whether they produced more or less. In 1611, new governor Sir Thomas Dale instituted land allotments to indentured servants who completed their terms satisfactorily. These allotments were increased by subsequent governors in 1618. Slivinski's settler-oriented analysis stops there as he draws the conclusion that these first steps toward 'private land ownership' were 'key to prosperity in the New World' (2010, 29), but I wish to press further in time to theorize the development of the settler colonial triad.

Despite the incentives of property, the indentured workforce was still not sufficient in number or productivity. Indigenous peoples could not be forced to work for them – settlers were outnumbered and out-of-place in the Tsenacommacah (Zinn

2005), and in the settler colonial logic set in motion by the political economy of tobacco for profit, the main job of Indigenous peoples was to disappear (Veracini 2011). Ultimately, captured and transported African slaves – because they were phenotypically distinct from settlers due to their skin color and not regarded by settlers as human – were the solution to the need for labor on tobacco plantations and to grow food for settlers to stay alive (Morgan 1975, 297). In 1619, the global slave trade came to the Tsenacommacah; 20 Africans were involuntarily transported to Jamestown and soon were brought in increasing numbers, from 6000 in 1700 to 170,000 in 1763 (Zinn 2005). Although they may have initially been listed as 'servants' on passenger lists, Africans were systematically differentiated from their white counterparts, who were also listed as 'servants,' with unequal treatment. They received harsher punishments for infractions, listed separately in lists of servants and denied access to arms and ammunition (Zinn 2005). Finally, even when and if they were granted freedom, they were denied the land allotments available to white indentured servants (Allen 1994). Increasing land allotments were instituted to discourage solidarity between white and black laborers and to create the distinction of race that was further reinforced by laws and policies favoring even propertyless white laborers (Allen 1994).

It was Indigenous peoples' job to disappear, the African slaves' job to work the land, and the settlers' entitlement to reap the profits and gain control over the land and people. The combination of these requirements establishes the settler colonial triad and provides the material basis for the legal and affective discursive maneuvers of Manifest Destiny.

## Remaking land into English property: legal discourse and practice

In *How the Indians Lost Their Land: Law and Power on the Frontier*, Banner (2007) meticulously examines primary settler texts and other sources to come to a nuanced interpretation of how Indigenous peoples lost land. He notes that both settler accounts and those of Indigenous people were inconsistent, and not just in predictable ways. Part of the problem, he reasons is that 'much of what has been written on Indian land acquisition implicitly assumes that conquest and sale are mutually exclusive alternatives that exhaust the possible methods of land transfer' (3). Banner argues that it is not so simple.

Recall that King James of England issued charters granting the Virginia Company 'full and exclusive rights to settle the land and enjoy its resources' (Haile 1998, 15). Despite this grand proclamation and the full confidence that 'land in North America was unowned and available for the taking' (Banner 2007, 15), there was doubt and debate about whether it was lawful to take land that already belonged to someone else. Minister William Crashaw argued in a sermon in 1609 that it was not: 'A Christian may take nothing from a Heathen against his will, but in faire and lawfull bargaine' (13). He goes on to qualify his point: 'We will *exchange* with them for that which *they may spare*, and we doe need … in so much as a great part of it lieth wild and inhabited of none but the beasts of the fielde, and the trees' (14). (This last point is an important qualifier that informs later developments.) Another minister, however, offered a different view; William Symonds raised the question of whether it is lawful to take lands by violence. He concludes that 'human history was largely a catalogue of invasions and wars, with the winners taking the land of the losers,' justifying outright conquest of the Tsenacommacah (14).

The Virginia Company published a list of reasons their claims to the land were justified. This list included an interesting variety of justifications, including living among the people to convert them to Christianity and establish partnerships, low population density, retribution for ambassadors killed by Indigenous peoples, and because they had purchased the land. While both claiming land that could be imagined as unused and forcibly taking land through violence were practiced by the English in the Tsenacommacah, it was the remaking of land into property according to English law that truly transformed both land and relations. Banner (2007) argues that '[m]ost colonists would have found it distasteful to think of themselves as conquerors' (84). By operating out of English property law, imagining it based in 'simple common sense,' '[t]he English could sincerely believe that Indian land was being purchased fair and square' (84). In this way, at least discursively, settler colonialism covered its tracks.

While King James and Virginia Company stakeholders back in England continued to view the land as uninhabited for the taking, people on the ground in Jamestown were divided (Banner 2007). Theories abounded justifying taking Tsenecommacah land. Some centered on the right of the English; for example, notions that Christians were justified in taking land from non-Christians and England could take land by right of conquest. Other theories focused on beliefs about the Tsenacommacah; for example, beliefs that they lacked a notion of land rights and that they were nomadic and didn't stay in one place long enough to rightfully claim property. Theories concerning the rights of the English were not supportable with English law, whereas theories concerning beliefs about the Tsenacommacah were contradicted by experience. The Tsenacommacah were clearly gardeners, not nomads. Despite claims by some to the contrary, not only did the Tsenacommacah practice agriculture, they recognized land rights, albeit not exactly like those of the English. John Smith, for example, notes: 'They all know their several lands, and habitations, and limits, to fish, fowle, or hunt in' (quoted in Banner 2007, 19).

In the early years of the colony, outright conquest was out of the question. Settlers were outnumbered and surrounded, so the English bought much of the land they acquired. Settlers reported that some among the Tsenacommacah were not happy with the English presence, but Percy recounts an early occasion on which

> … [T]he savages murmured at our planting in their country, whereupon this werowance made answer again, very wisely of a savage: 'Why would you be offended with them as long as they hurt you not, nor take anything away by force? They take but little waste ground which doth you nor any of us any good'. (Percy, 97)

Over time, Virginia settlers increased in numbers and exercised violence and force and made clear they had no intentions of sharing the land. As early as 1616, there were reports that the Tsenacommacah were experiencing food shortages brought on by their need to move their villages north to get out of the way of settlers and by constant vigilance and battles (Slivinski 2010). On 22 March 1622, the Tsenacommacah attacked Jamestown, destroying the settlement and killing many of the settlers (Vaughan 1978). Most analysts conclude that they had finally realized that the English were there to stay and hoped that a concerted effort to wipe them out would end the violent take-over of their land and means of livelihood. By this time, however, the settlers were too numerous and had taken over the governance of the land. Banner (2007) concludes that during the colonial era:

> [Indigenous people] sold much of the land under the overt or latent threats of English expropriation and ecological devastation. They sold some under the misapprehension that the English intended to share it with them. The English defrauded them out of some. And much of the land was sold by individuals who lacked the authority to sell … In the end the acquisition of land in North America is a story of power … a subtle and complex kind of power than would have been necessary to seize land by force. It was the power to supplant the Indian legal systems with the English legal system, the power to have land disputes decided by English officials using English law rather than Indian officials using Indian law. (82–83)

## Making savage

The supplanting of Indigenous law with English law was accomplished through an affective, discursive process of *making savage*, a process also key to the development of the cover story of Manifest Destiny. The word *savage* (sometimes spelled *salvage*) is used in almost all firsthand settler accounts when referring to the Tsenacommacah,[4] but it is not the use of the word itself that performs the task of *making savage*. The work of making savage is done through the detailed descriptions of the Tsenacommacah–how they dressed, their tattooing practices, their ceremonies, their rituals, how they lived, how they farmed, how they hunted, and so on. Early settlers acted as ethnographers, documenting and interpreting the lives of those they encountered. In a manner similar to nineteenth century English anthropologists in Australia, seventeenth century settlers of Jamestown attempted to provide the 'evidence' that the Tsenacommacah were a primitive people in an earlier stage of civilization than the English (Wolfe 1999). It might be possible to argue that the Jamestown narratives are ethnographic precursors to settler colonial anthropology and the theories of evolutionary anthropology that became integral to the discipline in the nineteenth century. There are many ways to investigate this possibility, but in the following discussion, I will focus only on a few examples of how the settler narratives produce the Tsenacommacah as savage in terms of land, land use, and agriculture.

Banner (2007) argues that the English viewed the Tsenacommacah through an anthropological lens as they compared Indigenous people with 'ancient peoples who had once inhabited Britain' (36). These comparisons led many observers to conclude that Indigenous people lived in a 'state of nature' or under 'natural law,' wherein they 'lacked property rights in their uncultivated land' (34). The English in England were going through a conversion of common fields used by many individual groups into enclosed private property that was owned exclusively by one individual. It was not that the English did not understand common property use such as the Tsenacommacah practiced, it was that English property law was moving toward exclusive rights, which was interpreted as a development toward progress. Even though the English understood the role of common and uncultivated land in the Tsenacommacah's land management practices, they began to speak of large tracts of uncultivated land as wasteful, explaining it in terms of England's high population density and high intensity food production practices (Banner 2007; Washburn 1959). With land use tied to profit, what became viewed as inefficiency was antithetical to proper capitalist enterprise, an affront to God's mandate of dominion, and further evidence that the Indigenous people were a less developed people and that seizure of 'empty' land was justified, even destined to happen.

The gendered division of labor as it was understood by the settlers was further evidence of savagery. Tsenacommacah women foraged for fruits and nuts in the forest and tended crops, growing corn, beans, squash, and melons all together in the same field. Men hunted and fished, cleared the fields for planting and grazing game, and, according to most accounts, were responsible for the cultivation of tobacco. It appeared to the English that the women did all the hard labor, while the men idled away their time. For example, Percy observes: 'I saw bread made by their women, which do all their drudgery. The men takes their pleasure in hunting and their wars, which they are in continually, one kingdom against another' (1998, 97). Strachey reports that the men never want 'to be seen in any effeminate labor, which is the cause that the women be very painful and the men often idle' (1998, 638). The perception that men of the Tsenacommacah had an easy life was quite an enticement to English indentured servants subjected to a life of labor and starvation in the colonies (Morgan 1975). Colonial leaders, frustrated by disappearing workers, circulated tales of the 'lazy Indian,' which became a prominent feature of Manifest Destiny discourse. Women of the tribes, despite the fact that they labored significantly less than English peasant women (Morgan 1975), were an affront to the ideal of the idle, ornamental wife of English nobility and gentry. These charges of barbarism also become part of the story of Manifest Destiny.

## Conclusion

Practices of farming large quantities of tobacco for export included appropriating more and more land, killing and displacing Indigenous people, disrupting sustenance food systems, introducing chattel slavery for labor, creating land ownership for indentured servants who completed their terms, and creating plantation agriculture, a forerunner to the monoculture, factory farming that is ubiquitous in the USA today. These practices, along with the discourses of English property law and Indigenous peoples' savagery, built the settler colonial triad and paved the way for evolutionary anthropology and an accompanying political economy of labor and land exploitation, necessitating disappearing Indigenous peoples and Indigenous peoples' sovereignty. Predicated on this triad and its discursive and material practices, Manifest Destiny became the cover story for English colonial settlement and expansion in Jamestown and other parts of Turtle Island at the expense of Indigenous people and land. Manifest Destiny did not just inspire the frontier, but rationalized its violence in the aftermath. In this regard, Manifest Destiny is a strategy with which settler colonialism seeks to 'cover its tracks and operate toward its self-supersession' (Veracini 2011, 3).

Contemporary discourses and practices of so-called Third World development carry on this legacy – still promoting monoculture of drug and other cash crops. These colonial enterprises by new names are informed by an evolutionary anthropology and political economies of exploitation that take so-called First World capitalist growth and expansion as the pinnacle of civilization in the new names of 'spreading democracy' and 'opening markets.' Environmental movements are often blocked, and environmental restrictions are overturned through the contemporary mobilization of Manifest Destiny ideology, state's rights, and property rights discourses (Brulle 1996). The discursive and material intra-actions of these dynamics have been devastating to people and environments, but it should be recognized that environmentalism is not innocent of these exploitative impulses cloaked in benevolence. Urban gentrification, for example, carries the legacy of Manifest Destiny. As Paperson theorizes in this special issue, the ghetto is recast as *terra sacer*, settler colonialism's 'internal frontier,' 'empire's outlawed life' (2014). Ghetto is seen as 'sacred wasteland that may be re-inhabited by anybody, with impunity' (2014). The 'clean up' of polluted urban environments is preceded by discursive maneuvers to *make savage* their inhabitants through aggressive policing and crime reporting. The inhabitants are cleared out through legal and illegal enactments of property law and practice, making way for the next wave of gentrifying settlers who will start anew to care for the 'abandoned' environment.

This example of an historical approach to land education has aimed to explore in detail the formation of the cover story for the settler colonial triad and its discursive and material practices, formations and practices that are instrumental in attempts to remake Turtle Island into the settler nation of the USA. Understanding historical and contemporary mobilizations of Manifest Destiny and its attending evolutionary anthropology and politico-economic dynamics is important to land education, especially in settler colonial contexts where it has been used to and continues to justify and even glorify eradication and displacement of people, crop over-production, and environmental devastation. It is just as important, however, to question what is done in the name of environmental redemption, especially when it involves the evolutionary logic of *making savage* the populations targeted for removal.

**Acknowledgments**

Previous versions of the article were presented at the American Educational Studies Association Annual Meeting, Denver, CO, October 2010; the International Congress on Qualitative Inquiry, Urbana-Champaign, IL, May 2011, the 32nd Annual Bergamo Conference on Curriculum Theory and Classroom Practice, Dayton, Ohio, October 201, and the American Educational Research Association Annual Meeting, Vancouver, BC, Canada, April 2012. The author wishes to thank Eve Tuck for careful readings and suggestions along the way and the *Environmental Education Research* reviewers for their insights and suggestions.

## Funding

Research for this paper was partially funded through a United University Professionals Professional Development Award Summer 2011, SUNY New Paltz, New York.

## Notes

1. This concept is introduced in a radio interview between Patrick Wolfe and K. Kehaulani Kauanui http://www.indigenouspolitics.org/audiofiles/2010/Wolfe%20Settler%20Colonialism%202010.mp3.
2. In a radio interview between Patrick Wolfe and K. Kehaulani Kauanui, Wolfe calls this 'franchise colonialism.' (http://www.indigenouspolitics.org/audiofiles/2010/Wolfe%20Settler%20Colonialism%202010.mp3.Patrick). Tuck and Yang (2012) characterize it as 'external colonialism' (4).
3. Adapted from Paula Gunn Allen's account in *Pocahontas: Medicine woman, spy, entrepreneur, diplomat* (2004). She is drawing from a sacred story of the Abenaki people collected by Natalie Curtis in *The Indians' Book* (1968). There are many North American Indigenous stories of the origin of tobacco. I chose to use this one because the themes work with the purpose of this paper and Allen's use of it in her book about the same era and geographical location.

4. It is beyond the scope of this study to investigate what that word might have meant to seventeenth century English settlers, but it seems possible that settler accounts helped to transform the meaning from 'people of the woods' toward its current meaning: 'a person belonging to a primitive society' (Merriam-Webster online dictionary, http://www.merriam-webster.com/).

## References


Allen, T. 1994. *The Invention of the White Race: Volume One: Racial Oppression and Social Control*. London: Verso.

Allen, P. G. 2004. *Pocahontas: Medicine Woman, Spy, Entrepreneur, Diplomat*. San Francisco, CA: Harper Collins.

Angrosino, M. V. 2003. "Rum and Ganja: Indenture, Drug Foods, Labor Motivation, and the Evolution of the Modern Sugar Industry in Trinidad." In *Drugs, Labor, and Colonial Expansion*, edited by W. Jankowiak and D. Bradburd, 101–116. Tuscon, AZ: University of Arizona Press.

Archer, G. 1998a. "A Relation of the Discovery of Our River from James Fort into the Main, Made by Captain Christofer Newport, and Sincerely Written and Observed by a Gentleman of the Colony." In *Jamestown Narratives: Eyewitness Accounts of the Virginia Colony: The First Decade: 1607–1617*, edited by E. W. Haile, 101–118. Champlain, VA: RoundHouse. Originally published in Public Records Office: Colonial Office 1/1–53, *Achaeologia Americana*, Transactions. Vol. 4, 1860d, 40.

Archer, G. 1998b. "The Description of the Now-discovered River and Country of Virginia, with the Likelihood of Ensuing Riches by England's Aid and Industry." In *Jamestown Narratives: Eyewitness Accounts of the Virginia Colony: The First Decade: 1607–1617*, edited by E. W. Haile, 118–121. Champlain, VA: RoundHouse. Originally published in Public Records Office: Colonial Office 1/1–53, *Achaeologia Americana*, Transactions. Vol. 4, 1860d, 59.

Banner, S. 2007. *How the Indians Lost Their Land: Law and Power on the Frontier*. Cambridge, MA: Harvard University Press.

Barad, K. 2007. *Meeting the Universe Half-way: Quantum Physics and the Entanglement of Matter and Meaning*. Durham, NC: Duke University Press.

Bond, E. L. 2001. *Damned Souls in a Tobacco Colony: Religion in Seventeenth-century Virginia*. Macon, GA: Mercer University Press.

Brulle, R. J. 1996. "Environmental Discourse and Social Movement Organizations: A Historical and Rhetorical Perspective on the Development of US Environmental Organizations." *Sociological Inquiry* 66 (1): 58–83.

Burns, E. 2007. *The Smoke of the Gods: A Social History of Tobacco*. Philadelphia, PA: Temple University Press.

Calderon, D. 2014. "Speaking Back to Manifest Destinies: A Land Education-based Approach to Critical Curriculum Inquiry." *Environmental Educational Research* 20 (1): 24–36.

Campbell, M. 1959. "Social Origins of Some Early Americans." In *Seventeenth-century America: Essays in Colonial History*, edited by J. M. Smith, 63–89. Chapel Hill, NC: University of North Carolina Press.

Coles, R. 2002. "Manifest Destiny Adapted for 1990s' War Discourse: Mission and Destiny Intertwined." *Sociology of Religion* 63 (4): 403–426.
Curtis, N. 1968. *The Indians' Book*. New York: Dover.
von Gernet, A. 2000. "North American Indigenous *Nicotiana* Use and Tobacco Shamanism: The Early Documentary Record, 1520–1660." In *Tobacco Use by Native North Americans: Sacred Smoke and Silent Killer*, edited by J. C. Winter, 59–80. Norman, OK: University of Oklahoma Press.
Ghosh, A. 2008. *Sea of Poppies*. New York: Farrar, Straus, and Giroux.
Gruenewald, D., and D. Smith, eds. 2008. *Place-based Education in the Global Age: Local Diversity*. Mahwah, NJ: Lawrence Erlbaum.
Haile, E. W., ed. 1998. *Introduction to Jamestown Narratives: Eyewitness Accounts of the Virginia Colony: The First Decade: 1607–1617, 1–82*. Champlain, VA: RoundHouse.
Harrison, P. 1999. "Subduing the Earth: Genesis 1, Early Modern Science, and the Exploitation of Nature." *The Journal of Religion* 79 (1): 86–109.
Jankowiak, W., and D. Bradburd, eds. 2003. *Drugs, Labor, and Colonial Expansion*. Tuscon, AZ: University of Arizona Press.
King James I of England, VI of Scotland. 1604. *A Counterblaste to Tobacco*. http://www.jesus-is-lord.com/kjcounte.htm.
Krech, S. 1999. *The Ecological Indian: Myth and History*. New York: W. W. Norton.
Matthee, R. 1995. "Exotic Substances: The Introduction and Global Spread of Tobacco, Coffee, Cocoa, Tea, and Distilled Liquor, Sixteenth to Eighteenth Centuries." In *Drugs and Narcotics in History*, edited by R. Porter and M. Teich, 24–51. Cambridge: Cambridge University Press.
Morgan, E. S. 1975. *American Slavery American Freedom: The Ordeal of Colonial Virginia*. New York: W. W. Norton.
Paperson, L. 2014. "A Ghetto Land Pedagogy: An Antidote for Settler Environmentalism." *Environmental Educational Research* 20 (1): 115–130.
Percy, G. 1998. "Observations Gathered Out of a Discourse of the Plantation of the Southern Colony in Virginia by the English, 1606. Written by That Honorable Gentleman, Master George Percy." In *Jamestown Narratives: Eyewitness Accounts of the Virginia Colony: The First Decade: 1607–1617*, edited by E. W. Haile, 85–100. Champlain, VA: RoundHouse. Originally published in Samuel Purchas *Hakluytus posthumus or Purchas his pilgrims, containing a history of the world in sea voyages and lande travels by Englishmen and others*, 1625d, 1685.
Slivinski, S. 2010. "Economic History: The Lessons of Jamestown." *Region Focus* first quarter: 27–29.
Smith, B. 2012. "Coffee Colonialism in Laos." *Daily Maverick*, June 19. http://www.dailymaverick.co.za/article/2012-06-19-coffee-colonialism-in-laos/.
Strachey, W. 1998. "The History of Travel into Virginia Britannia: The First Book of the First Decade." In *Jamestown Narratives: Eyewitness Accounts of the Virginia Colony: The First Decade: 1607–1617*, edited by E. W. Haile, 570–689. Champlain, VA: RoundHouse. Originally published in Bodleian Library: Ashmole 1758, folios 1–102.
Tuck, E., and K. W. Yang. 2012. "Decolonization is Not a Metaphor." *Decolonization: Indigeneity, Education and Society* 1 (1): 1–40.
Vaughan, A. T. 1978. "'Expulsion of the Salvages': English Policy and the Virginia Massacre of 1622." *The William and Mary Quarterly*, third series, 35 (1): 57–84.
Veracini, L. 2011. "Introducing Settler Colonial Studies." *Settler Colonial Studies* 1 (1): 1–12.
Wagner, G. E. 2000. "Tobacco in Prehistoric Eastern North America." In *Tobacco use by Native North Americans: Sacred Smoke and Silent Killer*, edited by J. C. Winter, 185–201. Norman, OK: University of Oklahoma Press.
Washburn, W. E. 1959. "The Moral and Legal Justifications for Dispossessing the Indians." In *Seventeenth-century America: Essays in Colonial History*, edited by J. M. Smith, 15–32. Chapel Hill, NC: University of North Carolina Press.
Waugaman, S. F., and D. Moretti-Langholtz. 2006. *We're Still Here: Contemporary Virginia Indians Tell Their Stories*. Richmond, VA: Palari.

Winter, J. C. 2000a. "Introduction to the North American Tobacco Species." In *Tobacco Use by Native North Americans: Sacred Smoke and Silent Killer*, edited by J. C. Winter, 3–8. Norman, OK: University of Oklahoma Press.

Winter, J. C. 2000b. "Traditional Uses of Tobacco by Native Americans." In *Tobacco Use by Native North Americans: Sacred Smoke and Silent Killer*, edited by J. C. Winter, 9–58. Norman, OK: University of Oklahoma Press.

Wolfe, P. 1999. *Settler Colonialism and the Transformation of Anthropology: The Politics and Poetics of an Ethnographic Event*. London: Cassell.

Zinn, H. 2005. *A People's History of the United States: 1492-present*. New York: Harper Perennial Modern Classics.

# Hoea Ea: land education and food sovereignty in Hawaii

Manulani Aluli Meyer

*Indigenous Knowledge, Maori University of New Zealand, Auckland, UK*

This short piece offers two literal and figurative snapshots of what land education looks like in action in Hawaii. The first snapshot depicts a contemporary example of Indigenous Hawaiian taro cultivation in the Limahuli valley on the island of Kauai. The second snapshot illustrates the food sovereignty movement in Waianae, Oahu located at the Kaiao Garden grown by the Hilo Boys and Girls Club.

E ho'omalu i ke kupa'a no ka 'aina.
Continue to be steadfast in your love for the land.
Joseph Nawahikalanaiopu'u

These lava-rock terraces of wetland taro (lo'i kalo) are found in Limahuli valley in the ahupua'a of Hā'ena on the island of Kauai in Hawaii. Limahuli means 'turning-hands' and infers a quality of work ethic needed to sustain this kind of intensive wetland cultivation. Taro is the common name for corms of several plants in the Araceae family. Native Hawaiians cultivated more than 200 varieties of the most common Colocasia and called the beloved plant kalo. Hawaii was the only Pacific nation to pound kalo/taro into a paste or poi, giving it a longlasting quality and unique viscosity. Kalo also plays a vital role in Hawaiian origin stories as Haloa-naka-lau-kapalili, the cosmological first man (Figure 1).

Wetland cultivation of food took place on stream banks, in marshy areas of freshwater springs, but most commonly in *lo'i* or irrigated pond fields. *Lo'i* came to occupy much of the flat, arable land in water-rich valleys of Hawaii. Building a *lo'i kalo* was labor-intensive and required constant maintenance and care. Kalo grows from previously harvested corms, cut into *huli* (leaf stalk consisting of a half-inch-thick slice of the top of the corm attached to 6–10 inches of the leaf-stem). The base of the *huli* was placed straight into the muddy pond or placed in man-made mounds and left for 6 to 12 months. Lo'i kalo is distinct from dry-land farming because of water. Flowing water in a lo'i kalo is vital as oxygen is needed for healthy corms. Mahi'ai or farmers were careful not to step on or around the developing corms yet managed to keep each pond weed-free. *Kalo* was planted at intervals to assure a daily or weekly harvest. Wetland *kalo* was primarily made into *poi* while leaves and stalks filled the Hawaiian diet with tasty soups, steamed greens, wrapped delicacies, and an infinite assortment of collaborations with sea and mountain fare.[1]

Image: Kaiao Youth Community Garden, Hilo
Ho'ea Ea: Food Sovereignty Movement in Hawaii

Figure 1. Kaiao Youth Community Garden, Hilo. Ho'ea Ea: Food Sovereignty Movement in Hawaii.

The ancient Hawaiians developed the ahupua'a system of resource management as a means to live sustainably in an island ecosystem. This system recognized the interconnection between the mountains and the ocean, and the roles fresh water, rain and ocean played in linking the two. By operating within this system, they were able to sustain a large and healthy population while maintaining the integrity of their natural resources. Ahupua'a were also unique land divisions that allowed for a diversity of plant and fish cultivation through uniquely constructed walls and ponds managed by distinct groups of people in kauhale/village settings. The Limahuli lava-rock terraces for growing taro (*lo'i kalo*) were built 700–1000 years ago. It is a focused and highly skilled commitment to cultivate this ancient Hawaiian staple food in Hawaii and as modern systems encroach on this ancient life style, Hawaiians are now looking toward international collaborations for help.

Ma ka hana ka 'ike.
Learning occurs through experience.

There is a food sovereignty movement in Hawaii! It began and is guided by MA'O Farm of Waianae, Oahu through their very first 'Hands Turned To The Soil' youth conference in 2003. Kaiao Garden at the Hilo Boys and Girls Club is one such project which is encouragingly inspired by MA'O Farm and maintained by community members living within walking distance of the garden. Kaiao is the 'dawning light' and infers an awakening process now nourishing the Downtown Hilo Association's edible sidewalk movement. Kaiao Youth Garden began in 2005 because a neighbor living beside the Boys and Girls Club noticed large tracts of unused lands and wondered if anything could be done. It was a community effort to secure, nourish and plant lands that eventually hosted more than 50 youth weekly in a variety of garden and Hawaiian cultural activities. Kaiao Garden was also uniquely situated in one of the oldest Kumiai of Hawaii Island. A Kumiai is a community association fashioned through Japanese culture and values. It is neighborhood-based and our Kumiai has

Figure 2. Limahuli, Kauai, Hawaiian Islands.

approximately 75 homes and families participating. The Kumiai now hosts annual picnics at the garden and produce is given to kumai members throughout our small neighborhood (Figure 2).

Why did Kaiao begin? Hawaii imports more than 90% of the food it eats! Kaiao Garden is a small link in the larger chain of gardens, communities and creative ideas surfacing in Hawaii's food sovereignty and Indigenous education movement. Kaiao is dedicated to the perpetuation of Hawaiian values and knowledge and brings this passion into daily use and practice. Kaiao is inspired by the values and impact of the Hawaiian Charter School movement, numerous cultural community initiatives and MA'O Farm. MA'O – Mala 'Ai Opio is the *nourishing of youth through food production.* MA'O is located in the Hawaiian community of Waianae, one hour from downtown Waikiki. It is a movement that helped awaken Hawaiian communities to develop and host youth projects dedicated to gardens, healthy eating and conscious relationship with lands, moon and each other. Kaiao Garden is a direct result from the love and care of MA'O farmers and visionaries. Friend, educator, and cultural practitioner, Pulama Collier of Maui, summarizes a native Hawaiian view of land:

> 'Āina momona/Fertile land. The land is our ancestor, teacher, parent, provider and nurturer continually shaping and defining us. Hawaii is an island nation protected, preserved and nurtured by our oceans, lands, sky and heavens. Land/'āina is abundant, rich, and living. We connect to our land as we connect to ourselves. To see our land as 'āina momona is to also see ourselves as full of life, fertile, abundant, and healthy. (Collier 2012)

Kaiao Youth Garden is fortunate to have the support of the Boys and Girls Club, the University of Hawaii at Hilo, and numerous community associations. It is truly a labor of aloha.

## Note

1. National Tropical Botanical Gardens. *Limahuli Garden and Preserve.*

## References

Collier, P. 2012. *Informal Discussions on Hawaiian Epistemology via E-mail*. Paia, Maui, Aotearoa, New Zealand, November 8.

National Tropical Botanical Gardens. *Limahuli Garden and Preserve*. http://ntbg.org/gardens/limahuli.php.

# Between the remnants of colonialism and the insurgence of self-narrative in constructing participatory social maps: towards a land education methodology

Michèle Sato, Regina Silva and Michelle Jaber

*Institute of Education, Federal University of Mato Grosso, Cuiabá, Brazil*

This article summarizes a social mapping project conducted by the Environmental Education, Communication and Arts Research Group from the Federal University of Mato Grosso. The primary goals of the project were to map the vulnerable social groups of Mato Grosso, and identify the social and environmental conflicts that put them in situations of risk. The conflicts and dilemmas these groups experience are typically caused by land and water disputes. In turn, the disputes can be traced to the continuance of colonialist forms of political, economic and ecological relations implicit in the prevailing model of development in the region. Supported by the reinvention and application of a new methodology for environmental education, namely the social map, the work illustrates the significance of group identities, self-narratives and interpretive frames, and discusses how social mapping might be used in land education to enable the construction of participatory forms of public policy.

## Territories of Mato Grosso

Mato Grosso is a land of unique beauty: of natural landscapes and Indigenous cultural expressions, of abundant rivers and local wisdom. Meyer (2001) identifies the latter with 'Xingu epistemology', preferring the notion of 'epistemology' to 'traditional knowledge' because it is an idea 'that barters within the currency of mainstream academia' (146). For Meyer, researchers of the land must provide spaces for Indigenous peoples to speak for themselves and their ways of knowing, avoiding the tendency of some anthropologists to 'ventriloquize the natives' (Wolfe 1999, 4). In other words, alongside the ecological and economic features of the land of Mato Grosso, research studies must recognize there is an epistemology of Indigenous and local inhabitants that emerges, develops and is contested within the bioregion, as it is built and rebuilt across the generations who live there.

Modern development, however, is transforming the landscapes of Mato Grosso. Broader senses of the culture and land are receding, such as those that combine rationality with spirituality noted above. Disruptions to culture and land in Mato Grosso are primarily associated with the relentless pursuit of economic growth since colonization, heavily focused on export-oriented agri-businesses. The territory is scarred by the parcelling of land for the purposes of modern and extensive farms devoted to monoculture crops. There have been violent practices of land concentration, converting vast amounts of forest into monoculture, cattle ranches and power plants, alongside other uses and activities that target immediate economic profit. These processes are accompanied by a constellation of uses of advanced technology, mechanization, irrigation, abusive use of pesticides and low-wage workers.

In spite of positive mass media representations that characterize the modern-day Brazilian economy as growing, across the states of Brazil the land is continuing to experience devastating environmental impacts and human rights violations. Other forms of life and livelihood are neglected, and there are significant social and environmental conflicts (Jaber-Silva 2012). Many social groups characterized by poverty and want are invisible in this process, while the media, government and bourgeoisie persist in keeping marginalized social groups out of the public eye (Silva 2011).

In an attempt to make visible what is happening in Mato Grosso, in 2008, we developed the project 'Mapping identities and territories of the State of Mato Grosso'. The project was proposed and implemented under the leadership of the Environmental Education, Communication and Arts Research Group (GPEA) of the Federal University of Mato Grosso (UFMT) with important contributions from various partners (mainly from civil society) and financial support from government agencies. We employed and redeveloped a methodology called *social mapping* to identify the social groups present in the state, including their identities and territories, and meaning-making practices. We also mapped conflicts and socio-environmental injustices to produce two inter-related maps: one of the social groups, the other of socio-environmental conflicts.

In this article, we illustrate our approach and the methodological considerations for the construction of these maps. The social mapping methodology seeks to recognize the Other, who has been historically erased in the process of land occupation and use, and is intended to both signify and represent matters of interest and concern from the other's perspective. In short, we use social mapping as a technique for developing a land education: to recognize and analyse identities of territorial resistance by recording the existence of various historically invisible social groups and understanding the socio-environmental conflicts they face in their lives.

## Remnants of the colonial world and the importance of land education

The prompt for developing and using social maps was borne from the recognition of the limitations of the planning instrument proposed by the Socioeconomic and Ecologic Zoning Committee of Mato Grosso (ZSEE), released in 2008. The ZSEE document is an instrument of the National Environmental Policy created in 1990, which aimed to set up a planning policy for Brazil starting with the Amazonian states. In the proposed zoning, although the term 'social' was present, a major weakness can be identified: the planning instrument ignores the conditions of invisible social groups and the socio-environmental conflicts they experience in relation to the current development model. This oversight has kept these groups and their struggles at the margins of history, including its contemporary manifestations in relation to land and cultural development priorities and considerations for the region.

The process of domination of territories and local cultures is historically present in Brazil and, consequently, in Mato Grosso. In brief, the modern state of Brazil arose from the colonialism imposed on the Americas unleashed in the fifteenth and sixteenth centuries, a heritage characterized by a mercantilist logic and colonialist processes that led to the destruction of natural resources as well as by the expropriation and genocide of various Indigenous peoples. The same hegemonic logics exerted on people across the Americas were also practiced over Brazilian biodiversity. According to Pádua (2002), for example, in the eyes of Europeans used to managing lands of much more modest dimensions, Brazilian biomes seemed like limitless horizons of inexhaustible nature. A letter (known as the 'birth certificate' of Brazil) written by Pêro Vaz de Caminha to Manuel I of Portugal in 1500, a member of Pedro Álvares Cabral's fleet that stumbled on Brazil en route to India, illustrates the contemporary perception: 'There is a great plenty, an infinitude of waters. The country is so well-favoured that if were rightly cultivated it would yield everything, because of its waters' (Pádua, 2002, 55 [translation by editor]).

The view that Nature is bountiful and replenishes itself has nourished the destruction of many ecosystems across several cycles of Brazilian economic history, including the export of products such as wood, gold, coffee, sugar-cane, latex rubber, livestock and, more recently, soybeans. These economic cycles are only possible because, and at the expense, of the local ecosystems. Yet, as ecosystems become depleted, the frontiers of exploration and exploitation have advanced toward those remaining and intact ecosystems. The states of Brazil, therefore, have become scarred with the violence meted out on the preceding habitats and their inhabitants.

Driven by this hegemonic conception of land and economic development, under the aegis of the capitalist mode of production, the production–consumption system of the modern Brazilian state still follows the modus operandi practiced in colonial Brazil. Oligarchies remain entrenched, assuring the perpetuation and near permanence of large land property owners controlling economic affairs. As with Porto-Gonçalves (2004), we can characterize this situation as that of a modern-colonial world, as distinct from a post-colonial form. The 'modern-colonial' was introduced by historians to signify the persistence of the rhetorical power of European universalism (Mignolo 2003, 2008), while according to Ashcroft, Griffiths & Tiffin (2001, 186), 'from the late 1970s the term has been used by literary critics to discuss the various cultural effects of colonization,' as distinct to closely related terms associated with the political and economic transitions primarily marked by some post-colonial theories (see the work of Fanon (1979), Bhabha (1994), Wolfe (1999, 2006), Anderson (2008) and Veracine (2011).

Applying the insights of modern colonialism and post-colonialism noted above to this situation, we can summarize that colonization as a set of practices still stands and has been stamped on Brazil, from the first wave of colonization by the Portuguese since the 1500s, and throughout the slower transition to a process of settler colonialism by Europeans mainly from Portugal and Spain in subsequent centuries. Many Indigenous people were enslaved by the colonists as chattels during the seventeenth and eighteenth centuries to service the agricultural economy, and those who resisted were often decimated in the name of Portuguese Crown. Throughout the eighteenth and nineteenth centuries, the Portuguese also introduced the bulk of African slaves to support the sugar economy, as well as cattle ranching and other foodstuff production, including coffee. While by 1888, Brazil was one of the last countries in the Western world to abolish slavery of both Africans and Iindigenous peoples.

Thinking and rewriting this history of the present from the point of view of its enslaved peoples, i.e. in subordinate social positions (Guha 1996), we recognize that the new settlers of Mato Grosso – large landowners and farmers, usually from the south of Brazil, which is abundantly colonized by Europeans – have continued these practices, perpetuating racial, social and economic inequalities, as well as incidences of slave labor. As noted by Quijano (2005), the end of colonialism did not mean the end of 'coloniality', for the dawn of the twenty-first century still sees numerous colonial atrocities being practiced. Thus, we argue we still face the brunt of a forceful and violent colonization process, imprinted in a predatory heritage in ways of relating to the environment, and in which land is understood by many as primarily commodity and resource.

In contemporary Brazil, this form of development is touted as the modernization of the countryside. However, such modernization is merely the reproduction of a modern-colonial world model, as it was and still is promoted, without changing the structure of land ownership. It makes itself dominant and, in this role, becomes the usurper of ecosystems and local cultures. It presents itself as 'new', but it remains very similar in principle and practice to the old colonial system of extraction of raw materials, centred on monocultures, favouring short-term actions for profit (with the same speed) and expropriation of native peoples. As Sartre (1979) observed, colonial violence is attributed to not only the objective of controlling those it dominates, it seeks to dehumanize them. Or as Freire (2000) asserts, it is a process that 'depeoplizes' men and women. Equally, when, for example, heavy machinery drags away trees to create monoculture plantations, an inhospitable landscape for local fauna and flora is created as far as the eye can see.

Land education in this context must take shape in response to the histories and present bio-political conditions in Brazil, most importantly in response to its incredibly diverse populations. In Brazil, there is a specific policy for 'traditional knowledge people,' including mainly Indigenous, *quilombolas*[1] or conventional groups (see detailed descriptions below). In the project we could not focus exclusively on one or another group, otherwise we would lose our commitment to broad social inclusion. We understood that each of these 65 groups has its own traditions, myths and organization models, which constitute how their identities are related to the land, work, ethnicity, philosophy of life or unexpected driving forces.

For example, the Indigenous group of Xingu call the planet 'Planet Water', because water constitutes most of their experience of the planet. Land is the portion on which they live, yet land is intrinsically connected with the other of Bachelard's (1994) 'elements' of space, that is to say, water, earth, fire and air. Xingu people understand their identity as intermeshed in a complex system that does not only involve ethnicity, but is strongly related to the land and its relations to other elements. Their educational system is based on oral knowledge, passed from one generation to another, and the learning process and curriculum is a very practical land education. Almost all of the origin stories over the world begin with water, as echoed in scientific descriptions of an organic 'soup'. But for some Indigenous groups, life begins inside a rock, with their place in the rock integral to their own cultural cosmologies. Each hollow in the rock gave birth to different ethnicities, and the sustainability of life is dependent on caring for the land (or piece of the rock) on which they live. Across these different cosmologies, it is clear that land is the most important dimension of learning, as it is inextricably related to air, fire and water.

## Methodological aspects of social mapping

The search for representing reality and its various interfaces by means of images and maps has always been present in civilization. Many cultures have created cartographic representations of their surroundings and spaces, either by cave paintings, making clay models, or by other means using common and sacred materials to delineate space and the uses, boundaries, inhabitants and migrants to territories.

Maps were, and still are, considered a language of power and legitimacy over land, supportive of the imperialist domination of spaces. According to Harley (2009, 5), like guns and warships, maps are key weapons of imperialism. Given that maps support colonial policies, when for example, territories are first claimed on paper before being effectively occupied, maps, in a certain way, anticipate empire. Harley addresses another important aspect of cartography in that he calls attention to the 'silences' of maps, highlighting not only what maps are expressing and valuing, but above all, what they are hiding. He points out that, 'in colonial maps, their silences can also be regarded as discriminatory against Indigenous peoples' (Harley 2009, 22).

Thus, we can appreciate that the process of mapping has never been ideologically neutral, being as it is necessary to rationally represent space and time but in ways that may also support the hegemonic power of the ruling classes. However, there is the counter possibility in the implicit processes of appropriating and representing territories reflected in mapping that can facilitate more democratic and inclusive relationships when ideologically committed to vulnerable social groups. Thus, we see maps as also being used as instruments of resistance, defence, subversion and complaint.

With these possibilities in mind, participatory mapping has often been developed to create meaningful alliances between popular movements and academic research interests. Such projects are developed *with* and mainly *by* the communities and groups involved. This is an important dialogic route for environmental education, particularly because it involves working with important themes such as environmental sustainability at the community level. Guided by this principle, we worked towards creating an innovative methodology for environmental education in the region, that is, *social mapping*, relying in this instance on *self-narratives* from members of a diverse range of social groups to create the content and ownership of the maps.

The choice to map groups and their social and environmental conditions is not random. Inspired by Bhabha (1994), we approached Mato Grosso from its margins, from the experiences of its minorities and their socio-environmental conflicts. We wanted to hear from the 'locals' to understand their narratives, including the essence of their identities and collective meanings in different territories. From 24 through 26 October 2008, GPEA and its partners promoted the first seminar on Social Mapping held in Cuiabá, the state capital. The seminar gathered 250 leaders, representing different social groups: *quilombolas*; Indigenous; traditional communities; rubber tappers; *extractivists*;[2] professional and amateur fishermen; *retireiros*;[3] *pantaneiros*;[4] *morroquianos*;[5] and many others, totalling 65 social groups represented in the seminar.

We collected data during the seminar using semi-structured interviews. These were preceded by dynamic activities in working groups, recording the participants' self-definitions and narratives. We interviewed 115 representatives across 12 working groups organized according to the regions planned for Mato Grosso. We sought to highlight and document their perceptions of identity and territory. Interviewees were asked to indicate the identification and geographic location of their groups and of their communities in a printed map of the region, according to the proposed planning. The maps were made available at 1:900,000 scale. Following these activities, GPEA continued to examine secondary data, field studies, and to produce state maps of 'social groups' and '*socio-environmental* conflicts', in addition to holding several meetings that led to the second seminar.

The second seminar was held in 2010 at UFMT. More than 250 participants attended and they chose to form groups based on the expression of their identities and territories. Six working groups were formed: *Pantaneiro*, *Cerrado*, Indigenous, *Quilombolas*, *Retireiros* of Araguaia and small farmers. Data collection was guided by a script of questions in a semi-structured interview format. We interviewed 124 people. The working dynamic again included pointing out their geographic location in printed maps of the state. The map used was that of the political administrative and territorial division of the State of Mato Grosso (2010), at 1:1,500,000 scale. The data gathered and organized during the first seminar in 2008 were made available to all participants to validate and complement their responses.

Across both seminars, we interviewed 239 people from diverse social groups with the aid of a facilitator and rapporteur. The facilitator conducted group discussions supported by an interview script, directing the activities and instigating debates around the questions and issues raised by the group. Some of the prompts included: Do you belong to a particular social group? How do you identify yourselves? Are there other groups you know? Who are they? Did changes in your place cause any problem (*socio-environmental* conflicts)? What conflicts? Which social groups are involved in these conflicts? Are there any clear signs of violence? What signs? Are there life threatening warnings? The rapporteur took notes during the discussions, noting the main topics raised by the groups and reporting back to the groups with written reports.

Data from the written reports of each working group were supplemented with video recordings and photographs of activities that occurred during the seminars. In addition, some research subjects representing different social groups were individually interviewed; these interviews were video recorded.

In total, the two seminars brought together approximately 500 participants. They came from 54 municipalities. Seventy native Indians of 19 Indigenous ethnicities and Indigenous lands were represented: *Apiaká, Bakairi,Bororo, Chiquitano, Kamaiurá, Kanela, Karajá, Kayabi, Kaiapó, Yudjá* (*Juruna*), *Munduruku, Panará, Paresi, Rikbaktsa, Terena, Trumai, Txucarramãe, Umutina* and *Xavante*. The participation of the Landless Rural Workers Movement and the Pastoral Commission for Land was important too, as it enabled the participation of squatters and small farmers settled in various regions of the state, particularly from municipalities of the Amazon region. While in both seminars, we had representatives of rubber tappers, and of those affected by dams,[6] as well as *retireiros* of Araguaia.

In addition to interviews and other data gathering associated with each seminar, we conducted field research with participatory observations, semi-structured and non-structured interviews, workshops and in-loco meetings with some of the social groups participating in the project. It was also possible to conduct some longer interviews, guided by a script aligned to the goals of social mapping, as well as open-ended interviews, talking as if we were old friends and evoking memories of childhood, the places they played, their favourite meals or what they did with their leisure time.

The fieldwork conducted with the Maroon community of Mata Cavalo illustrates this feature of the project. The Maroon community is composed of approximately 420 families who have been struggling for more than one hundred years to assert their rights over an area of approximately 14 thousand hectares (Simione 2008). The roots of the contemporary land allotment arrangements date back to 1889, and are linked to the death of Mrs Ana da Silva Tavares whose will released her slaves and donated part of the land she owned to them. Since that time, they have been free and continued living on their land, planting and harvesting their food. Since 1890, attempts have been made by neighbouring farmers who bought land or invaded nearby lands to evict the former slaves from the land they had inherited. Many of these families were forced to sell their rights to the land or to abandon their lands, owing to the lack of political support and state bureaucratic neglect. This legacy endures to this day. Without land ownership, the *Quilombolas* of Mata Cavalo face constant threat of eviction and death threats (Simione 2008).

For GPEA–UFMT, environmental education is not only promoted in schools, but also through popular education (Freire 1992). We also approach the curriculum of school and the curriculum of life from a phenomenological position (Passos and Sato 2002). In this sense, every educational curricula can be designed as a trajectory, road or path that can reveal our moral existence. In other words, every pedagogical proposal that attempts a land education should be designed by teachers and students, with both learning and teaching through an open dialogue.

Grounded in the history and contemporary experience of this community, and working with the students registered in the Youth and Adults Education program at Saint Benedict School, we therefore co-constructed a local socio-environmental map to document their territories and identities, socio-environmental conflicts and vulnerabilities. In order to develop these maps, we implemented 'edu-communicative' interventions with multimedia resources, including videos, magazines, photographs, newspaper clippings and art. The co-construction process is deliberately designed to be participatory and enable community members to realize and recognize themselves as the main agents of their story. A short script, developed collaboratively with participants, serves as a guide in the collective construction of the map. The map's role then is to raise awareness using concrete evidence from daily life and from the interface between that and historical background, the processes of colonization and decolonization, and the everyday realities shaping current ways of living.

The mapping work developed in the community of Mata Cavalo shows similarities with Berhe's approach (2004), who in her study of the conflicts, territories and identities of Ethiopia argues that identifying and understanding conflicts can build the identity of a nation through careful and critical interpretation of the narratives of the conflicting groups (Bhabha 1994). Equally, in surfacing and voicing the colonial history of Ethiopia, Berhe believes that the deconstruction and reconstruction of identity can also help mitigate a sense of victimization and encourage citizenship.

Drawing on these insights, we suggest that a Social Mapping methodology can be a powerful tool for land education because in the process of mapping identities, it recognizes land as an epistemological basis for understanding people's lives. Indeed, according to Jennings, Swidler, and Koliba (2005, 45), land-based education is not the opposite of standards-based education; however, 'when standards are set apart from the communities, local initiative is killed, local ownership is killed'.

## Social mapping – actions and reflections

In our project, we emphasized each group's own history over and against the dominant metanarratives that traditionally privilege individualized and universal knowledge to the detriment of local culture (Bhabha 1994). We utilized Buber's (2001) conception of human relationships, which stresses self-identity is always created in relation to the existence of another, and the Other. Therefore, identities are outlined in this encounter with others, again to emphasize the importance of collective organization against the driving forces which cause socio-environmental conflicts.

The maps resulting from the processes and analyses in this study were not intended to exhaustively delineate the set of conflicts and actors that make up the identities of resistance in Mato Grosso. Consequently, mapping offers a history in the making: dynamic and woven with continuities and discontinuities. Equally, we did not produce a census, but a panoramic view of the current situation, a portrait – always temporary – of identities and their conflicts.

The project sought to interpret the self-narratives and build meanings together with the agents of the stories. In both social mapping seminars we recorded the existence of 52 social groups or movements, totalling 47 Indigenous ethnicities, and identified 99 mapped identities in the territories of the state. To describe these identities, we grounded the work in line with Porto-Gonçalves' (2001) perspectives, which suggest that collective identities are constructed in relation to three dimensions: social conditions, ethnic relations with nature and so-called 'big projects' (related to hydro electrical dams, roads or large buildings, usually built in the name of 'development'). Through the seminars, we identified five themes related to collective identity constructions:

(1) cultural tradition,
(2) cultural place and habitat,
(3) labour, work and production,
(4) driving forces and development, and
(5) choices, alternatives or philosophy of life.

The *cultural tradition* theme refers to identities that are derived from traditional conditions, social or ethnic, such as the case of Indigenous peoples, *quilombolas*, gypsies and the groups who emphasized regional and cultural expressions, such as the *Siriri* group, the *Caruru* and the Congo Dance.[7] The *cultural place and habitat* theme includes groups whose identities are primarily attributed to rootings in place, such as those groups intrinsically connected to land and still dependent on the habitat they belong to, such as the *pantaneiros*, *mimoseanos*,[8] *morroquianos*, *beiradeiros*[9] and riparian people. The third dimension, *labour, work and production*, includes identities principally associated with those relationships of work that are closely related to nature or to livelihoods, for example, the rubber tappers, the *extractivists,* the *retireiros,* the artisans, the professional and amateur fishermen, the family farmers, the organizers of solidarity economy, the Landless Rural Workers Movement and so on. The fourth dimension includes identities indexed to a function of *driving forces and development,* that is, people affected by large development projects, such as dams, the squatters,[10] the settlers and so on. The fifth dimension, *choice and/or philosophy of life*, includes groups that have identities built around identification with some social movement, religion, leisure, art or philosophy of life, such as ecologists, pro-nature artists, hippies, the black movements, liberation theology advocates and groups with expressions linked to other spiritualties, among others.

We did not intend to create rigid boundaries with these classifications; therefore, we emphasize that the five dimensions are dialectically interconnected, as many identities collide and reshape themselves in their plurality and fluidity.

In this 'coming-to-being' of several groups and movements, we also mapped the existence of old and new social actors, and, literally, put them on the maps we created for the social groups of the State of Mato Grosso (Figure 1).

Concomitant with this richly mapped mosaic, the project also showed the consequences of the settler-colonial model that directly affects social groups, especially those whose livelihoods and resistance are strongly connected to the environment in which they live, as they fight for the survival of the local environment and their local culture. Mapping *socio-environmental* conflicts, numerically, registered 194 sites with 359 causes, wherein 68 of these sites have life threatening conditions and 12 of these sites engage in inhumane slave labour. Conflicts and conditions such as these highlight the social and ecological unsustainability of the established settler colonial model, as shown in the map of *socio-environmental* conflicts of Mato Grosso (Figure 2).

Concerns about sustainability necessarily link environmental, social, cultural, economic and many other factors. However, in Mato Grosso, the weighting given to economic factors overrides all others. The social mapping revealed that the main driving forces of socio-environmental conflicts are land disputes, water uses, deforestation, forest burning, abusive use of pesticides and illegal mining. The narratives

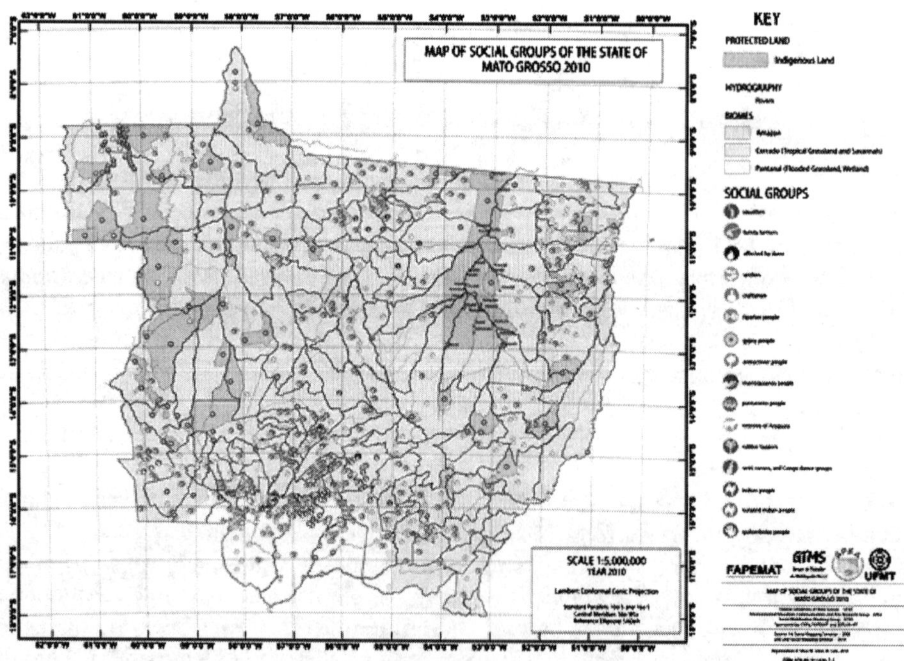


Figure 1. Mapping of social groups of the State of Mato Grosso, 2010.

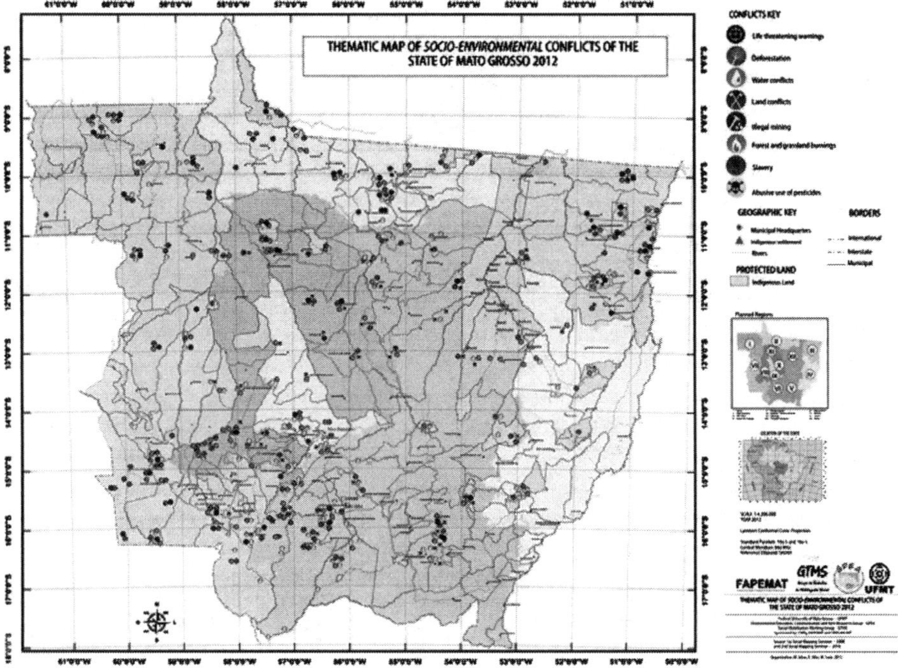


Figure 2. Thematic mapping of socio-environmental conflicts of the State of Mato Grosso, 2010.

indicate that the agents who incite conflict are, in most cases, related to agribusiness activities such as large farms. In contrast, the agents of resistance are mainly Indigenous, *Quilombolas* and small farmers.

Socially mapped environmental conflicts typically correlate with trends in development policies, such that increases in their magnitude often mirror society's demands for a given product. For example, soy production has become a main driving force of conflict in the region, coinciding with growing populations in industrialized countries, increases in per capita income, and diversification in food spending as associated with the increased consumption of protein, services and industrialized goods. To meet this market demand in developing countries, deforestation and bush-fires are encouraged and financed by the State, which supports the conversion of forest areas into pastures, and the development of grain crops which are overwhelmingly exported to developed countries.

## Signs of hope: land education in use

The conflicts mapped in this project have not exhaustively represented the many confrontations that exist. Some are not yet visible, but the maps do gesture toward the magnitude of the problems resulting from the imposition of major projects, as well as illustrate a large and important array of cases and conflicts. These are expressions of the settler colonial model that leads to ecosystem destruction and annihilation of particular ways of life. These territories, identities and temporalities are entangled in webs and mosaics, intrinsically interwoven in relation to culture and land, interconnected in such a way that the loss of one implies the disappearance of another.

Galeano (1971) states that to change any unjust reality, we must first know it. By studying the political face of conflicts, Guerin (2004) suggests that the examination of groups in conflict can be analysed by maps, diagnostics or case studies, but in all situations, whatever they are, it is necessary to have historical knowledge of the *socio-environmental* context. Guerin also suggests that people do not need to resolve these conflicts, but the studies must be widely available for in public policy development to protect the groups involved. Thus in the process of decolonization, land education teaches us to fight against the forces of the oppressors, to be able to choose our freedom, promote education to respond to the question of *for* whom we are practicing environmental education, and essentially *against* whom we need to shape land education (Freire 1992).

Consequences of this social mapping project are already evident. Publication of preliminary results (Silva 2011) in the form of maps and reports has been consulted in public policy development for the state. For example, the social mapping was used as input for drafting the State Report on Human Rights. Moreover, it has also been used as the basis for creating a 'Long Term Plan for Mato Grosso' and introduced as a core consideration for decision-makers. Finally, the maps have served as the basis for studies and purposeful measures of understanding conflict for the Prosecutor's Office of Justice and Environmental Protection, and the Urban Order of the State Prosecutor.

In closing, this project sought to use research and education methods to struggle against injustices and foreground an environmental education that is guided by a phenomenologically focused land education. The research was carried out simultaneously with an educational process, asking not only for whom we are planning the education, but also against whom we have to be prepared to fight. We expect that social mapping can be used to positively transform the status quo that these 'invisible' groups have faced. We also hope to build public policies that guarantee these groups the right to retain their territories and their identities, and ensure that they have the freedom to make their decisions and choices for happiness.

## Funding

INAU – Wetlands Institute for Science and Technology and CNPq – Brazilian Council for Research and Development.

## Acknowledgements

To Tom Marcinkowski, Kate McCoy and Alan Reid for the reading, help and patience.

## Notes

1. These are black communities and descendants of runaway slaves. They only had their territories and culture recognized recently.
2. It is important to note that *extractivism* (collecting forest products without killing the ecosystem) came with Chico Mendes' struggle. He spoke against the notion of property, stating that rubber tappers were able to live without private property, but could continue to maintain their livelihood from common land. After their fight, many extractive reserves were created in Brazilian territories, mainly in the Amazon region.

3. These are communities that move cattle from wetlands during the flood season and return them to pasture in the dry season, following the dynamics of the Araguaia river, northwest of the Mato Grosso wetland region.
4. These are inhabitants of one of the most conserved wetlands of the world, the Pantanal.
5. These communities inhabit a fragile ecosystem region with low hills or slopes (*morro*), the root of the word *morroquiana.*
6. Hydropower plants are the main sources of energy in Brazil. Although considered clean, this technology is not socially fair, nor is it environmentally harmless or free of harmful impacts. Generally, people affected by dams are riparian populations, Indigenous, and economically disadvantaged communities, who in having their land acquired by the state or energy company, are displaced to other territories. With their social and environmental dilemmas worsened, these communities have associated with one another, under the banner of those 'affected by dams'.
7. *Siriri, Cururu* and Congo Dance are typical dances featured in festivities of Mato Grosso communities.
8. Those from Mimoso, a locality of Pantanal.
9. These are the people who live on the margins of rivers.
10. These are landless communities. Aiming for some quality of life, they often invade non-used lands usually from huge farms.

## References

Anderson, B. 2008. *Comunidades imaginadas: reflexões sobre a origem e a difusão do nacionalismo* [Imagined Communities: Reflections on Origin and Nationalism Diffusion]. Tradução Denise Bottman. São Paulo: Companhia das letras.

Ashcroft, B., G. Griffiths, and H. Tiffin. 2001. *Post-colonial Studies: The Key Concepts.* London: Routledge.

Bachelard, G. 1994. *The Poetic of Space*. Boston, MA: Beacon Press.

Berhe, A. 2004. "Of Land and Identity: Territorialization of the Eritrean National Identity." *Eritrean Studies Review* 4 (1): 55–82.

Bhabha, H. 1994. *The Location of Culture*. Oxford: Routledge.

Buber, M. 2001. *Eu e tu* [Thou and I] [Tradução Newton Aquiles Von Zuben [Translation of Newton Aquiles Von Zuben]]. São Paulo: Centauro.

Fanon, F. 1979. *Os condenados da terra* [The Wretched of the Earth]. 3rd ed. Rio de Janeiro: Civilização Brasileira.

Freire, P. 1992. *Pedagogia da esperança* [Pedagogy of Hope]. Rio de Janeiro: Paz e Terra [Peace and Earth].

Freire, P. 2000. *Ação cultural para a liberdade e outros escritos* [Cultural Action for the Freedom and Other Essays]. Rio de Janeiro: Paz e Terra [Peace and Earth].

Galeano, E. 1971. *As veias abertas da América Latina* [Open veins of Latin America]. Tradução de Galeno de Freitas. 12th ed. Rio de Janeiro: Paz e Terra [Peace and Earth].

Guerin, B. 2004. "Political Facets of Conflict." In *Conflict Resolution*, edited by K. Hipel, 1–14. Oxford: UNESCO Encyclopaedia of Life Support Systems.

Guha, R. 1996. "The Small Voice of History." In *Subaltern Studies*, Vol. IX, edited by S. Amin and D. Chakrabaty, 1–12. Delhi: Oxford University Press.

Harley, B. 2009. "Mapas, saber e poder [Maps, Knowledge and Power]." *Confins* 5. Accessed 20 October 2011. http://confins. revues.org/5724

Jaber-Silva, M. 2012. "O mapeamento dos conflitos socioambientais de Mato Grosso: denunciando injustiças ambientais e anunciando táticas de resistência. Tese Doutorado e Ciências [Socio-environmental Conflicts Mapping of Mato Grosso: Denouncing Environmental Injustices and Advertising Tactics of Resistance]." PhD thesis., Federal University of São Carlos, Ecology Post Graduation Programme, 253.

Jennings, N., S. Swidler, and C. Koliba. 2005. "Place-Based Education in the Standards-Based Reform Era – Conflict or Complement?" *American Journal of Education* 112 (1): 44–65.

Meyer, M. A. 2001. "Our Own Liberation: Reflections of Hawaiian Epistemology." *The Contemporary Pacific* 13 (1): 123–198.

Mignolo, W. 2003. *The Darker Side of the Renaissance: Literacy, Territoriality, and Colonization*. Michigan: University of Michigan Press.

Pádua, J. 2002. *Um sopro de destruição: pensamento político e crítica ambiental no Brasil escravista, 1786–1888* [A Breath of Destruction: Political Thought and Environmental Critics on Brazilian Slavery, 1786–1888]. Rio de Janeiro: Jorge Zahar.

Passos, L. A., and M. Sato. 2002. "Educação Ambiental: o currículo nas sendas da fenomenologia merleaupontyana [Environmental Education: The Curriculum in the Pathways of Merleau-Ponty Phenomenology]." In *Sujets choisis en éducation relative à I'environnement. D'une Amérique à l'autre* [Chosen Texts on Environmental Education – from one America to Another], edited by L. Sauvé, I. Orellana, and M. Sato, 129–135. 1st ed., 1 vol. Montréal: ERE-UQAM.

Porto-Gonçalves, C. 2001. *Amazônia, Amazônias* [Amazon, Amazons]. São Paulo: Context.

Porto-Gonçalves, C. 2004. *O desafio ambiental* [The Environmental Challenges]. Rio de Janeiro: Record.

Quijano, A. 2005. "Colonialidade do poder, eurocentrismo e América Latina [Colonialism of Power, Euro-centrism and Latin America]." In *A colonialidade do saber: eurocentrismo e ciências sociais Perspectivas latino-americanas* [The Colonialism of Knowledge: Euro-centrism and Social Sciences. Latin American Perspectives], edited by E. Lander, 227–278. Buenos Aires: CLACSO.

Sartre, J. 1979. "Prefácio a Fanon [Preface to 1961 Edition]." In *Os condenados da terra* [The Wretched of the Earth], edited by F. Fanon, 15–36. Rio de Janeiro: UFJF.

Silva, R. 2011. "Do invisível ao visível: o mapeamento dos grupos sociais do estado de Mato Grosso – Brasil [From Invisibility to Visibility. The Mapping of Social Groups in Mato Grosso State, Brazil]." PhD thesis., Federal University of São Carlos, Ecology Post Graduation Programme, 221.

Simione, R. M. 2008. *Mata Cavalo's Territory: Identities in Motion on Environmental Education*. Cuiabá: Federal University of Mato Grosso, Education Post Graduation Programme (Master of Education), 189.

Veracine, L. 2011. "Introducing Settle Colonial Studies." *Settler Colonial Studies* 1: 1–12.

Wolfe, P. 1999. *Settler Colonialism and the Transformation of Anthropology: The Politics and Poetics of an Ethnographic Event*. London: Cassell.

Wolfe, P. 2006. "Settler Colonialism and the Elimination of the Native." *Journal of Genocide Research* 8 (4): 387–409.

# A ghetto land pedagogy: an antidote for settler environmentalism

La Paperson

*Department of Ethnic Studies, University of California San Diego, La Jolla, USA*

A ghetto land pedagogy begins with two axioms that align it with land education more broadly, and that distinguish it from the general umbrella of environmental education. First, ghetto colonialism is a specialization of settler colonialism. Second, land justice requires decolonization, not just environmental justice. A ghetto land pedagogy thus attends to an analysis of settler colonialism, offers a critique of settler environmentalism, and forwards a decolonizing cartography as a method for land education. This article discusses 'storied land' as a critical cartographic method for land education, illustrated through a discussion of land in the San Francisco Bay Area.

and Coyote sprinkles corn pollen in the four directions
to thank the tribal people
indigenous to what some call the state of California
the city of Oakland
for allowing use of their land. Esther Belin (1999)

This article presents ghetto land pedagogy as an analysis of and intervention into settler colonialism. First, I analyze an Urban Ecology lesson as an illustration of how settler environmentalism employs the logic of *terra sacer*, or sacred/accursed land, to describe ghettos as wastelands ripe for rescue by ecological settlers. Second, I interrogate 'Occupy' as settler signifier for social justice, an extension of the settler pursuit of land. Third, I discuss land in the San Francisco Bay Area, where I have been educator, researcher, settler. In contrast to *place* as a site of settler belonging and identity, this discussion heeds Goeman's (2013) call to think through 'storied land' as an antidote to settler colonial vanishing. Storied land offers a method of land education, by extending critical cartography's spatial analysis with a temporal analysis implied by Indigenous struggle and Black resistance: the when of land, not just the where of place. A ghetto land pedagogy thus attends to an analysis of settler colonialism, offers a critique of settler environmentalism, and forwards a decolonizing cartography as a method for land education.

## Ghetto colonialism as twenty-first century settler colonialism

Known as the 'master builder' of New York City, Robert Moses was responsible for nearly half of a century's worth of urban planning in North America's most populous city. Moses' parkway network laid waste to Black and working class neighborhoods where, in the wake of bulldozers, he erected the iconic towers that have come to symbolize the housing projects of the East Coast North American ghetto. He said unapologetically, 'more people in the way, that's all … When you operate in an over built metropolis, you have to hack your way with a meat ax' (quoted in Berman 1982, 134). Similar to the 'founding fathers' in American settler history, Moses is often narrated as a complicated, controversial, and yet necessary leader in the progress of the settler nation. Unlike those founding fathers, Moses was a twentieth century power broker, and his actions are illustrative of how settler colonialism has continued, and how it is has evolved.

Ghetto colonialism is a specialization of settler colonialism in North America. Settler nations are those where colonial invaders never leave but instead claim to have become the new native, and to possess absolute sovereignty over all life and land within a territory. Of primary interest to this writing is the USA as a settler nation built upon slavery. Land is a predominant concern in settler colonialism, and thus, people are arranged – raced, classed, gendered, sexualized, dis/abled, il/legalized – into triadic relations to land: the settler whose power lies in shaping the land into his wealth, the Indigenous inhabitant whose claim to land must be extinguished, and the chattel slave who must be kept landless (for more on settler colonialism, see Tuck and Yang 2012). In North America, whiteness is intimately co-constructed as settler entitlement. Specifically, whiteness[1] emerges as a racial category of entitlements: the right to claim land and sometimes people as property, and conversely, the right not to be bound by borders nor bonded as property. Indian-ness is invented as a form of racial disappearance; yet Indian-ness is also made an object of possession that settlers can acquire through blood, marriage, or cultural appropriation. For example, it was not simple disguise that motivated Boston Tea Party participants to masquerade as Natives, but a way for those British settlers to claim a native-ish American identity against their British counterparts. In North America, blackness is invented as enslavability, illegality, murderability. Black labor was essential for settler colonialism, yet the Black person is an excess of that labor who must be bridled, caged, killed. Indeed, chatteling and not the chattel's labor is the business of slavery, that is, the business of enslaving, dislocating people from places, disembodying them from themselves, and disposing of their bodies (Wilderson 2003). Ghetto colonialism takes place at this intersection between Indigenous displacement and black dislocation.

For settlers seeking new frontiers, the ghetto serves as an interior frontier to be laid waste in order to renew. It is a *terra sacer*, doubling as sacred and accursed land, a murderable nonplace always available for razing and resettlement. Here, I am drawing from Agamben's (1998) examination of the outlaw life of the *homo sacer* – the sacred or accursed man – a person who may be killed by anybody, with impunity. Not necessarily urban nor necessarily inhabited by people of color, the ghetto serves as a dislocation for blackness, intimate to and yet necessarily cast out from the great metropolises of the empire (Paperson 2010). If Native land is imperialism's frontier, the 'outpost, the fort and the port' (Smith 1999, 22), then the ghetto is imperialism's interior frontier: the outcast, the alley and the underground. It is empire's outlawed life. Settler colonial eyes see the ghetto as sacred wasteland that may be re-inhabited by anybody, with impunity.

*Terra sacer* is a virulent variation of the setter colonial ideology of *terra nullius,* the colonial fiction of 'empty land' or 'land not legally belonging to anyone.'[2] *Nullius* is the justification for the doctrine of discovery: that one can stab a flag into the earth or a needle into a person's tissue and claim a colony. It is the founding covenant for settler colonial states. The problem is that no land is empty.[3] It must be made empty forcibly and ideologically. The Americas, under sixteenth to eighteenth century colonialism, were made *terra nullius* by declaring Indians uncivilized, the land uncultured, and the relationship between Native people/land as 'primitively' unsubscribed to capitalist exploitation. Throughout the nineteenth and twentieth centuries, *terra nullius* was reinvented through frontier violence, military force, removal, Indian boarding schools, land acts, tribal termination, and citizen/naturalization acts that re-raced Indians into 'white men' and 'white women,' thereby converting tribal lands into settler commonwealth and private property.

The duality of land as desecrated, in pain, in need of rescue; and land as sacred, wild, and preserve-able; are contemporary discourses that justify re-invasion. They collapse Native land and black space together, leading once again to re-settlement. In this futuristic settler vision of land,

- Land is sacred yet desecrated – one could say sacredly injured.
- Indigeneity is metaphorized into the settler's own adoption of and by the land.
- Settlers rewrite them/ourselves as ecological stewards.
- Re-inhabitation – a sustainable (settler) future – is the goal.

In this ecological dystopia, Indigenous Americans are largely extinct through regrettable genocide,[4] or survive spectrally through the settler's Indian heart. Indigenous vanishing is essential for the twenty-first century ecological settler to become the new adoptive 'native', and thus rightful re-inhabitant of Native land. *Terra sacer* is a proxy for settler humanity; like the land, settlers view them/ourselves as traumatized yet healable. This is the settler adoption fantasy (see Tuck and Yang 2012) – that they/we can adopt the land and be adopted *by* the land – leading Spokane/Coeur d'Alene poet, Alexie (1996) to sardonically observe:

> In the Great American Indian novel, when it is finally written, all of the white people will be Indians and all of the Indians will be ghosts.

### *Pain, rescue, and place in settler environmentalism*

Environmental education research has made important critiques of the ecological destruction that has accompanied settler colonialism, of environmental racism, of 'nature' as rape-able, and of 'development' as the normalized aim of modernity. In these regards, eco-pedagogical approaches align with anti-racist, feminist and Indigenous education principles. However, eco-pedagogies can miss the core of Indigenous relationships to lands and communities, particularly the complex relationships between *urban* Indigenous land and life (Friedel 2011), not to mention between Indigenous, Black, and ghettoized communities. Moreover, environmental education has been largely silent on land, that is, silent on the settler colonial recasting of land into 'environment,' and silent on broader Indigenous understandings of land as ancestor, as sovereign, as people-places with their own politics and identities.

As an illustration, this brief vignette of an Urban Ecology unit at an Oakland high school draws from a one-year ethnographic study of youth resistance to education in 1999–2000. Taught by guest instructors from a nonprofit organization in a US history class, the unit aimed to develop young people's critical awareness of city planning policies and their impact on sustainability. Students role-played board members at a mock county transportation board meeting, as well as special interests: a bicycle collective, a neighborhood road improvement organization, Alameda County (AC) Transit, a pedestrian group, and the Freeway Development Corporation.

On the first day of the lesson, instructors discussed environmental racism, showed a video on the growth of urban transportation and the concurrent growth of pollution; in particular, they highlighted the negative consequences of the automobile. As an instance of pain curriculum, it set the stage for a performance of environmentalist rescue. Next, each special interest group was given a set of concerns, and a proposal that required funding from the agency. They were also handed scripted arguments, such that students could literally read their opinions from a paper during their mock board meeting.

The board received a one million-dollar budget and a cost breakdown of the proposals. Coincidentally, the budget was just large enough to fund either *only* the enlargement of an existing freeway, or nearly *all* of the other proposals. By design, the lesson compelled students to 'choose' not to enlarge the freeway. Students detected this agenda early on. 'It's like we're doing them a favor,' one student observed.

The roles for the five-member board were assigned to Nina, Zola, Hanifa, Amber and Marcus – all African American students except for Nina (Mexican-American), and all young women except for Marcus. Zola told me they were all outspoken students and speculated that as the reason they were chosen. Unlike the special interest groups, board members received no scripts. They began to improvise questions that were informed by their perspectives as residents of the city. For example, after a presentation about building bike lanes for the downtown area, Marcus raised the question below.

Marcus: What if our city wanted to promote business, how would they be able to keep parking spaces for people that come and aren't able to ride their bikes to shop at our stores? If we eliminate parking spaces?

Concerned about reaching the conclusion of the lesson, one instructor stepped in and prohibited questions from the board. This upset Zola in particular, who wanted to ask a question to AC Transit about their desire to extend a rapid commuter bus service from downtown Oakland to San Francisco. 'Well, how are we going to make a judgment if we don't have time for questions?'

When the board went into the hallway to deliberate, they dwelled on the rapid commuter bus proposed by AC Transit, the issue that Zola was unable to query. They felt it was a good presentation with sound arguments.

Hanifa: No, I mean she did make a good point though. I mean with the fifty-four people thing [A bus would reduce the number of cars by fifty-four].

However, they drew from their own experiences with the poor service provided to the poorer communities of color, away from downtown, by AC Transit. Some excerpted talk follows below:

| | |
|---|---|
| Zola: | The bus takes hell of fucking long. You are stuck on this bus that smells like shit and … They make us pay hella money everyday and walk on, get on their bus. |
| … | |
| Marcus: | By where I live … the 64, the 64 doesn't run on the weekend. |
| … | |
| Zola: | I don't like County Transit. Why do they want to increase the thing to San Francisco? … We already got BART![5] |

As they deliberated, they grew increasingly angry about the narrowly conceived options before them, and the obvious directive to vote in favor of the host of alternative transportation reforms. They shifted their performance into a satire of how government policy meets the needs of people with privilege and in power.

| | |
|---|---|
| Amber: | I'm gonna say sorry, but we all need new offices downtown so screw you guys. |

Ending deliberation, they re-entered the classroom/meeting hall.

| | |
|---|---|
| Marcus: | By popular demand, we're giving the money to the Freeway Development Corporation – |
| Instructor: | Really? |
| Zola: | And the rest of the money goes to buy our office supplies because – |
| Marcus: | because we all in the suburbs and – |
| Hanifa: | and we need an easy way to work and um – |
| Marcus: | So we never really cared about your situation, it's nothing personal |
| … | |
| Paul (a student not on the board, representing AC Transit): You're ugly | |
| Marcus: | We're all Republicans, Paul. We don't really care about your issues so – |
| Hanifa: | So we chose what was best for us and Freeway Corp is what's most beneficial. |
| Paul and other students: | New board! New board! |
| Instructor: | That's the first time that's happened. |
| Board: | [laugh] |

Learning from youth resistance moves us away from individualizing the critique to the guest instructors' teaching ability and cultural competency. Rather, youth resistance reveals key differences between what Keeling (2007) terms a 'ghettocentric commonsense' and commonsense environmentalism. The youth did not dispute the ecological advantages of bike lanes and public transportation.

However, they understood ghetto colonialism from a lived perspective, specifically how city planning has always disposed of poor communities of color. Bike lanes and buses, not to mention BART,[6] falsely promised a 'public' transportation system because they worked differently for white[7] cosmopolitans than for ghettoized peoples. Further, the youth detected the metanarrative within the lesson's cartography of Oakland's places and peoples. Downtown matters. Commuters count. Indeed, this urban ecology unit invited students to participate in their own disappearance: lend your voice to fixing the ghetto wasteland by paving bikeways and funding rapid commuter lines for the cosmopolitan citizen.

By contrast, the students' comments reflected everyday tales of dispossession within the very solutions of public infrastructure meant to 'repair' the ghetto wasteland.

Youth rejected the settler environmentalist moral through a parody of power. They pulled out the meat ax, and pointed at it with glee. *We never really cared about your situation. You are just people in the way.* Their performance foreshadowed a future reality. A few years later, then-Mayor Jerry Brown would successfully redevelop downtown Oakland into expensive lofts and condos. When pressed on the costs of gentrification, he replied that Oakland had 'discriminated' far too long against middle and upper middle class people. The commuter bus would be extended to SF, and bike lanes put in place. Youth indeed began to disappear – from over 50,000 to fewer than 40,000 school-age youth in five years. Despite developments toward a greener city, urban youth and their communities would not fare any better.

Urban educators have few tools for engaging settler colonialism because *terra sacer* often under-girds environmental education in urban schools. Environmental education offers three limited social justice frameworks: environmental racism – a framework that focuses on pain; green curriculum – a framework that focuses on rescue; and place-based curriculum – a framework that focuses on inclusion, and thus, the replacement of Native land/people with a multicultural immigrant nation. Despite their social justice intentions, and their ecological truths, when strung together, such pedagogies concerning US ghettos contain a settler colonial teleology.

Pain curriculum[8] highlights, legitimately, the disproportionate toxification of air, soil and water in poor, urban, communities of color. However, reducing ghettos to pain-filled sites of environmental toxicity in need of salvation, echo the settler colonial logics of *terra sacer* – wasteland whose inhabitants lack the liberal capitalist insights and technological know-how to properly occupy a city.

Rescue curriculum follows logically from pain curriculum. It presents green solutions in the form of urban gardens, recycling, clean fuels, etc. It leans explicitly on green technologies and implicitly on the technologies of government. The hidden curriculum of rescue naturalizes city planning, urban redevelopment, and de-ghetto-fication as inevitable remedies for pain. It positions ghettoized communities as wards under settler colonial sovereignty. Rescue curriculum promotes green cities, a wealth of green consumption through which the multicultural cosmopolitan citizen earns his/her/our right to be the nouveau settler. Enter place-based curriculum.

Place-based curriculum helps write the master narrative of future, green, metropolitan neo-colonies. Often inclusive, multicultural, and celebratory, such curriculum highlights the urban as a place of diversity, flavored by communities of color. (And wouldn't you like to live here too?) Claiming the urban as a contact zone or multicultural home – whether by people of color, or by white people – violently erases Indigenous understandings of that land and place. If Native people are mentioned at all, they are almost always only as a premodern population who were pleasantly 'one with nature,' or ecological Indians so few in number that the ecological settler becomes a 'good neighbor' or benevolent reinhabitant. Such a representation inscribes settler colonialism as a done deal, renders urban Native youth as inauthentic Indians, and denies contemporary Native relationships to urban land and place (Friedel 2011). The hidden curriculum of place-based pedagogy lies in its teleology. Native people used to live here. White people settled here; they fled. People of color replaced white people; they suffer. Coming up, the multicultural cosmopolitan citizen will replace people of color. *When the Great American City is finally built, all the white people will be colorful, and all the colored people will be gone.*

## Occupy, no there there

> what was the use of my having come from Oakland it was not natural to have come from there yes write about it if I like or anything if I like but not there, there is no there. (Stein 1993, 298)
>
> There was an occupation. (Stein 1997, 32)

Settler environmentalism describes efforts to redeem the settler as ecological, often focusing on settler identity and belonging through tropes of Indigenous appropriations – returning to the wildman or demigoddess, claiming of one's natural or 'native' self and thus the land, again. For example, 'off the grid' does not describe a place, but a set of redemptive behaviors – it is a *terra nullius* imaginary of a somewhere, nowhere, neverplace where one is no longer a settler. In using the term settler environmentalism, I am deliberately ambiguous about critical environmentalisms, such as movements in eco-feminism, deep ecology, and antiracist environmental justice. These are important trajectories in critical scholarship and activism around environmental justice, and ought to inform any decolonizing framework. However, antiracist, feminist, and environmental justice work are not automatically the opposite of settler colonialism. Decolonization might be incommensurable with projects more generally thought as social justice (see Tuck and Yang 2012).

In the previous ethnographic example, greening the ghetto can mask a neoliberal curriculum of whitening[9] the ghetto with 'better-educated,' ecologically 'responsible,' global citizens. More radical environmentalisms can also uphold the settler fantasy of sacred 'wilderness' – another form of unpeopled land – that must be restored or preserved. Even the progressive concept of land as Commons to be occupied, collectively shared and stewarded, may require the negation of Indigenous sovereignty. 'The people still speak of the sacredness of places now claimed by the parks services for instance' (Goeman 2008, 32). Occupying land for the Commons assumes that all prior, indeed current as well as future relations between people and land are null and void. 'In other words,' writes Sandy Grande, 'both Marxists and capitalists view land and natural resources as commodities to be exploited, in the first instance, by capitalists for personal gain, and in the second by Marxists for the good of all' (2004, 27). Social justice endeavors *all* take place on Native land. In this vein, I now turn to the Occupy movement.

Behind every great American city is a great crime. Oakland was founded on occupation and land theft. In 1850, a coterie of Yankee businessmen began building a port in what would become Oakland's Jack London Square, developing and selling land unbeknownst to landlord Luis Peralta, who was granted 48,000 acres for his service to the Spanish army. Indeed, the Native Ohlone still lived in the land 'owned' by the Peraltas, as well as Miwok and other Indigenous people who had migrated as a result of historic relationships between tribes and efforts to escape the Mission system. The Peraltas sued, and in 1856, the US Supreme Court upheld their claim, but maintained that it was too late to reverse – as deeds and titles had exchanged hands so many times that there was no undoing – and because Oakland was now occupied.

Occupy Oakland, which began in October of 2011, was an active part of the movements that began with Occupy Wall Street. Occupy itself was a diverse set of movements and dialogues not reducible to a single name or a campaign. Various queer, people of color and Indigenous groups participated in or sympathized with Occupy and recognized its importance as a meeting space, a node, for struggle. However, many of these groups had serious points of difference, most notably in the problematic name, 'Occupy.'

On 28 October 2011, a group of Indigenous and non-Native intellectuals/activists introduced 'The Memorandum of Solidarity with Indigenous Peoples' at the General Assembly of Occupy Oakland.

> WHEREAS, those participating in 'Occupy Oakland' acknowledge that Oakland is already occupied land; Oakland being the historical territory of the Chochenyo Ohlone people; and
>
> . . .
>
> RESOLVED, that those participating in 'Occupy Oakland' seek the genuine and respectful involvement of indigenous peoples in the rebuilding of a new society on their ancestral lands; and
>
> As a signal to the national 'Occupy Wall Street' movement and the indigenous peoples here and there who have felt excluded by the colonialist language of occupation used to name this movement, it shall be declared that 'Occupy Oakland' aspires to 'Decolonize Oakland' – to 'Decolonize Wall Street' – with the guidance and participation of indigenous peoples;

The memorandum points to difference as a modality of organizing, a source of strength and political possibility rather than as simply a curtailment of common struggle. Most importantly, the memorandum makes explicit the moral and political leadership of Indigenous peoples in any decolonial effort in North America. Significantly, the first signature of memorandum is by Chochenyo Ohlone educator Corrina Gould.

The memorandum was passed, but not without controversy. One of the signers, Joanne Barker (Lenape) posted in her blog, *Tequila Sovereign,* that several people approached the group with serious anxieties about decolonization.

> Ultimately, what they were asking is whether or not we were asking them, as non-indigenous people, the impossible? Would their solidarity with us require them to give up their lands, their resources, their ways of life, so that we – who numbered so few, after all – could have more? Could have it all?

And this is the rub about decolonization: it forces people to confront their complicity in settler colonialism and the ongoing violence of empire. It immediately unsettles the utopian vision of wealth redistribution and collectively owned Commons. It exposes how numerical the conceptualization of social justice remains – the 99% is a 'deserving' supermajority that renders Indigenous peoples (a super-minority) completely illegible. Barker goes on to write,

> I have a dream that the people of 'Occupy Oakland' will not see the affirmation of indigenous peoples' rights to self-government, territorial restoration, and cultural autonomy as a threat to their own; that they will see solidarity with indigenous peoples as an affirmation of their humanity and justice.

Barker's assertion reflects how 'sovereignty' as an Indigenous word is spoken with a different inflection than its cousin in the settler nation's lexicon. It echoes the questions posed by Watson, writing from an aboriginal Australian perspective:

> Is aboriginal sovereignty to be feared by Australia in the same way as Aboriginal people fear white sovereignty and its patriarchal model of the state – one which is backed by power or force? Or is aboriginal sovereignty different … for there is not just one sovereign state body but hundreds of different sovereign aboriginal peoples. Aboriginal sovereignty is different from state sovereignty because it embraces diversity, and focuses on inclusivity rather than exclusivity. (Watson 2007, 20)

A little over a month later, another proposal came before the General Assembly – to change the movement's name to Decolonize Oakland. This time, the proposal did not pass. Christine Cordero (who does not identify as Native) posted on Facebook a few of her responses to the arguments made against the name change, including 'Decolonize is divisive.' To which she responded, 'Occupy is divisive already and not including whole swaths of people. Decolonize and liberate are TRANSFORMATIVE. Difference, diversity, and change aren't divisive.'

Occupy Oakland means to Occupy *Ohlone*. Because Ohlone is both people and land/place simultaneously, you cannot occupy Oakland without also trespassing on the bodies and spirits of those who live/d there. Land is 'more than a site *upon* which humans make history or as a location that accumulates history' (Goeman 2008, 24), more than a site to occupy.

## Storied land and critical cartography as method

> Waterplace it was called, which was why, before some scientist come in and named us Pomo, the other tribes in these parts called us Waterplace – people by the water. That's how it was in the old times: You was where you lived. (Sarris 1998, 57)

Critical cartography is the mapping of structural oppression, as well as the critique of mapping as an exercise of power. Although it uses tools from traditional cartography, it also redirects our gaze back onto the master narrative of maps. Mapping creates taxonomies of land, water, and peoples. It generates false territories and also false temporalities, as land becomes property in a linear history of shifting ownerships. Mapping is knowledge generated in the service of empire. Thus, maps are not in themselves critical, even if they document social injustice. It is the surrounding narrative, the story that is told about maps, that may be critical. In other published work (Paperson 2010), I explored maps of Oakland – homicides, liquor stores, grocery stores, and other indicators of violence – as a way of examining how violence is spatialized within the ghetto, and also how the master stories (using the same maps!) advocate for managing violence through the eradication of the ghetto. Critical cartography is an essential method for understanding the coloniality of space.

However, critical cartography is not by itself a decolonizing method, just as deconstructing coloniality is *not* the same as decolonization (Tuck and Yang 2012). A decolonizing methodology (Smith 1999) repatriates Indigeneous land and life as they have survived before, during, and beyond colonialism. Decolonization is not just symbolic; its material core is repatriation of Native life and land, which may be incommensurable with settler re-inhabitation of Native land. It is *not* a stance that grants an easy solidarity with more inclusive social justice projects – even if they are antiracist, feminist, or environmentalist.

Land is not generalizable the way space and place are generalizable. Land is both people and place, that is, Native people constitute and are constituted by Native land. *You was where you lived.* Indigenous place-based education is *land* education. Place-based education, from a settler perspective, is far more inclusive – place becomes something everyone can claim, can tell a story about. Place-based education leads to restorying and re-inhabitation, whereas land education leads towards repatriation.

Storied land moves place back, between, and beyond to Native land, providing a transhistorical analysis that unroots settler maps and settler time (Goeman 2008). It offers a method that is temporal and spatial. As an illustration, storying the land and waters of San Francisco Bay disrupts the settler maps as well as settler time:

The ceiling in Mission Dolores in San Francisco is adorned by several thousand chevrons, hand-painted by Bay Indigenous peoples in Ohlone motif of ochre, white, red, and blue-gray. The cemetery outside 'is the final resting place of some 5000 Ohlone, Miwok, and other First Californians who built Mission Dolores.'[10] Grave markers date from 1830 to about 1898. Across the Bay, on the shores near Point Richmond, the Chevron refinery overlooks the water, an oil works first established in 1902.[11]

Oil and Native life are often written as different epochs in American settler history. I deliberately juxtapose these times and landmarks to position Native resistance to colonialism squarely within modern California history, rather than in some distant pre-national past.

San Quentin penitentiary, where all death sentences in California are carried out, is situated in Bay waters north of San Francisco and west of Point Richmond, on a point of land bearing the same name as the prison. Its namesake: Miwok captain Quintín, who fought the Spanish until his capture on that point in 1824. The California state prison at San Quentin was completed 1853. It lies within Marin County, the wealthiest county in California and the priciest county in the United States (Forbes.com 2008), named after El Marinero (Chief Marin), Quintín's leader and elder, who continued to skirmish with the Spaniards until 1833. In the middle of the Bay is Alcatraz Island, which became a military reservation in 1850, and its history as a prison began shortly thereafter. In 1894, Alcatraz housed Hopi from Arizona, imprisoned for refusing to surrender their children to federal boarding schools. In 1969, it became the site of reclaimed land for 19 months by the United Indians of All Tribes. As a parody of power, they seized it for 'occupation'[12] under the 'Right of Discovery.' Crossing east again over the water, we find Oakland, a city founded upon land theft made legally excusable through Yankee occupation between 1850 until its incorporation in 1852.

Indian resistance is often narrated as a lost cause of a vanishing race and a dying culture (e.g. Bray 2003). In settler history, Quintín is imagined to have disappeared with his capture, signifying the completion of the colonial period, and the close of an unfortunate chapter for the settler nation. The naming of his place of capture, *Punto de Quintín*, helps to re-present the glory of colonialism through its might, because genocide is what seals the deal for settler colonialism. Settler violence upon land is often a 'historical element … monumentalized and claimed by the state.'

> Many prisons are placed on historical sites of confrontation, though the Indigenous narratives, stories and land are buried, such as the Hopi incarcerated at Alcatraz or the site of the oldest maximum security prison in Auburn, NY (1817) which is raised at the site of a burned Seneca village. (Goeman 2008, 28)

For the countless ships that passed the point in the 1849 rush for gold in the Sierras, San Quentin serves as a monument to genocide. The American Indian Holocaust, although a regret for the settler nation, is also the premise for its existence.

Therefore, the refusal of modern Native peoples to disappear is threatening to any occupation.

On that note, Quintín did not die at San Quentin. To avoid execution, he successfully played the mission priests against the Spanish military by converting to Christianity and laboring at Mission Dolores (Bray 2003). I imagine that his hands cleaned those very chevrons on the ceiling. Afterwards, he went into service for the Spanish military, helping them navigate the difficult tides of the Golden Gate. El Marinero also pledged himself to the Spanish god in order to avoid execution, but then escaped Mission Dolores and kept up armed resistance for the next nine years. When captured for the last time in 1833, he again 'converted,' and essentially retired at Mission San Rafael – a stone's throw away from Punto Quintín.

Both Marin and Quintín were raised in the mission system, yet still had enough aboriginal mastery of Bay waters to carry out military maneuvers against a far larger and better-armed foe. They were evidently fluent enough in Spanish colonial society to exploit the loophole of Christian clemency. Their tactics show that Bay Indigenous people were neither isolated primitives nor powerlessly assimilated into European colonial society. They were modern actors, strategically engaging their oppressors to best ensure the survival of their tribes. Despite their exploitative conditions, the Missions at their apex under Spanish rule allowed Miwok, Ohlone and other California Indian tribes to access different technologies and modest protection from murderous settlers, while maintaining a relationship to their lands. Missions also presented an opportunity to build communities with other Bay tribes. As the mission system withered with the decline of the Spanish empire after the Mexican Independence in 1821 and the increasing presence of Yankee settlers, tribal leaders like Marin and Quintín found the missions to have lost much of their strategic value. They made war upon the same missions that had sought to 'civilize' them.

Despite being narrated as ghosts, as people long-gone, Indians are enough of a corporeal problem for the settler agenda that California has never stopped trying to legislate them out of the land. The 1850 Act for the Government and Protection of

Indians and its amendments, also known as the Indian Slave Acts, allowed any person to request an Indian child for indenture and allowed for the removal of Indians from their land. Such legislation, which remained in effect until 1937, fueled a business of kidnapping and selling of Indian children and murder of their parents. Between 1850 and 1860, over *one billion dollars* in state appropriations were used to fund expeditions against Indians in California. The on-going history of settler colonial interdiction on Native life prompted Senator John L. Burton to request a report from California Research Bureau in 2002 (Johnston-Dodds 2002).

These modalities of state and settler violence, technologies of elimination, and cartographies of containment are recommissioned for use upon black bodies. San Quentin, Alcatraz, Mission Dolores, Point Richmond and Oakland as a carceral city are contracted out to manage outlawed life. Therefore, land serves as an important connecting node between Indigenous struggle and Black resistance.

In 2004, 2005, and 2006, young men from East Oakland Community High School (EOC) – a social justice school that I helped to found – took 'classes' from men on life sentences in San Quentin. Rudy Corpuz, former inmate, and founder of United Playaz youth leadership and violence prevention organization, helped to make these connections possible. I will not say more about these experiences, except that such programs connecting young men and women to their incarcerated elders provided outlawed wisdoms to be transmitted in the only form possible: storytelling. 'Jail is an odd place to find freedom, but that was the place I first found mine' (Newton 2002). Organizations like United Playaz enact the spirit of freedom in jail described by Huey Newton, who co-founded the Black Panther Party in Oakland in 1966. Such stories teach about being free under the most extreme states of unfreedom.

Within these walls of San Quentin, Newton's comrade George Jackson, Black Panther leader and author of *Soledad Brother*, was shot and killed in an alleged attempt to escape in 1971. James Baldwin wrote: 'No Black person will ever believe that George Jackson died the way they tell us he did' (Baldwin, quoted in Jackson 1994, x). When Johnny Cash sang, 'San Quentin, I hate every inch of you' in San Quentin in February 1969, George Jackson had just been transferred to Soledad Prison for a stint before returning to die at San Quentin. He spent nearly a decade of his life at San Quentin for robbing a liquor store at age 18, for which Youth Authority assigned him the sentence of *one year to life* in prison.

While EOC youth were learning from life in San Quentin, they were also sharing that land with death row inmate Stan 'Tookie' Williams. He was the co-founder of the Los Angeles Crips gang, turned antigang advocate and author of multiple books for children and youth. Regardless of our assumptions of Williams' guilt or innocence of his conviction for four murders in a robbery in 1979, in the ghettocentric commonsense Tookie Williams was a voice that resonated with the realities of many urban youth.

EOC youth, some 'gang-affiliated,' were also convening gang unity summits and organizing to combat violence under the guidance of various community educators. One such innovative program was titled *N/Sur/Gentes* (North/South/Peoples), led by poet, activist, educator, Cesar Cruz. Cruz's mode of organizing was rooted in storytelling that connected urban youth lives to Indigeneity across continents and temporal scales, and to the very ghetto land in which youth lived, claimed blocks, and all too frequently died. He taught youth to seek the sacred in between the cracks of desecration. More about these stories I will not tell in this writing, only to say that within them, the coloniality that dislocated black/brown/red/yellow/white peoples became their node of convergence as people relocated to Ohlone land.

Tookie Williams was executed by lethal injection in the early minutes of 13 December 2005 inside the walls of San Quentin. Many EOC youth, educators, and multiple Oakland community leaders gathered outside at the vigil on the night of Williams' execution. One reason that then-California Governor Arnold Schwarzenegger gave for denying his pardon was the inclusion of George Jackson in the dedication of Williams' (2001) book, *Life in Prison*.

## Conclusion

Since 2005, Indian People Organizing for Change has organized Shellmound Peace Walks to the shellmound burial sites around the ancestral, unceded Ohlone lands: covering nearly 300 miles over 3 weeks at 18 miles a day, from Vallejo to San Jose to San Francisco. As of this writing, the Muwekma Ohlone Tribe, comprised of surviving lineages from Missions Dolores, Santa Clara, and San Jose have been fighting for federal recognition since the 1980s. The Bay intertribal community 'and Coyote,' have always recognized them.

Indigenous presence in urban areas like Oakland is 'more like ironic immigration from tribal nation to tribal nation' (Belin 1999). Even before relocation, the Bay Area was a place of transboundary relationships among different Ohlone and Miwok people. After relocation, the Intertribal Friendship House in Oakland – one of the oldest of such urban centers in the country – was established out of support, solidarity, and sociality of various urban Native communities. *Urban Voices* is a collaboratively written collection of the voices of tribal elders in Oakland across multiple generations before and after relocation (Intertribal Friendship House and Lobo 2002) and expresses an Indigenous relationship to the urban as Native land. Not an urban Commons to be re-inhabited, but Ohlone land, a social place, a place from which one misses home and a place to which one can enact some desires to leave home. As an intertribal place, Native-Native relations to Ohlone land and to each other can teach us valuable lessons in re-imagining ethical forms of solidarity beyond the ecological Commons.

Storied land is a partial answer to the question, 'How do we uproot settler maps that drive our everyday materiality and realities?' (Goeman 2008, 170). A poetics of land learns from human resistance to mapping, from peoples' and nature's transgressions of maps, and from land itself as a bearer of memory. 'Land is a resistance to a conception of fixed space; Indigenous artists, storytellers, word warriors, elders, youth, medicine men and women, and scholars utilize the word land differently with vital and various meanings' (Goeman 2008).

Why Huey Newton became free in prison, while Johnny Cash hated every inch of San Quentin, has to do with a fundamental colonial difference between people who see themselves as constituted by versus dwelling in accursed/sacred space. Each year at un-Thanksgiving, a gathering of Indigenous tribes conduct a sunrise ceremony on Alcatraz Island: 'a recognition that they were connected with the Native land under the layers of cement' (Goeman 2008, 28). Describing Tuscorora scholar, Vera Palmer's work with Native prisoners at Mt. Auburn prison on Cayuga land, Goeman writes:

> They were able to roam through the bars of imprisonment by recognizing a new horizon – that the land beneath them was Indigenous land and connected them with others. (28)

Geronimo Pratt, Black Panther leader and survivor of 27 years of incarceration for a murder conviction that was overturned in 1997, spoke about his time in solitary confinement in sacred terms of connection with the earth and sky. He described initially despising the ants who would come into his cell. Through humility, he learned to learn from the ants, who offered a connection to the earth through the cracks in the prison. According to Pratt, the ants loved him back, bringing him food and providing him company. He died on 3 June 2011, in an Imbaseni village, 15 miles from Arusha, Tanzania, where he spent the last five years of his life.

A poetics of land *is*, because outlaw life and outlaw land inherently disrupt propertied life and land as property. As storied land contends with the current condition, settler colonialism, it elucidates pathways of de/colonization of land and people. What are the colonial pathways that bring our people into this land? Where do our pathways diverge from Indigenous pathways? Where do they converge with settler colonial ones? In other words, what is our relationship to settler colonialism, to Indigenous survivance and tribal sovereignty?

**Acknowledgments**

Kate McCoy, Eve Tuck, and Marcia McKenzie for the push. Aries Yumul for mutually constitutive. Angie Morrill for of course the ghetto has land. Cesar Cruz for NSurGentes. C. Ree for the red button. Members of the Land Pedagogy panel at AESA 2010. Ohlone, where this is written: thank you.

## Notes

1. Whiteness and blackness refer to socially (colonially) constructed racial structures beyond phenotype. People of color can be settlers, and can invest in whiteness. Native Americans can be, and have been enslaved, and are incarcerated at some of the highest rates – in other words subject to black subjection. In general, I capitalize Black, Indigenous, etc. when referring to identities, and use lowercase when referring to the colonial structuring of blackness, indigeneity, whiteness, etc.
2. Dictionary definition accessed http://www.allwords.com/word-terra + nullius.html.
3. Even if we accept the pretext that some land is uninhabited by humans, ice sheets are traversed, islands visited, mountain peaks gazed upon, even it they are not 'occupied' by Indigenous peoples (Fujikane 2012). Regardless of inhabitation, land nonetheless constitutes memory, time, and cosmology.
4. Genocide, though real, was not successful in making Native Americans extinct. Indians-as-extinct is ideology rather than actuality; settler guilt/remorse is part of this ideology of extinction.
5. Bay Area Rapid Transit, an expensive commuter monorail that services San Francisco, Oakland, and the suburbs surrounding Oakland.
6. For more about this difference in public transportation, see *Fruitvale Station* (2014), a film based on Oscar Grant's murder by a BART police officer on 1 January 2009.
7. Cosmopolitan 'whiteness' here refers to spatial and embodied entitlements not limited to 'white' phenotype, e.g. bourgeois multiculturalism (Paperson 2010).
8. See Tuck (2009), Suspending Damage: A Letter to Communities.
9. Whitening refers to a process of settlement that can include people of color.
10. Mission Dolores website, http://missiondolores.org/old-mission/visitor.html.
11. Chevron website, The early years 1902–1914, http://www.chevron.com/products/sitelets/richmond/about/history_early_years.aspx.
12. Alcatraz might be more precisely called a De-occupation, symbolic of a movement to unsettle and repatriate tribal lands. 'We will purchase said Alcatraz Island for twenty-four dollars in glass beads and red cloth.'

## References

Agamben, G. 1998. *Homo Sacer: Sovereign Power and Bare Life*. Stanford: Stanford University Press.

Alexie, S. 1996. "How to Write the Great American Indian Novel." In *The Summer of Black Widows*, edited by Sherman Alexie, 94–95. Brooklyn, NY: Hanging Loose Press.

Belin, E. 1999. "Blues-ing on the Brown Vibe." In *From the Belly of My Beauty: Poems*, edited by Ester Belin, 3–6. Tucson: University of Arizona Press.

Berman, M. 1982. *All that is Solid Melts into Air: The Experience of Modernity*. New York: Simon and Schuster.

Bray, P. 2003. "Miwok Indian leaders Chief Marin and Quintin fought for a Doomed Way of Life in Northern California." *Wild West* 16 (2): 68–69.

Cash, J. 1969. *Johnny Cash at Folsom Prison and San Quentin*. New York: Columbia Records.

Forbes. 2008. *Complete List: America's Richest Counties*. http://www.forbes.com/2008/01/22/counties-rich-income-forbeslife-cx_mw_0122realestate_slide_2.html.

Friedel, T. 2011. "Looking for Learning in all the Wrong Places: Urban Native Youths' Cultured Response to Western-oriented Place-based Learning." *International Journal of Qualitative Studies in Education* 24 (5): 531–546.

Fruitvale, Station. 2014. *Directed by Ryan Cooper*. New York: The Weinstein Company, Blu Ray.

Fujikane, C. 2012. "Mapping Mauna a Wākea: Against Anti-Genealogical and Other Fragmenting Fictions of the Settler State." Paper presented at the annual meeting of the Native American and Indigenous Studies Association, Uncasville, CT, June 3–6.

Goeman, M. 2008. "From Place to Territories and Back Again: Centering Storied Land in the Discussion of Indigenous Nation-building." *International Journal of Critical Indigenous Studies* 1 (1): 23–34.

Goeman, M. 2013. *Mark my Words: Native Women Mapping our Nations*. Minneapolis: University of Minnesota Press.

Grande, S. 2004. *Red Pedagogy: Native American Social and Political Thought*. Lanham, MD: Rowman & Littlefield.

Intertribal Friendship House (Oakland, CA), and S. Lobo. 2002. *Urban Voices: The Bay Area American Indian Community*. Tucson: University of Arizona Press.

Jackson, G. 1994. *Soledad Brother: The Prison Letters of George Jackson*. Chicago, IL: Lawrence Hill Books.

Johnston-Dodds, K. 2002. *Early California Laws and Policies Related to California Indians. CRB-02-014*. Sacramento, CA: California Research Bureau, California State Library.

Keeling, K. 2007. *The Witch's Flight: The Cinematic, the Black Femme, and the Image of Common Sense*. Durham: Duke University Press.

Newton, H. P. 2002. "Freedom." In *The Huey P. Newton Reader*, edited by H. P. Newton, D. Hilliard, and D. Weise, 28–43. New York: Seven Stories Press.

Paperson, L. 2010. "The Postcolonial Ghetto: Seeing Her Shape and His Hand." *Berkeley Review of Education* 1 (1): 5–34.

Sarris, G. 1998. *Watermelon Nights: A Novel*. New York: Hyperion.

Smith, L. T. 1999. *Decolonizing Methodologies: Research and Indigenous Peoples*. London: Zed Books.

Stein, G. 1993. *Everybody's Autobiography*. Cambridge, MA: Exact Change.

Stein, G. 1997. *Tender Buttons: Objects, Food, Rooms*. Mineola, NY: Dover.

Tuck, E. 2009. "Suspending Damage: A Letter to Communities." *Harvard Educational Review* 79 (3): 409–428.

Tuck, E., and K. W. Yang. 2012. "Decolonization is not a Metaphor." *Decolonization: Indigeneity, Education & Society* 1 (1): 1–40.

Watson, I. 2007. "Settled and Unsettled Spaces: Are We Free to Roam?" In *Sovereign Subjects: Indigenous Sovereignty Matters*, edited by A. Moreton-Robinson, 15–32. Crows Nest: Allen & Unwin.
Wilderson, F. 2003. "Gramsci's Black Marx: Whither the Slave in Civil Society?" *Social Identities* 9 (2): 225–240.
Williams, S. T. 2001. *Life in prison*. New York: SeaStar Books.

# Eco-heroes out of place and relations: decolonizing the narratives of *Into the Wild* and *Grizzly Man* through Land education

Lisa Korteweg and Jan Oakley

*Faculty of Education, Lakehead University, Thunder Bay, Canada*

Eco-heroic quests for environmental communion continue to be represented, mediated, and glorified through film and media narratives. This paper examines two eco-heroic quests in the Alaskan 'wilderness' that have been portrayed in two Hollywood motion pictures: the movies *Grizzly Man* and *Into the Wild*. Both films vividly document and re-inscribe heroic status to the stories of Timothy Treadwell (*Grizzly Man*) and Christopher McCandless (*Into the Wild*), their tragic encounters with nature, and the pivotal experiences that gave them both eco-heroic identities in the American imagination. As is often the case for Greek and Shakespearean dramas, each hero met a tragic, unnecessary death in Alaskan 'wilderness', but in the process reiterated a settler colonial narrative. We argue that an Indigenous-focused Land education and its counter-narratives of holistic relations are sorely needed. It is Indigenous Land education that can break the cycle of Eurocentric celebrations of solitary heroism, rugged individualism, and ignorance of place. In order to forge Indigenous/non-Indigenous relations in our cultural imaginations and to address compounding environmental struggles, we need to turn to Indigenous stories and teachings that are already in place, in deep relation with the Land, water, animals and plants on Indigenous territory. We need to turn to Land education that is currently not in place or acknowledged in environmental education.

> If this is your land, where are your stories? (Gitskan Elder, land claim meeting, Gitskan territory, northwest British Columbia)

Eco-heroic stories for environmental communion or salvation continue to be represented, glorified, and communicated through film and media narratives. As such, eco-heroic stories are informing place-based educational models, environmental education conceptualizations, and indicate a new 'field of green' (McKenzie et al. 2009). This paper examines two eco-heroic quests in the Alaskan 'wilderness'[1] that have been portrayed in Hollywood motion pictures: the movies *Grizzly Man* and *Into the Wild*. Both films vividly document and inscribe eco-heroic status to the stories of Timothy Treadwell (*Grizzly Man*) and Christopher McCandless (*Into the Wild*) by glorifying wild places. While 'wilderness' is an omnipresent character in most environmental films or media, assumptions about land as pristine and 'wild' ignore the traumatic histories of colonization, including the removal of people from the Land, resulting in displacements and deaths of Indigenous peoples. And in the dominant discourses of environmental film narratives (such as *Into the Wild* and *Grizzly Man*), Alaska (as wilderness) is cleansed of human tragedy and historical contamination in order to be recast as a *place* full of sunlight, pristine nature, and new promise (Cronon 1995, 1996). Yet, all of North America (including Alaska) is not simply a place of trees, animals, and lakes. It is also the *place* of ongoing land-based struggles by Indigenous peoples who are forced to assert their rights to land claims, land entitlement, and self-determination on their own homelands.

Colonization inflicts multiple damages – socially, psychologically, physically, and psychically. In a North American context, colonization has meant damages by one dominant oppressor group, the Euro-settlers, onto the local people of the 'newly discovered' land, the Indigenous peoples. Kulchyski (2005) states that colonization is evident when 'colonial power can be identified with any process that "totalizes," working to reshape Indigenous peoples and their Lands so that they will come to embody and reflect the colonized' (17). And, in the history of North American settlement, two colonial damages have occurred simultaneously: environmental damages to the land/animals (through resource extraction, animal extinction, land clearance, and pollution) intertwined inextricably with sociocultural genocide to the Indigenous peoples of the Land.

Graveline (1998) contends that 'Our degradation as humans is vitally interconnected with the continuing destruction of our Mother Earth, upon whom our existence depends' (7). Initially, colonization displaced Indigenous peoples from their traditional lands, which were in turn cleared for settlement and resource exploitation to feed rapidly growing populations and the consumptive desires of Imperial Europe (Rasmussen 2001). The devastation of the Land jeopardized Indigenous traditional ways of life (e.g. hunting, fishing, gathering medicines, and ceremonies) and Indigenous knowledge, which had sustained the people and the Land for thousands of years (Adams 1999). Environmental education has the power to shift social perceptions and cultural imaginations and needs to actively grapple with this dual issue of colonization: environmental destruction and species extinction with the cultural genocide of Indigenous peoples by Eurocentric or cognitive imperialism (Battiste 2005). One cannot be effectively addressed without the other.

To address such linked environmental and cultural damages, it is important to understand the contested histories of the places in which those damages have and continue to occur. Places, according to the environmental place-based theorist Somerville (2007, 2010), are those spaces of contested stories and values, often between settlers and Indigenous peoples. Given that all of North America is the traditional territory of Indigenous peoples, then all of Alaska is contested place, full of complex and traumatic stories of the relationship between Indigenous people and non-Indigenous settlers on Indigenous Land. We suggest that environmental education, whether through films, TV shows, or popular media, needs to confront the contested histories represented in these 'places' (such as the Alaskan 'wilderness') in order to tell new stories of environmental relations as Land education.

In this paper, we specifically indicate the ways in which media and media analysis can function as Land education through the confrontation of such contested place histories and then reconciliation through new stories that braid Indigenous and non-Indigenous peoples into better relations. Our objects of decolonization are two major motion pictures – *Grizzly Man* and *Into the Wild* – that we believe continue to impact the cultural and environmental imaginations of North American settler youth with their powerful, yet neo-colonial, stories of American eco-heroes Timothy Treadwell and Christopher McCandless. In both films, these heroes are cultural symbols of urban and societal alienation who find their redemptions and deaths by acting out their fantasies of 'wilderness' or eco-quests in Alaska. In their quests, wilderness is personified through national parks or uninhabited places of Alaska – yet, this Alaskan 'wilderness' is itself a highly problematic construct, marinated in colonization, displacement of Indigenous peoples, their loss of self-sufficiency rights to hunt/fish and self-determination. It is a historical tragedy that is rarely recognized or accounted for in North American history textbooks, stories or film narratives. We felt compelled to deconstruct the neo-colonialism of these films in order to explore the damages that are replayed or re-embedded onto the North American cultural psyche as stories where Indigenous peoples are absent, erased, or avoided on their Land. We also want to extend the critical readings of these films (e.g. Brinks 2008; Conesa-Sevilla 2008; Schutten 2008) to encourage the birth of new media representations that could address the cultural complexities of de/colonization in eco-film narratives, as well as shift this 'naturally ready' education discipline (McKeon 2012) towards Land education.

Through our decolonizing deconstruction of *Grizzly Man* and *Into the Wild*, we are trying to provoke a new kind of environmental education reading of film narratives, one that does not rely on Eurocentric cultural desires for 'wilderness' and eco-heroes. In its *place*, we imagine a counter-narrative of how environmental educators would enter into respectful relations with Indigenous peoples to protect Indigenous Land. Our discussion holds relevance for those in environmental education because our central concern is that the Indigenous knowledge, politics, struggles and resilience of Indigenous peoples are quite inseparable from an education for a better planet and sustainable practices. When environmental education ignores or erases Indigenous peoples from places or does not recognize Indigenous Land as critical sites of environmental struggle, the environmental education story loses depth, longevity, and ethical righteousness. Environmental education itself becomes more assimilated or colonized to unsustainable industrial-corporate greed than it was originally conceived to oppose as an educational solution. These films provide useful illustrative entry points into discussing Eurocentric (cognitive) imperialism than still directs environmental stories of wilderness in much environmental education curriculum and can assist the field to reorient itself towards Indigenous Land education.

## *Grizzly Man* (Timothy Treadwell)

Timothy (Dexter) Treadwell, a failed actor and recovering alcoholic living in Malibu, escaped the chaos of his life in the human world to find refuge in what he considered an Eden-like sanctuary in the Alaskan wilderness. An environmental advocate and self-styled 'defender' of bears, he spent 13 summers living and interacting with grizzlies in Katmai National Park, which boasts the world's largest population of Kodiak brown bears (Alaska Bear Tours 2011). Over the course of his last five summers, Treadwell recorded 100 h of video footage, intending to produce a film of his crusade. Herzog's (2005) documentary of Treadwell is assembled through interviews of close friends, family, various professionals, and Treadwell's own video footage. Herzog, who edited and narrated the film, chronicles Treadwell's story up until and including Treadwell's death in 2003, when he and his girlfriend Amie Huguenard were killed by one of the bears Treadwell vowed to protect.

The promotional rhetoric in the movie's advertising portrayed Treadwell as a 'grizzly activist', but this must be called into question. The bear poaching that Treadwell was ostensibly preventing was never a reported problem during the years he was in Alaska: although Treadwell claimed to be saving the bears from poachers seeking trophies, gall bladders, and other parts destined for Asian markets, the reserve is in fact federally protected land and no poaching incidents have been reported there since the 1970s (Lapinski 2005). It has thus been suggested that Treadwell's militant eco-warrior persona was largely a fabrication, created to lend him a heroic stance and rationale for illegally camping in a national park.

Herzog, for his part, has established a career as a classic auteur director who has a penchant to tackle 'madness' in both his fiction and non-fiction films. He is driven to understand and portray what he likes to call an 'ecstatic truth' about people, society, and the environment (Prager 2007). As a filmmaker, his talent lies in recognizing and taking existing materials, such as the 100+ h of film footage by Treadwell, and transforming it into something uniquely intimate, quirky, and sublime. As Herzog narrates in *Grizzly Man* (2005):

> Having myself filmed in the wilderness of jungle, I found that beyond a wildlife film, in his [Treadwell's] material lay dormant a story of astonishing beauty and depth. I discovered a story of human ecstasies and darkest inner turmoil. As if there was a desire in him to leave the confines of his humanness and bond with the bears. Treadwell reached out and seeked a primordial encounter. But in doing so, he crossed an invisible borderline.

The strength in Herzog's filmmaking is his passion to portray and interpret personal stories without heavy-handed judgments. Herzog follows the narrative arc of a man who shuns civilization for a more authentic and meaningful existence in the wild with bears, but leaves interpretive doors open for multiple audiences. For example, eco-psychologists approve of the manner in which Treadwell's existential malaise and abusive addictions were 'cured' by the bears, the outdoors, and his devotion to bear protection: 'This is the first clue and reassurance [for] those who are involved in adventure and outdoor education, of the power of raw nature, and its symbol the grizzly, to heal if not transform the psyche' (Conesa-Sevilla 2008, 139). In contrast, cultural critics understand Treadwell quite differently, portraying him as a feral child living a romanticized Garden of Eden fantasy and refusing to accept the responsibilities of adult life:

> The dangers and violence in the wilderness may in the end be more a substitute than an alternative to those of Los Angeles; yet they have a longer history of being romanticized, and Treadwell invest[ed] the Alaskan wild with a quality of kindness and nurture able to undo the toxic effects of urban misery. (Brinks 2008, 308)

Yet, whether Treadwell is interpreted as an individual seeking to heal himself or trying to escape from adult responsibilities and relationships, his ecological identity (Thomashow 1995) is worth unpacking to understand its construction and contribution to environmental education thought.

## *Into the Wild* (Christopher McCandless)

Based on a Jon Krakauer book with the same title, Sean Penn's *Into the Wild* (2007) tells the real-life story of Christopher McCandless, a 24-year-old Virginia college graduate who, propelled by a mixture of grandiosity and grievance, decided to leave civilization and head out, alone and unaided, as far away as he could go. In a remote reach of Alaska, he met a tragic end from eating a poisonous plant and subsequently starving to death. The film alternates scenes from an abandoned bus, where McCandless spent his last months attempting to survive as a hunter-gatherer, with episodes of road travels from the preceding year and a half and occasional cuts to his family, consumed by sorrow over his disappearance, back East.

Krakauer (1996), like Herzog, is fascinated with extreme characters seeking out the harshness of nature and risking their lives due to some great drive. Beyond the risks of extreme outdoor adventure, Krakauer perceived a ferocious passion in McCandless to seek ultimate answers, an intense asceticism, and a religious zeal for solitude in nature. Penn's (2007) film tends to glorify McCandless's wanderings of the American west and the Alaskan wilderness through majestic mountain panoramas, slow-motion shots in deep forests, and aerial plunges down river canyons. The film emphasizes McCandless's idealism and inner disappointment with his parents' hypocrisy, which fueled his drive to seek out a wilderness monastery.

McCandless traveled with Western classic literature as sources of solace. Narratives of close communion with nature and wilderness were his inspiration: he carried Thoreau's *Walden Pond*, Jack London's *The Call of the Wild*, and Leo Tolstoy's writings in his backpack, often referring to this literature in journal entries and correspondence with friends. These Western classics are narratives of autonomy and libertarian independence that only exceptional Western men, such as the authors themselves, might possess in order to thrive in the wilderness. The texts seemed to serve as bibles to quench McCandless's existential thirst, guides in seeking out wilderness as the remedy to his flight from social commitments, and testimonies to his extreme confidence in his own autonomy. They were the books by which he lived and, sadly, died. And, it turned out that McCandless's death was especially needless and tragic as there was an undiscovered park rangers' cabin (within 10 miles of his bus) stocked with emergency supplies.

## Film analysis for decolonizing eco-heroic place-based stories

Films are particularly powerful in their capacity for changing or shifting the stories of wilderness/nature in our environmental imaginations and consequently, environmental education. Braun (2002) states that, 'there is no place *outside* such cultural practices [*film*] from which nature [*wilderness*] can be objectively known. Even when our relation to nature seems most immediate, it is profoundly shaped by the narrative, knowledges, and technologies that enable experience' (15, italicized words in brackets added). There is no mention in these movies that this region of Alaska is not in fact the 'wilderness', but rather the homeland and traditional territory of the Alutiiq/Yupik/Inuit peoples who have lived there since time immemorial. The Alutiiq/Yupik/Inuit have lived on the land with all wild animals, including grizzly bears, for thousands of years and have accumulated critically important Indigenous knowledge of how to survive and thrive in this harsh environment and to not become meat (Schutten 2008) or prey of the grizzlies. Their language, stories,

Elders, and ancestors all combine, interconnect, and intertwine with the non-human world of plants, animals, trees, and water to become Land and to be able to teach their children a holistic Land education (see Barnhardt and Kawagley 2005; Battiste 2005; Cajete 1999; Graveline 1998).

Both Treadwell (*Grizzly Man*) and McCandless (*Into the Wild*) arrived in Alaska for communion and purification with the environment, special places, and animals. Each man ran away from an American urban center where he felt sickened or imprisoned by a madness of civilization that would not stop contaminating him, and both sought out extreme conditions in the 'pure wilderness' of Alaska. Treadwell's idea of the zealous spiritual quest for salvation through an animal can be understood as a neo-colonialist representation of how poor or irrelevant conventional religion has become. Having become so estranged from wilderness and the outdoors in urban depravity, it is romanticizing of the animal-other that appears as the new frontier of spirituality and salvation. It was Timothy Treadwell's colonial misery that drove him to the bears to find communion by literally touching them and, at times, physically transforming himself to act as a bear. His only 'constructed' or 'imagined' enemies were White men (park officials and hunters/poachers), and though there was an Indigenous museum and local Indigenous communities nearby, he never spoke about or indicated in his own media that they would have something to offer his fieldwork or advocacy for the bears. The question we grapple with, as environmental and social justice educators, is how Treadwell could spend 13 summers in Katmai National Park and never once communicate with or acknowledge the traditional territory of the Alutiiq people and their knowledge of the Kodiak bear. As a grizzly advocate and self-described educator, was it not Treadwell's passion and commitment to learn as much about the bears as he could, including how they have been understood by the people, the Alutiiq, with whom they have harmoniously shared the same land for thousands of years?

Indigenous Alaskans are strikingly absent from *Into the Wild* (2007), an absence that is echoed in McCandless' hapless attempts to live on the Land. McCandless referred to the day he killed a moose as one of his worst of his life because he could not harvest the meat before it rotted. Using a mere tourist guidebook to model his butchering, he lost the majority of the moose meat to maggots. His lack of knowledge of edible plants was, of course, even worse and dire in consequences: guided by a wild plants book with one small photo and a textual description of the plant in its prime, he mistook a poisonous plant for wild potatoes. When he figured out he had committed a lethal error, he called out and wrote for help from fellow, though absent, human travelers, and it was then that he perhaps realized his other fatal flaw: that he had cut himself off completely from all human relations. As he wrote in his copy of Doctor Zhivago, 'HAPPINESS ONLY REAL WHEN SHARED' (Krakauer 1996, 189), a declaration that he finally understood relations or relationality with others as the means for durable contentment. McCandless was the ideal Western, purest Euro-American eco-hero: 'he rejected conformity and materialism in order to discover what was authentic and what was not, to test himself, to experience the raw throb of life without a safety net' (Krakauer 2013). He was well read but imperviously ignorant of an Indigenous worldview or Indigenous knowledge of plants as the critical piece of Alaska's Land. Wilderness was his abstract monastery, devoid of humans, constructed with texts wherein McCandless could think and experience pure autonomy. He was a monk without religion but with fervent conviction that a 'wilderness place' would assuage and cure his existential malaise. He did not pursue a new social world but a strict individualist code of self-reliance – no personal *relations* with animals, family, people, spirits, or community. As a highlighted passage from his copy of Doctor Zhivago suggests, he sought to commit himself to 'something absolute', such as 'life or truth or beauty', instead of 'man-made rules' (Krakauer 1996, 102). Clearly, this commitment is not reflective of an Indigenous worldview in any territory or a central teaching of Land education. Rather, it is a Eurocentric mindset that is distinctly *out of place* in Alaska and other Indigenous Lands. And it is a mindset that ultimately cost McCandless his life.

We question these films and their compromised approach or avoidance of Indigenous peoples in the film stories. Herzog (2005), for example, asserts that there is a 'line between bear and human', and that line is 'something that has always been respected by native communities of Alaska'. Yet instead of articulating what that 'line' is, or investigating the construction of 'nature/environment' by Indigenous peoples, he cuts to Sven Haarkanson, Alutiiq museum director, who notes that Treadwell died while trying to *be* a bear. Haarkanson explains:

> For us on the island, you don't do that. You don't invade on their territory … For him to act like a bear the way he did, to me it was the ultimate in disrespecting the bear and what the bear represents … I think he did more damage to the bear, because when you habituate the bears to humans, they think they are safe. He tried to be a bear, to act like a bear and for us on the island you don't do that … If I look at him from my culture, Timothy Treadwell crossed a boundary that we have lived with for 7000 years; it's an unspoken, an unknown boundary, but when we know we crossed it, we pay the price.

Herzog's reference to Haarkanson appears inclusive of an Indigenous Alaskan perspective at best, or another 'angle' for understanding Treadwell's tormented quest, a token statement at worst. The existence of Indigenous knowledge in Alaska of how to survive on the Land and in sustainable relations with animals demonstrates an American cultural ignorance that was, ironically, the way of life that both men were desperately trying to eschew. These eco-heroes' greatest quest, to rid themselves of their civilization or cultural contamination, became their greatest liability in the wilderness. Both men were unaware or imperviously ignorant of local Indigenous peoples (McCandless), unwilling to acknowledge or learn local Indigenous knowledge of bear/human relations (Treadwell), when doing so might have saved each man from tragic failure.

When we armchair travel into these Alaskan *places* as if they were politically neutral, environmentally pristine and spiritually divine, we are buying into and perpetuating neo-colonial narratives of 'wilderness'. *Grizzly Man* and *Into the Wild* create representations of places that are untainted by Western or settler exploits of injustice, domination and colonialism. The romanticized beauty and goodness of the Alaskan wilderness as special *place* then somehow absolves us of any guilt about the appropriation of Land from the Indigenous peoples of Alaska and the concurrent contamination of their traditional practices, Indigenous language and knowledge systems. By ignoring or denying the presence and knowledge of Indigenous peoples in Alaska, Treadwell and McCandless were continuing to exert a type of neo-colonial oppression and ignorance upon the Land and the Indigenous people of the Land. The American view of wilderness as special *place* and eco-heroic identities as a cultural project that articulates itself through film are intimately and inextricably linked to what the films, and Treadwell and McCandless ignored: Indigenous presence

(Bordo 1992), Indigenous homelands or traditional territory, and Indigenous knowledge.

## Land education is Indigenous knowledge in relation to Land

Borne out of more than 7000 years of relations, observations, experiences, and knowledge with animal communities (including the Kodiak grizzly bear), Indigenous and Inuit Alaskans know their place and the place of animals in both spiritual and material spheres. As Alaskan scholar Ray Barnhardt and Yupik scholar Oscar Kawagley (2005) emphasize, 'Indigenous knowledge rooted in the long inhabitation of a particular place offers lessons that can benefit everyone, from educator to scientist, as we search for a more satisfying and sustainable way to live on the planet' (9). Through ongoing deep respect and reverence, Indigenous Alaskans have figured out and related through stories and teachings, the psychic, spiritual, and concrete practices of Land education that maintains harmony and peaceful co-existence of human and more-than-human beings (Brant Castellano 2000; Cajete 1994; LaDuke 1997; Smith 2000).

Unlike the eco-heroes of the two films, an Indigenous worldview does not recognize individual identity as separate or distinct from family and community. As McGregor (2009) describes:

> Traditionally, Anishnaabe people understood their relationship with Creation and assumed the responsibilities given to them by the Creator. The relationship with Creation and its beings [land, animals, non-animate entities] was meant to be maintained and enhanced, and the knowledge that would ensure this was passed on for generations over thousands of years. The responsibilities assumed by individuals, communities and nations as a result of having this knowledge ensured the continuation of Creation (what academics now refer to as 'sustainability'). (33)

In other words, Indigenous knowledge can be characterized as a collective, in-relation, accumulative process of responsibilities of ancient wisdom and spiritual teachings, as a life-long learning path or embedded way of being in/on/with the land. Or, as Battiste (2005) explains:

> All Indigenous knowledge flows from the same source: the relationship of Indigenous peoples with the global flux, their kinship with other living creatures, the life energies as embodied in their environments, and their kinship with the spirit forces of the earth. (128)

Globally, Indigenous peoples regard the Land as a totality with people, trees, animals, water, rocks, and spirits/ancestors all embedded into this entity. Connection to, or embeddedness in, the Land is at the core and very essence of Indigenous belief structures (Battiste and Henderson 2000; Grand Chief Beardy 2009; LaDuke 1999). This remains true despite dispossession, displacement, and genocide of Indigenous cultures since colonization (Godlewska, Moore, and Bednasek 2010) and needs to have profound implications for a new settler understanding of relationship to *place*. Environmental scholars and researchers cannot begin to articulate a position about place without confronting the historical trauma and current complex political realities of the Indigenous – non-Indigenous relationship on Indigenous Land (Somerville 2010).

## Place-based and environmental education learning from Indigenous Land education

Place-based theorist Gruenewald (2003) has argued that reinhabitation through environmental place-based theories means learning how to live well in place, how 'to identify, recover, and create material spaces and places that teach us how to live well in our total environments' (9). Thomashow (1995) describes ecological identities and narratives as emerging from the ways people perceive themselves *in relation* to place, as manifested in character, values, action, sense of self, and direct experiences with nature. Or, as Orr (1992) describes it: 'Good inhabitance is an art requiring detailed knowledge of a place, the capacity for observation, and a sense of care and rootedness' (130). In the film narratives of *Grizzly Man* and *Into the Wild*, McCandless and Treadwell could be interpreted as place-based eco-heroes who learned how to live well in place, identifying and recovering spaces and places of animals and forests. Certainly, McCandless and Treadwell were successful at a sense of care and appreciation of the animals and the beauty of these Alaskan wild *places*.

Yet, a deep failure to recognize Indigenous presence and Indigenous knowledge embedded in this Land were also evident. With these two film narratives, we question how an eco-heroic quest story can be focused on place and yet remain a colonizing, imperviously ignorant narrative – or, how living to re-inhabit a place (wilderness) can be interpreted as both heroic and damaging.

In our view, Greenwood (2010) presents a limited approach to environmental education through the processes he terms *reinhabitation* and *decolonization* because it does not yet take into account Land education or the Indigenous knowledge of these places:

> Decolonization involves learning to recognize disruption and injury in person-place relationships, and learning to address their causes. … Reinhabitation involves maintaining, restoring, and creating ways of living that are more in tune with the ecological limits of a place, practices that are less dependent on a globalized consumer culture that values profits and conveniences more than people and places. (19)

In the heroic narratives of *Grizzly Man* (Treadwell) and *Into the Wild* (McCandless), we see two eco-heroes living a 'good inhabitance' of place, according to most place-based and environmental educators, but simultaneously, being completely unaware of any notion of de/colonization for the Indigenous peoples of that Land, on Indigenous traditional territory, holding, and maintaining Indigenous language, knowledges, and practices.

With the powerful depictions in the two films come decolonizing and re-inhabitation (place-based) responsibilities. We acknowledge that both films detail the tragic endings of each eco-hero's death, yet we worry that Treadwell and McCandless remain as role models or exemplars for desperate young White males to copy-cat or model their own treatment of urban alienation and 'nature deficit disorder' (Louv 2005). We should not celebrate or idealize the stories of Treadwell and McCandless through film, except as cautionary tales of doom when disrespecting Indigenous knowledge and perpetuating a neo-colonial mindset of the White settler eco-hero in a mythological place called 'wilderness'. On the contrary, what needs to be *in place*, and the subject of artistic representation and deep cultural re-storying, is the commitment and dual address of reconciling socio-cultural human rights and ecological injustices.

In our unpacking the representations in *Grizzly Man* and *Into the Wild*, it is evident that Treadwell and McCandless imparted colonial Western values onto their relationship with nature while knowing little of the social histories of 'disruption and injury' (Greenwood 2010) of the lands on which they travelled. For Treadwell and McCandless, travelling to Alaska was a balm for the deep existential dissatisfaction they felt in urban American society, yet in seeking wild salvation by abandoning their *relations* – their commitments, families, and social lives – in Malibu (Treadwell) and Virginia (McCandless), to live on little more than their wits in Alaska, these film portrayals continue to glorify narratives of settler eco-heroes who were dangerously *out of place* or disconnected from the Land, tragically ignorant of the Indigenous peoples who understand and continue to be *in relation* with that Land. When we watch these eco-quest films and do not deconstruct their colonial meanings, we are equally participating in hegemonic narratives that sustain the settler mythology of the Alaskan 'wilderness' as non-Indigenous or White places.

## Land education is learning from Indigenous continuous relation with the Land

There are two principles of *being* for the Nishnawbe Aski Nation (NAN) people:

> (1) Our special relationship with the Creator.
> (2) Our special relationship with the land.
> That is who we are as Indigenous (NAN) people.
>
> (Stan Beardy, NAN Grand Chief, Treaty #9 Conference, February 2011, Lakehead University)

Frustrated at what they perceived as a selfishness and human-centered hypocrisy in the world, and turning toward extreme nature as its antithesis, Treadwell and McCandless discovered in Alaska a *place* to reinvent themselves. Yet the act of abandoning their communities, families, and social lives – their *relations* – needs to be critiqued and deconstructed, rather than passively consumed or celebrated. While we applaud the films for bringing environmental stories and eco-heroic narratives to mass audiences (especially those audiences who live unsustainable, disconnected, or alienated lives in urban centers and suburbs), we do think there are more important Indigenous stories of land that deserve to be told as Land education for all – stories that demonstrate sustainable, eco-centric ways of living, embedded in social and natural communities holistically in relation and since time immemorial.

We understand how powerful these films are in demonstrating the intense disconnectedness of young White North American men as they question the lack of nature or place connectedness in their lives, along with a lack of meaning. Certainly, youth can feel out of place in the cities where they have grown up, and many dream of Alaska's wilderness as a promise for a new beginning or an existence with deeper meanings. There are Indigenous people, however, to contend with in this Alaskan wilderness, living on the very Land now coded as desirable for urban White youth as their 'wilderness' that will cure their existential angst. The absence or erasure of Indigenous peoples, along with their rich consciousness of Land (their accumulated Indigenous knowledge over millennia), only perpetuates the false Western ideal of rugged individualism and the Eurocentric man vs. nature binary. In decolonizing these film narratives, we hope that a 'Land education' approach focused upon epistemological and cosmological *relations* between all peoples, land, water, and flora and fauna will take *the place* of (Eurocentric) place-based environmental education. In the face of mass audience settler seduction by these types of place-based film narratives, and as non-Indigenous environmental educators, we wish to be 'idle no more' in our responses and actions (see #idle no more).

We must not forget that Indigenous peoples *are* the Land, because they have the stories, the language, and the eco-centric (harmonious) practices of Land education. Films and movies can begin to acknowledge, celebrate and embed these Land education images in our Western cultural imaginary. They can remind us that we cannot be an eco-hero in any place unless we share and respect the Land, the common stories, the experiences, and respectful relationships with the resident Indigenous peoples. It is these Indigenous peoples who are the eco-heroes in their Land, and non-Indigenous people have never been in *a place* where we needed their stories, good relations and Land education more than right now.

## Acknowledgments

We wish to acknowledge the Anishinaabe people of the Fort William First Nation on whose traditional territory we live as settlers and who have been the environmental caretakers of this Land since time immemorial. We also wish to honor the elders and teachers who have shared their stories and knowledge with us–Elder Agnes Hardy, Elder Dolores Wawia, and Tesa Fiddler.

## Note

1. See Cronon's pivotal essay (1996) that traces the historical consciousness of 'wilderness' and 'frontier' as culturally constructed (Eurocentric) ideals that became the embodiment of affluent White (male) desire for freedom and liberation from social constraints.

## References

Adams, H. 1999. *Tortured People: The Politics of Colonization*. Penticton: Theytus Books.

Alaska Bear Tours. 2011. *Bear Viewing Tours in Katmai National Park, Alaska*. http://www.alaskabeartours.com.

Barnhardt, R., and A. Kawagley. 2005. "Indigenous Knowledge Systems and Alaska Native Ways of Knowing." *Anthropology and Education Quarterly* 36 (1): 8–23.

Battiste, M. 2005. "You Can't be the Global Doctor if You're the Colonial Disease." In *Teaching as Activism*, edited by P. Tripp and L. Muzzin, 121–133. Montreal: McGill Queen's University Press.

Battiste, M., and J. Y. Henderson. 2000. *Protecting Indigenous Knowledge and Heritage: A Global Challenge*. Saskatoon: Purich.

Bordo, J. 1992. "Jack Pine: Wilderness Sublime or the Erasure of the Indigenous Presence from the Landscape?" *Journal of Canadian Studies* 27 (4): 98–128.

Brant Castellano, M. 2000. "Updating Indigenous Traditions of Knowledge." In *Indigenous Knowledge in Global Contexts*, edited by G. Dei, B. Hall, and D. Rosenberg, 23–24. Toronto: University of Toronto Press.

Braun, B. 2002. *The Intemperate Rainforest: Nature, Culture, and Power on Canada's West Coast*. Minneapolis: University of Minnesota Press.

Brinks, E. 2008. "Uncovering the Child in Timothy Treadwell's Feral Tale." *The Lion and the Unicorn* 32 (3): 304–323.

Cajete, G. 1994. *Look to the Mountain: An Ecology of Indigenous Education*. Durango, CO: Kivaki Press.

Cajete, G. 1999. "Reclaiming Biophilia: Lessons from Indigenous Peoples." In *Ecological Education in Action: On Weaving Education, Culture and the Environment*, edited by G. Smith and D. Williams, 180–206. Albany: State University of New York Press.

Conesa-Sevilla, J. 2008. "Walking and Dying with Bears: An Ecopsychological Case Study of Timothy (Dexter) Treadwell." *The Trumpeter* 24 (1): 136–150.

Cronon, W. 1995. "The Trouble with Wilderness: Or, Getting Back to Wrong Nature." *Environmental History* 1 (1): 7–28.

Cronon, W. 1996. *Uncommon Ground: Rethinking the Human Place in Nature*. New York: W. W. Norton.

Godlewska, A., J. Moore, and C. D. Bednasek. 2010. "Cultivating Ignorance of Aboriginal Realities." *Le Géographe Canadien* [Canadian Geographer] 54 (4): 417–440.

Grand Chief Beardy. 2009. "Keynote Speech." In *Nishnawbe Aski Nation Treaty #9 Conference*, Thunder Bay, Ontario.

Graveline, F. 1998. *Circle Works: Transforming Eurocentric Consciousness*. Halifax: Fernwood.

Greenwood, D. 2010. "Nature, Empire, and Paradox in Environmental Education." *Canadian Journal of Environmental Education* 15: 9–24.

Gruenewald, D. 2003. "The Best of Both Worlds: A Critical Pedagogy of Place." *Educational Researcher* 32 (4): 3–12.

Herzog, W. 2005. *Grizzly Man*. Santa Monica, CA: Lion's Gate.

Krakauer, J. 1996. *Into the Wild*. New York: Random House.

Krakauer, J. 2013. "How Chris McCandless Died." *The New Yorker*. http://www.newyorker.com/online/blogs/books/2013/09/how-chris-mccandless-died.html.

Kulchyski, P. K. 2005. *Like the Sound of a Drum: Indigenous Cultural Politics in Denendeh and Nunavut*. Winnipeg: University of Manitoba Press.

LaDuke, W. 1997. "Voices from White Earth: Gaa-waabaabinganikaag." In *People, Land and Community*, edited by H. Hannum, 22–37. Great Barrington, MA: E. F. Schumacher Society.

LaDuke, W. 1999. *All Our Relations: Native Struggles for Land and Life*. Cambridge, MA: South End Press.

Lapinski, M. 2005. *Death in the Grizzly Maze: The Timothy Treadwell Story*. Guilford, CT: The Globe Pequot Press.

Louv, R. 2005. *Last Child in the Woods: Saving Our Children from Nature-deficit Disorder*. Chapel Hill, NC: Algonquin Books.

McGregor, D. 2009. "Honouring Our Relations: An Anishnaabe Perspective on Environmental Justice." In *Speaking for Ourselves: Environmental Justice in Canada*, edited by J. Agyeman, P. Cole, R. Haluza-DeLay, and P. O'Riley, 27–41. Vancouver: UBC Press.

McKenzie, M., H. Bai, P. Hart, and B. Jickling, eds. 2009. *Fields of Green: Restorying Culture, Environment, and Education*. Cresskill, NJ: Hampton Press.

McKeon, M. 2012. "Two-eyed Seeing into Environmental Education: Revealing its 'Natural' Readiness to Indigenize." *Canadian Journal of Environmental Education* 17: 131–147.

Orr, D. 1992. *Ecological Literacy*. Albany: State University of New York Press.

Penn, S. 2007. *Into the Wild*. Hollywood, CA: Paramount/Vantage.

Prager, B. 2007. *The Cinema of Werner Herzog: Aesthetic Ecstasy and Truth*. Brighton: Wallflower Press.

Rasmussen, D. 2001. "Qallunology: A Pedagogy for the Oppressor." *Canadian Journal of Native Education* 25 (2): 105–116.

Schutten, J. 2008. "Chewing on the Grizzly Man: Getting to the Meat of the Matter." *Environmental Communication: A Journal of Nature and Culture* 2 (2): 193–211.

Smith, G. 2000. "Protecting and Respecting Indigenous Knowledge." In *Reclaiming Indigenous Voice and Vision*, edited by M. Battiste, 209–224. Vancouver: University of British Columbia Press.

Somerville, M. 2007. "Place Literacies." *Australian Journal of Language and Literacy* 30 (2): 149–164.

Somerville, M. 2010. "A Place Pedagogy for 'Global Contemporaneity'." *Educational Philosophy and Theory* 42 (3): 326–344.

Thomashow, M. 1995. *Ecological Identity: Becoming a Reflective Environmentalist.* Cambridge, MA: MIT Press.

# Index

Note: Page numbers in **bold** represent figures
Page numbers followed by 'n' refer to notes


Aboriginal sovereignty 12, 123
activism 121
actors 109; social 110
Africa 13, 71, 75–8
African Americans 76–7, 118
African Diaspora 72–3, 76–8
African-centered approach: to environmental education 75–8; to land education 70–81
Africana Studies 2–4, 70, 74–9
Agamben, G. 116
Agyeman, J. 79n
Akulukjuk, T.: and Rasmussen, D. 12
Alaska (USA) 2, 12, 133–6, 140
Alexie, S. 117
Alfred, T. 49
Allen, P.G. 86, 94n
Amazon 107, 112n
*America: Pathways to the Present* (Cayton *et al.*) 32
American Civil War (1861–5) 32
*American Odyssey: The United States in the 20th Century* (Nash) 30
*American Vision, The* (Appleby *et al.*) 30, 32
*Americans: Reconstruction to the 21st Century, The* (Danzer *et al.*) 31, 32
anthropocentrism 43–5
anthropology: evolutionary 85, 92–4; settler colonial 92
*apook* (tobacco) 87–8
Arabs 78
Araguaia River (Brazil) 107, 113n
Archer, G. 86
Ashcroft, B.: Griffiths, G. and Tiffin, H. 104
Asia 30
Australia 1–2, 11, 29, 92; Aboriginal sovereignty 12, 123; Cape York 56–8, 62–6; Council for Aboriginal Reconciliation 58; environmental education 56–69; Great Barrier Reef 56, 62, 65–6; *Melbourne Declaration on Educational Goals for Young Australians* 62; Queensland 58, 61, 66
Australian Curriculum Assessment and Reporting Authority (ACARA) 62–3, **62**
autonomy 135–6
axioms 115

Bachelard, G. 105
Bacon, F. 85
Baldwin, A. 16
Bang, M.: *et al.* 3, 9–10, 13, 18, 37–55
Banner, S. 90–2
Barad, K. 83
Barker, J. 122–3
Barnhardt, R. 138
Barrett, M.J.: *et al.* 3, 18, 56–69
Battiste, M. 138
*Becoming Native in this Place* (Jackson) 16
Belin, E. 115
Berhe, A. 108
Bernal, D.D. 25
Berthold-Bond, D. 49
Bhabha, H. 106
Bible 83
biodiversity 58
blackness 128n
Blackwater, A. 14
Blimkie, M.: Styres, S. and Haig-Brown, C. 9–10

Boston Nature Center (USA) 73
Boston Tea Party (USA) 116
Boston (USA) 73, 79
Botswana 11
bourgeoisie 103
Bowers, C.A. 40, 44
Brandt, C.B. 27
Braun, B. 135
Brazil 1, 5, 11
British colonization 60–1
British Empire 60
Brooks, L. 12
Brown, J. 120
Buber, M. 109
Burkhart, B.Y. 10, 44, 49
Burton, J.L. 126

Calderon, D. 2–3, 10, 16, 24–36
California (USA) 5, 115, 124–6; Malibu 133; Oakland 115–25, 128n; San Francisco Bay 5, 11, 115, 124
*Call of the Wild, The* (London) 135
Canada 2, 10–11, 14, 19, 33
*Canadian Journal of Environmental Education* 14
Cape York (Australia) 56–8, 62–6
Caribbean 83
Carroll, K.K.: and Engel-Di Mauro, S. 4, 70–81
cartography 2, 106, 120, 126; critical 2, 18, 123–7; decolonizing 115
Casey, E. 44
Cash, J. 126–7
Chambers, C. 13
chattel slavery 88–90
Chicago (USA) 3, 8, 18, 37–55; Shkaakwa 38–9
Chicana pedagogy 25–6
Chigeza, P.: *et al.* 3, 18, 56–69
Chilsa, B. 11
China 82
Christianity 88, 91, 125; Protestant 4, 85
citizenship 24–9, 34n
civilization 84, 92, 106–8, 135–6
class: middle 120; working 83, 116
coffee colonialism 83
cognitive imperialism 13
Cole, P.: and O'Riley, P. 13
Collier, P. 100
colonial identity 28
colonial ontology 33–4n, 56–69
colonial teleology 120
colonial world 103–5
colonialism 5–6, 11–13, 57–60, 102–14, 124–5, 137; coffee 83; exploitation 6, 83; external 6, 94n; ghetto 9, 115–21; neo- 133; settler 1–19, 20n, 24–33, 60–6, 71–4, 78
colonialist epistemology 57
coloniality 105, 124–6
colonies: English 4
colonization 6–7, 63–4, 82, 102–5, 138; British 60–1; European 61
Columbus, C. 7, 88
commonsense environmentalism 119
communalism 15, 75
communion 136
communities: ghettoized 120; Indigenous 11, 33, 42, 75, 136; local 25
community-based design research (CBDR) 45–6
community-based education 15
Cook, Capt J. 7
Cook-Lynn, E. 11
Corbett, M. 44
Cordell, J.: and Fitzpatrick, J. 59
Cordero, C. 123
Corpuz, R. 126
cosmology 3, 76, 105; cultural 105; Indigenous 1, 8–11, 27, 37, 56, 83
Council for Aboriginal Reconciliation (Australia) 58
counterculturalism 15
Crashaw, W. 90
critical cartography 2, 18, 123–7
critical curriculum inquiry 24–36
critical pedagogy 70–1
cultural cosmology 105
cultural sustainability 26
culture-nature dichotomy 72–4, 77
Curley, L.: *et al.* 3, 9–10, 13, 18, 37–55
Curtis, N. 94n

Dale, T. 89
decolonization 3–5, 13–18, 20n, 24–8, 122–4, 132–3
decolonizing: cartography 115; perspectives on place 1–23

deforestation 111
Deloria, V. 25–7; and Lytle, C.M. 42
Descartes, R. 10, 44, 85
design-based research (DBR) 45
developing countries 111
diaspora: African 72–3, 76–8
dichotomy 71; culture-nature 72–4, 77; people-nature 74
Diop, C.A. 74
direct colonial rule 73
Donald, D. 13

eco-feminism 121
eco-heroes 131–43
eco-heroic identity 131, 137
eco-pedagogy 117
ecological imperialism 47
ecology 59; urban 115–20
economic growth 102
ecosystems 44, 58, 70–3, 99, 104, 111, 113n; Great Lakes 38
Eden 86
education: community-based 15; environmental 1–23, 56–69, 75–8, 84; place-based 1, 6, 14–17, 24–7, 72–4, 139–40
eighteenth century 59, 104, 117
Engel-Di Mauro, S.: and Carroll, K.K. 4, 70–81
England 83–92; King James I (1566–1625) 87–91
English colonies 4
English language 12, 47
English people 83, 91–3
enlightenment 85
enslavement 76
entrepreneurialism 26
Environment Education Communication and Arts Research Group (GPEA) 103, 107
environmental education: Australia 56–69; research 1–23, 84
environmental racism 72, 79n
environmental sustainability 58
environmentalism 2, 11; commonsense 119; settler 115–30
epistemology 3, 13, 39, 48–50, 85, 102; colonialist 57; Indigenous 39, 46–9; Western 47; Xingu 102; zero point (ZPE) 41–3

Ethiopia 108
ethnicity 105; Indigenous 107–9
ethnography 2, 18; land-based 11
Euro-settlers 132
Eurocentric universalism 13
Eurocentrism 4, 72
Europe 31, 47, 75–7, 89; Imperial 132
European colonization 61
European universalism 1, 13
evolutionary anthropology 85, 92–4
exploitation colonialism 6, 83
external colonialism 6, 94n
extractivism 112n

Facebook 123
famine 86
Fanon, F. 20n
feminism: eco- 121
fifteenth century 103
First Man 86
First Woman 86–7
First World 93
Fitzpatrick, J.: and Cordell, J. 59
food: security 83; sovereignty 2–5
Freire, P. 105
Friedel, T.L. 10
frontier 141n

Galeano, E. 112
Genesis 85
genocide 71, 125, 128n, 138
gentrification 5, 94, 120
geography 1–4
Gernet, A. von 87
ghetto: colonialism 9
ghetto-fication 120
ghettocentric commonsense 119
ghettoized communities 120
Ghosh, A. 82
Girls Club (Hawaii) 98–100
global warming 46
globalization 25, 37, 40
Goeman, M. 115, 127
Grande, S. 121
Graveline, F. 132
Great Barrier Reef (Australia) 65
Great Barrier Reef Marine Park Authority (GBRMPA) 56, 62, 66; *Sea Country Guardians* programme 56, 65–6

Great Britain 92
Great Lakes ecosystems 38
Green Belt Movement (Kenya) 73
Greenwood, D. 139
Griffiths, G.: Tiffin, H. and Ashcroft, B. 104
Griffiths, J. 44
*Grizzly Man* (2005) 131–43
Gruenewald, D. 15–17, 26, 40–4, 50n, 139; and Smith, D. 16, 42, 84
Guerin, B. 112
Gussow, A. 15
Gutiérrez, K.D.: and Vossoughi, S. 45

Haarkanson, S. 137
Haig-Brown, C.: Blimkie, M. and Styres, S. 9–10
Harley, B. 106
Harrison, P. 85
Hawaii 4–5
hegemonic power 106
hegemony 7
heroes: eco- 131–43
heroism 131
Herzog, W. 133–4, 137
hierarchy 33–4n
Hilo Boys (Hawaii) 98–100
Hollywood movies 5
*How the Indians Lost Their Land* (Banner) 90
human migration 87
human rights 103
human tyranny 85
humanity 75, 123
humanness 134
hydropower plants 113n

identity: colonial 28; eco-heroic 131, 137; self- 109; settler 25–7, 33, 121; social 5, 59
ideology 7, 25–7, 30–2, 77, 82, 128n; Northern Cradle 74, 77; racialized 31; settler 25, 29, 33; settler colonial 73, 117
immigrants 30
Imperial Europe 132
imperial power 83
imperialism 5, 106, 116, 133; cognitive 13; ecological 47
India 6, 82–3
Indian-ness 116
*Indians' Book, The* (Curtis) 94n
Indigenous land 3–7, 14–17, 20n, 27–8, 37–55, 82–3, 132–3, 139–40; rights 11–12
Indigenous people;
Indigenous peoples 1–3, 16–19, 20n, 27–32, 34n, 38–41, 64–6, 104–9, 128n, 140–1; communities 11, 33, 42, 75, 136; cosmology 1, 8–11, 27, 37, 56, 83; epistemology 39, 46–9; ethnicities 107–9; knowledge 10–14, 24–8, 31, 71; non- 19, 39; ontology 39, 44, 49, 56–69; perspectives on place 1–23; realities 27–8; sovereignty 12, 20n, 121
individualism 75, 79, 131, 140
industrialized countries 111
institutionalization 71
interconnectedness 75
intra-activity 83
irrigation 103
Islam 78

Jaber, M.: Sato, M. and Silva, R. 5, 11, 18, 102–14
Jackson, G. 126–7
Jackson, W. 16–17
James I, King of England (1566–1625) 87–91
Jamestown (Virginia) 4
Jennings, N.: Swidler, S. and Koliba, C. 108

Kaiao Garden (Hawaii) 98–100, **99**
Kauai (Hawaii): Limahui valley 4, 98–100, **100**
Kauanui, K.K. 94n
Kawagley, O. 9–12, 138
Keeling, K. 119
Kemit (Egypt) 75
Kenya 73; Green Belt Movement 73
Kessel, A.: *et al.* 3, 9–10, 13, 18, 37–55
Keto, C.T. 77
knowledge: Indigenous 10–14, 24–8, 31, 71
Koliba, C.: Jennings, N. and Swidler, S. 108
Korteweg, L.: and Oakley, J. 5, 131–43; and Russell, C. 14
Kovach, M.E. 11
Krakauer, J. 135
Kulchyski, P.K. 132

La Paperson (Yang, K.W.) 5, 9–11, 18, 94, 115–30
land: Indigenous 3–7, 14–17, 20n, 37–55, 82–3, 132–3, 139–40; native 116–17, 121

land pedagogy: ghetto 115–30
land-based ethnography 11
land-based pedagogy 10, 37, 45
Le Grange, L. 13
legitimacy 41, 106
liberal multiculturalism 49
liberalism: neo- 40
liberation 141n
*Life in Prison* (Williams) 127
Limahui valley (Kauai) 4, 98–100, **100**
Loban, F. 59
local communities 25
Locke, J. 85
London, J. 135
Los Angeles (USA) 134
Lowe, K.: and Yunkaporta, T. 63
Lytle, C.M.: and Deloria, V. 42

Mabo, E.K. 61
McCandless, C. 131–6, 139–40
McCoy, K. 4, 7, 10, 82–97; Tuck, E. and McKenzie, M. 1–23, 57
McGregor, D. 138
McKenzie, M.: McCoy, K. and Tuck, E. 1–23, 57
MacLean, E.A. 12
Malibu (California) 133
Manifest Destiny 24–36
MA'O Farm (Waianae) 99–100
mapping/maps: identities 103; Mercator 77; social 2, 5, 18, 102–14
Marin, A.: *et al.* 3, 9–10, 13, 18, 37–55
Marker, M. 40
mass migration 76
materialism 136
Mato Grosso (Brazil) 5, 11, 102–3
*Melbourne Declaration on Educational Goals for Young Australians* 62
Mercator map 77
metaphysics 25–7
metropolitan neo-colonies 120
Mexico 87
Meyer, M. 4–5, 9, 57, 74, 98–101, 102
middle class 120
Mignolo, W.D. 41, 47; and Tlostanova, M.V. 47
migration 30, 76; human 87; mass 76
modernism 4
modernity 13, 85, 117
modernization 105
monoculture 82–4, 93, 103–5; large-scale 82
Mooka, A. 58
Morgensen, S.L. 7, 15
mortality 88
Moses, R. 116
multicultural settler society 20n
multiculturalism 33; liberal 49
Muskrat theories 37–55

Nakata, M. 65
nation-state 6, 13, 20n, 28
National Tropical Botanical Gardens (Hawaii) 100n
nationalism: settler 30–1
native land 116–17, 121
natural world 85
neo-colonialism 120, 133
neo-liberalism 40
New World 83, 88–9
New York (USA) 116
New Zealand 8, 11, 29
Newton, H. 126–7
*Nicotania* (tobacco): *rustica* 87; *tabacum* 88–9
nineteenth century 10, 31, 82–5, 92, 104, 117
Nishnawbe Aski Nation (NAN) 140
non-anthropocentrism 43
Non-Indigenous peoples 19, 39
non-profit organizations 118
North America 8–9, 19, 30, 48, 87–92, 116, 132
Northern Cradle 74–5, 77–8

Oahu (Hawaii): Waianae 98–9
Oakland (California) 115–25, 128n
Oakley, J.: and Korteweg, L. 5, 131–43
ontology 3, 9–10, 13, 16, 34n, 39–40, 44–50; colonial 33–4n, 56–69; Indigenous 39, 44, 49, 56–69; relational 58, 64; Western 63
organizing ideas (OIs) 63–4
O'Riley, P.: and Cole, P. 13
Orr, D. 139
O'Sullivan, J. 84
Other 31, 103, 109
oxygen 98

Pacific Ocean 31
Pádua, J. 104
Palmer, V. 127
Papua New Guinea 61

parochialism 71
participatory social maps: constructing 102–14
Peaches, A. 1
pedagogy 2, 15, 26, 40–1, 46–9, 65, 120; Chicana 25–6; critical 70–1; eco- 117; ghetto land 115–30; land 115–30; land-based 10, 37, 45; place-based 13, 70, 120; relational 9
Peña, D.G. 27
Pendleton Jiménez, K. 25–6
Penn, S. 135
people-nature dichotomy 74
Percy, G. 86, 91–3
Peters projection 77
place: perspectives on 1–23; settler-colonial discourse 40–1
place-based education 1, 6, 14–17, 24–7, 72–4, 139–40
*Place-Based Education in the Golden Age* (Gruenewald and Smith) 16, 42, 84
place-based pedagogy 13, 70, 120
*Pocahontas* (Allen) 86, 94n
political economy 84
Porto-Gonçalves, C. 104, 109
Portugal 104
post-colonial perspectives: on place 1–23
postcoloniality 72
poverty 103
power: hegemonic 106; imperial 83; relations 4
Pratt, G. 128
profitability 71
Protestant Christianity 4
Protestantism 85
purification 136

Queensland (Australia) 58, 61, 66
Quijano, A. 105

racial minority 34n
racialized ideology 31
racism 72, 76; environmental 72, 79n
Rasmussen, D.: and Akululjuk, T. 12
rationality 102
realities: Indigenous 27–8
relational ontology 58, 64
relational pedagogy 9
research: community-based design (CBDR) 45–6; design-based (DBR) 45; environmental education 1–23, 84
rights: human 103; Indigenous land 11–12
Rolfe, J. 89
Rose, D.B. 59
Russell, C.: and Korteweg, L. 14

San Francisco Bay (California) 5, 11, 115, 124
San Francisco (USA) 118–19, 124–7, 128n
San Quentin penitentiary (USA) 124–7
Sartre, J. 105
Sato, M.: Silva, R. and Jaber, M. 5, 11, 18, 102–14
savagery 93
Schwarzenegger, A. 127
*Sea Country Guardians* programme (Great Barrier Reef Marine Park) 56
*Sea of Poppies* (Ghosh) 82
security: food 83
self-determination 50n
self-identity 109
Sellwood, J.: *et al.* 3, 18, 56–69
settler colonialism 1–19, 20n, 24–33, 60–6, 71–4, 78; anthropology 92; discourse on place in education 40–1; ideology 73; triad 82, 88–90, 93–4
settlerism 27
settlers: colonization of Sea Country 60–2; environmentalism 115–30; Euro- 132; identity 25–7, 33, 121; ideology 25, 29, 33; multicultural society 20n; nationalism 30–1; sustainability 5; territoriality 30; typology 7
seventeenth century 4, 85, 92, 95n, 104
Shava, S. 13
Silva, R.: Jaber, M. and Sato, M. 5, 11, 18, 102–14
Singe, J. 58
sixteenth century 104, 117
Skikaakwa (Chicago) 38–9
slave labor 105
slavery 4, 71–2, 93, 104, 116; chattel 88–90
slaves 82, 108
Slivinski, S. 89
Smith, D.: and Gruenewald, D. 16, 42, 84; and Sobel, D. 25, 73
Smith, J. 8, 91
Smith, L.T. 3, 11, 19, 25
Sobel, D.: and Smith, G.A. 25, 73
social actors 110

social constraints 141n
social groups 103–7, 110, **110**
social identity 5, 59
social mapping 2, 5, 18
social movements 11–12
Socioeconomic and Ecological Zoning Committee of Mato Grosso (ZSEE) 103
*Soledad Brother* (Jackson) 126
Somerville, M. 132
Southern Cradle 74–5, 79
sovereignty 2, 11–13, 33, 42, 116, 123; Aboriginal 12, 123; food 2–5; Indigenous 12, 20n, 121; settler colonial 120; state 12, 123; white 123
Spain 89, 104
spirituality 75, 102
state sovereignty 12, 123
stories: decolonizing eco-heroic place-based 135–8
Strachey, W. 86–8, 93
Strack, G.: *et al.* 3, 9–10, 13, 18, 37–55
Styres, S.: Haig-Brown, C. and Blimkie, M. 9–10; and Zinga, D. 9
supremacy: white 30–3, 84
sustainability 26–8, 56–7, 105, 110, 118; cultural 26; ecological 26; environmental 58; settler 5
Suzukovich III, E.: *et al.* 3, 9–10, 13, 18, 37–55
Swayze, N. 17
Swidler, S.: Koliba, C. and Jennings, N. 108
Symonds, W. 90

Tanzania 128; Arusha 128
teleology 121; colonial 120
*Tequila Sovereign* 122
territorialism 30–1
territoriality 26–33, 84; settler 30
Third World 93
Thomashow, M. 139
Thoreau, H.D. 135
Tiffin, H.: Ashcroft, B. and Griffiths, G. 104
Tlostanova, M.V.: and Mignolo, W.D. 47
tobacco 38–45; *apook* 87–8; *Nicotania rustica* 87; *Nicotania tabacum* 88–9
Tolstoy, L. 135
Torres Strait: *Ailan Kaston* (Island Custom) 3–4, 56–61, 64–5; Creole language 59; Sea Country 3–4, 8, 18, 60–2
Treadwell, T. 131–6, 139–40
triad: settler colonial 82, 88–90, 93–4
Tsenacommacah 83, 84–93
Tuck, E.: McKenzie, M. and McCoy, K. 1–23, 57; and Yang, K.W. 20n, 42, 72, 83, 94n
twentieth century 60, 116–17
twenty-first century 65, 105, 116–21
Two-Cradle Theory (Diop) 74
tyranny: human 85

United Indians of All Tribes 124
United States of America (USA) 1–4, 25–32, 34n, 50n, 71–3, 77–8, 116, 124; African Americans 76–7, 118; Alaska 2, 12, 133–6, 140; Boston 73, 79; Boston Nature Center 73; Boston Tea Party 116; California 5, 115, 124–6; Chicago 3, 8, 18, 37–55; Civil War (1861–5) 32; Los Angeles 134; New York 116; Occupy Wall Street 122; San Francisco 118–19, 124–7, 128n; San Quentin penitentiary 124–7; Virginia 4, 7, 82–97, 140
universalism: European 1, 13
urban ecology 115–20
urban gentrification 94
urbanization 19

Veracini, L. 7, 46, 83
victimization 108
Virginia (USA) 4, 7, 82–97, 140
Vizenor, G. 12
Vossoughi, S.: and Gutiérrez, K.D. 45

Waianae (Oahu) 98–100; MA'O Farm 99–100
*Walden Pond* (Thoreau) 135
Watkin Lui, F.: *et al.* 3, 18, 56–69
Watson, I. 123
Weitzer, R. 29
West 32; epistemology 47; ontology 63
West Indies 89
wetlands 37–8, 46–50, 98, 113n
Whap, G. 59
white sovereignty 123
white supremacy 30–3, 84
Whitehouse, H.: *et al.* 3, 18, 56–69
whiteness 128n
wilderness 141n
Williams, T. 127

Wilson, S. 11
Wolfe, P. 29–30, 60, 72, 83, 94n
working class 83, 116
*World Geography* 77–8

xenophobic worldview 75
Xingu epistemology 102

Yang, K.W. 5, 9–11, 18, 94, 115–30; and Tuck, E. 20n, 42, 72, 83, 94n
Yunkaporta, T.: and Lowe, K. 63

zero point epistemology (ZPE) 41–3
Zinga, D.: and Styres, S. 9
Zone of Confluence 74